ARMINIAN THEOLOGY

Myths and Realities

ROGER E. OLSON

IVP Academic
An imprint of InterVarsity Press
Downers Grove, Illinois

InterVarsity Press
P.O. Box 1400, Downers Grove, IL 60515-1426
World Wide Web: www.ivpress.com
E-mail: email@ivpress.com

InterVarsity Press® is the book-publishing division of InterVarsity Christian Fellowship/USA®, a student movement active on campus at hundreds of universities, colleges and schools of nursing in the United States of America, and a member movement of the International Fellowship of Evangelical Students. For information about local and regional activities, write Public Relations Dept., InterVarsity Christian Fellowship/USA, 6400 Schroeder Rd., P.O. Box 7895, Madison, WI 53707-7895, or visit the IVCF website at <www.ivcf.org>.

Design: Cindy Kiple

Images: The Dordt Synod by Bernard Picart (1729)

ISBN-10: 0-8308-2841-9

ISBN-13: 978-0-8308-2841-8

Printed in the United States of America ∞

Library of Congress Cataloging-in-Publication Data

Olson, Roger E.
  Arminian theology: myths and realities/Roger E. Olson.
  p. cm.
  Includes bibliographical references and indexes.
  ISBN-13: 978-0-8308-2841-8 (cloth: alk. paper)
  ISBN-10: 00-8308-2841-9 (cloth: alk. paper)
  1. Arminianism   I. Title.
BX6195.O47   2006
230'.49—dc22

                        2006020859

P	19	18	17	16	15	14	13	12	11	10	9	8	7	6	5
Y	22	21	20	19	18	17	16	15	14	13	12	11	10	09		

Contents

Arminian Theology Is the Opposite of Calvinist/Reformed Theology

Jacob Arminius and most of his faithful followers fall into the broad understanding of the Reformed tradition; the common ground between Arminianism and Calvinism is significant.

A Hybrid of Calvinism and Arminianism Is Possible

In spite of common ground, Calvinism and Arminianism are incommensurable systems of Christian theology; on issues crucial to both there is no stable middle ground between them.

Arminianism Is Not an Orthodox Evangelical Option

Classical Arminian theology heartily affirms the fundamentals of Christian orthodoxy and promotes the hallmarks of evangelical faith; it is neither Arian nor liberal.

The Heart of Arminianism Is Belief in Free Will

The true heart of Arminian theology is God's loving and just character; the formal principle of Arminianism is the universal will of God for salvation.

Arminian Theology Denies the Sovereignty of God

Classical Arminianism interprets God's sovereignty and providence differently than Calvinism without in any way denying them; God is in charge of everything without controlling everything.

Preface

I HAVE ALWAYS BEEN AN ARMINIAN. I WAS raised in a Pentecostal preacher's home, and my family was most definitely and proudly Arminian. I don't remember when I first heard the term. But it first sunk into my consciousness when a well-known charismatic leader of Armenian background rose to prominence. My parents and some of my aunts and uncles (missionaries, pastors and denominational leaders) distinguished between *Armenian* and *Arminian*. I probably heard it even before that, however, as some of my relatives were faithful members of Christian Reformed Churches, and behind their backs my parents and other relations discussed their Calvinism and contrasted it with our Arminianism. I recall sitting in a college theology class and the professor reminded us that we are Arminians, to which one student muttered loudly, "Who would want to be from Armenia?" In one class we read Arminian theologian Robert Shank's books *Life in the Son* and *Elect in the Son* (both from Bethany House, 1989). I had trouble understanding them, partly, I think, because of the author's Church of Christ theology. So I got my hands on a couple other books on Arminian theology in an attempt to figure out "our" theology. One was Nazarene theologian Mildred Bangs-Wynkoop's *Foundations of Wesleyan-Arminian Theology* (Beacon Hill Press, 2000). Another was Nazarene theologian H. Orton Wiley's one-volume summary of Christian doctrine titled *Introduction to Christian Doctrine* (Beacon Hill Press, 1946). Eventually I felt I had a fairly good grasp on the subject and laid it aside. After all, everyone around me was Arminian (whether they knew it or not), and there was no particular need to defend that point of view.

Things changed when I enrolled in an evangelical Baptist seminary and began to hear *Arminian* used in a pejorative sense. In my studies there my own theology was equated with the heresy of semi-Pelagianism. Now I had to find out what that was! One of my professors was eminent evangelical Calvinist James Montgomery Boice, who was then pastor of Tenth Presbyterian Church in Philadelphia. We sparred a little over Calvinism and Arminianism, but I perceived he had already made up his mind that my church's theology was heretical. Boice stimulated me to study the matter further and also to subscribe to *Eternity* magazine, which was the leading evangelical alternative to *Christianity Today* in the 1970s. I was an avid reader of both publications. There, in both of these evangelical magazines, I found a fascinating irony. Their unofficial editorial policies were clearly guided by Reformed theology; most of the theologians who wrote for them were Calvinists. Both also, however, included Arminian voices from time to time and tried to be irenic about the theological differences among evangelicals. I felt affirmed—and somewhat marginalized.

Only after Clark Pinnock, one of my theological mentors from a distance (we later became friends), very publicly switched from Calvinist theology to Arminianism did a new round in the old Calvinism versus Arminianism battle flare up within evangelical ranks. By then I was an aspiring evangelical theologian and realized that my options were somewhat limited by my Arminianism. The reaction to Pinnock's change of mind by evangelical Calvinists was swift and sharp, and increased as he edited two volumes of essays defending classical Arminian theology. I read them with great interest without finding there or anywhere else a straightforward, one-volume exposition of classical Arminian theology in all its dimensions and aspects. Throughout the 1980s and 1990s as my own career evolved I discovered that my evangelical world was being affected by what one Reformed friend called "the revenge of the Calvinists." Several evangelical authors and publications began to attack Arminian theology very caustically, and with misinformation and misrepresentation. I heard and read my own form of evangelicalism called "humanistic" and "more Catholic than Protestant." My family and church always considered ourselves Protestants!

The idea for this book was formulated when I read the May-June 1992 issue of an exciting new magazine titled *Modern Reformation*. It was entirely dedicated to the critique of Arminianism from a Reformed perspective. In it I found what I considered to be serious misrepresentations and most ungenerous portrayals of my own theological heritage.

Around that time a student made an appointment to talk with me. In my office he announced most sincerely, "Professor Olson, I'm sorry to say this, but you're not a Christian." This was in the context of an evangelical liberal arts college that did not have an official confessional position on Arminianism or Calvinism. In fact, the denomination that controlled the college and seminary had always included Calvinists and Arminians within its ranks. I asked the student why, and he responded, "Because my pastor says Arminians aren't Christians." His pastor was a well-known Calvinist who later distanced himself from that statement. Similar events within my evangelical world made clear to me that something was afoot; what my Reformed friend sarcastically called "the revenge of the Calvinists" was leading to a widespread impression among evangelicals that Arminianism is at best subevangelical and at worst outright heresy. I determined not to wilt under the pressure but to speak out on behalf of an evangelical heritage nearly as old as Calvinism itself and just as much a part of the historical evangelical movement as Calvinism. I wrote an article for *Christianity Today,* which was given the unfortunate title "Don't Hate Me Because I'm Arminian." I felt the title falsely portrayed the article and myself as overly defensive. I never thought that critics of Arminianism hate us! But I was finding that some evangelical leaders were increasingly misunderstanding classical Arminianism. One labeled himself a "recovering Arminian," as he moved from his own Holiness (Wesleyan) background toward Reformed theology under the influence of a leading evangelical Calvinist theologian. One of the authors I had read with great appreciation in *Eternity* magazine labeled Arminians "barely Christian" in one of his books in the 1990s. A pastor in my own Baptist denomination began to teach that Arminianism is "on the precipice of heresy" and "profoundly mistaken." A colleague who attended that pastor's church asked me if I had ever considered the possibility that my Arminianism was evidence of latent humanism in my thinking. I noticed that many of my Arminian friends were dropping the label in favor of "Calminian" or "moderately Reformed" in order to avoid conflict and suspicion that might hinder their careers in teaching and publishing.

This book was born out of a burning desire to clear the good Arminian name of false accusations and charges of heresy or heterodoxy. Much of what is said about Arminianism within evangelical theological circles, including local congregations with strong Calvinist voices, is simply false. That is worth pointing out. My hope is that this book will not come across to readers as overly defensive; it is not my wish to be defensive, let alone offensive. I want to clear up confusion about Arminian theology and respond to the main myths and misconceptions about it that are widespread in evangelicalism today. I believe that even if most people who call themselves Arminian are really semi-Pelagian (which will be explained in the introduction), that does not make Arminianism itself semi-Pelagian. (Would Calvinists like Calvinism to be defined and understood by the ill-informed beliefs of some Reformed laypeople?) I believe in turning to history for correct definitions and not allowing popular usage to redefine good theological terms. I will turn to leading Arminian theologians past and present to define true Arminianism. My hope and prayer is that readers will approach this project with an open mind and be guided in their opinions of Arminianism by the evidence. I hope even the most diehard Calvinist opponents of Arminian theology will at least be willing to reconsider what true Arminians believe in light of the evidence marshaled here.

The Nature of This Book

Some chapters in this book repeat some information and arguments found in earlier chapters because I expect that not every reader will read straight through the book from beginning to end. If this occasional repetition annoys those of you who read the whole book, I apologize to you in advance. My goal is to make this book as reader friendly as possible in spite of the fact that the subject matter can be quite complex at times. Some scholarly reviewers may be put off by this. My aim, however, is to reach as wide an audience as possible, so the book is not written primarily for specialists (although I hope they will benefit from and enjoy reading it). I have purposely held back from following tangents too far away from the main arguments of the book. Readers who expect more discussion of, for example, middle knowledge or open theism (see chap. 8) will no doubt be disappointed. But this book has one main purpose: to explain classical Arminian theology as it really is. And I have intentionally kept it relatively brief in order to make it accessible to a larger audience.

This project came to fruition with the help of many friends and acquaintances. I want to thank my many Calvinist friends for their contributions via e-mail-based discussions and face-to-face conversations. I also thank my Arminian friends for their help. Over the past decade I have participated in many lively and sometimes heated discussions and debates with proponents of both camps within the evangelical movement. They have pointed me to good sources and provided me with their scholarly insights and opinions. I especially thank William G. Witt, who graciously corresponded with me about his Ph.D. research at the University of Notre Dame; his dissertation was for me an invaluable resource. He is innocent of any errors I have made. I also thank the administration and regents of Baylor University and Dean Paul Powell and Associate Dean David Garland of George W. Truett Theological Seminary (Baylor's seminary) for providing me with summer sabbaticals and a research leave. In addition, I thank Keith Johnson and Kyle Steinhauser for creating the name and subject indexes.

This book is dedicated to three theologians who died while I was researching and writing it. Each one contributed in a very material way to it by offering insights and criticisms. They are my colleague in theology A. J. (Chip) Conyers; my first theology teacher, Ronald G. Krantz; and my dear friend and collaborator Stanley J. Grenz. They died within months of each other and left me impoverished by their absences. But they left me enriched by their presence in my life, and to them I most gratefully dedicate this volume.

Introduction

A Primer on Arminianism

THIS BOOK IS FOR TWO KINDS OF PEOPLE: (1) those who do not know Arminian theology but want to, and (2) those who think they know about Arminianism but really don't. Many people are included in those two categories. Every student of theology—lay, pastoral and professional—should know about Arminian theology because it has a tremendous influence on the theology of many Protestant denominations. Some of you who are deciding whether to read this book are Arminians, but you don't know it. The term *Arminian* is not all that commonly used in the twenty-first century.

The recent surge of interest in Calvinism has produced a great deal of confusion about Arminianism; many myths and misconceptions swirl around it because both its critics (mostly Reformed Christians) and many of its supporters misunderstand it. Because of the surge of interest in Calvinism and Reformed theology, Christians on both sides of the issue want to know more about the controversy between those who embrace belief in absolute, unconditional predestination and those who don't. Arminians affirm predestination of another kind; they affirm free will and conditional predestination.

This book attempts to fill a gap in current theological literature. To the best of my knowledge no book currently in print in English is devoted solely to explaining Arminianism as a system of theology. Some of Arminianism's harsher critics (who are numerous among evangelical Calvinists) no doubt regard this gap as a good thing. However, after my article "Don't Hate Me Because I'm An Arminian" appeared in *Christianity Today* in 1999, I received numerous communications asking for more information about Arminianism and Arminian theology.[1] Many inquirers wanted to read an entire book about the subject. Unfortunately none are in print, and those that exist in libraries are generally old volumes that go into much more depth than the average student of theology desires. Arminians, or those who suspect they might be Arminians, want the gap filled. Many Calvinists also want to know about Arminianism from the proverbial horse's mouth. Of course they have read individual chapters about Arminianism in books of Calvinist theology (which is the only source many Calvinists have on the topic), but out of fair-mindedness they would like to read a full-blown Arminian self-description. That is all to the good. Every theology student should read books by proponents of the various theologies rather than merely read about those theologies by their critics.

A Brief Overview of This Book

First we need to clear up one important point. Arminianism has nothing to do with the country of Armenia. Most people mispronounce the word as if it were somehow associated with the central Asian country Armenia. The confusion is understandable because of the purely accidental similarity between the theological label and the geographical one. Arminians are not from Armenia. Arminianism derives from the name Jacob (or James) Arminius (1560-1609). Arminius (whose birth name was Jacob Harmensz or Jacob Harmenszoon) was a Dutch theologian who had no ancestral lineage in Armenia. Arminius is simply the Latinized form of Harmensz; many scholars of that time Latinized their names, and members of the Harmensz family looked back with reverence to a Germanic chieftain named Arminius who resisted the Romans when they invaded central Europe.

Second, Jacob Arminius is remembered in the annals of church history as a controversial Dutch pastor and theologian who wrote numerous works, filling three large volumes, defending an evangelical form of synergism (belief in divine-human cooperation in salvation) against monergism (belief that God is the all-determining reality in salvation, which excludes free human participation). Arminius was certainly not the first synergist in Christian history; all of the Greek church fathers of the first Christian centuries and many of the medieval Catholic theologians were synergists of some

---

[1]Roger E. Olson, "Don't Hate Me Because I'm An Arminian," *Christianity Today,* September 6, 1999, pp. 87-94. The unfortunate title was assigned to the article by the magazine's editors and was not my choice.

kind. Furthermore, as Arminius and his earliest followers, known as the "Remonstrants," loved to point out, many Protestants before him were synergists in some sense of the word. (Like most theological terms, *synergism* has multiple shades of meaning, not all of which are positive; here it merely means any belief in human responsibility and the ability to freely accept or reject the grace of salvation.) Philip Melanchthon (1497-1560), Martin Luther's lieutenant in the German Reformation, was a synergist, but Luther wasn't. Because of Melanchthon's influence on post-Luther Lutheranism, many Lutherans throughout Europe adopted a synergistic outlook on salvation, eschewing unconditional predestination and affirming that grace is resistible. Arminian theology was at first suppressed in the United Provinces (known today as the Netherlands) but caught on there later and spread to England and the American colonies, largely through the influence of John Wesley and the Methodists. Many early Baptists (General Baptists) were Arminians, just as many are today. Numerous denominations are devoted to Arminian theology, even where the label is not used. These include all Pentecostals, Restorationists (Churches of Christ and other denominations rooted in the revivals of Alexander Campbell), Methodists (and all offshoots of Methodism, including the large Holiness movement) and many if not most Baptists. The influence of Arminius and Arminian theology is deep and broad in Protestant theology. This book is not about Arminius per se but about the theology that stems from his theological work in Holland.

Finally, the context of this book is the controversy between Calvinism and Arminianism. While both are forms of Protestantism (even if some Calvinists deny that Arminianism is authentically Protestant), they take very different approaches to the doctrines of salvation (soteriology). Both believe in salvation by grace through faith alone *(sola gratia et fides)* as opposed to salvation by grace through faith and good works. Both deny that any part of salvation can be based on human merit. Both affirm the sole supreme authority of Scripture *(sola sciptura)* and the priesthood of all believers. Arminius and all of his followers were and are Protestants to the core. However, Arminians have always opposed belief in unconditional reprobation—God's selection of some persons to spend eternity in hell. Because they oppose that, they also oppose unconditional election—the selection of some persons out of the mass of sinners to be saved apart from anything God sees in them. According to Arminians the two are inextricably linked; it is impossible to affirm unconditional selection of some to salvation without at the same time affirming unconditional selection of some to reprobation, which, Arminians believe, impugns the character of God.

The controversy that raged around Arminius in his day continues into the twenty-first century, especially among evangelical Protestant Christians throughout the world. The thesis of this book is that Arminianism is at a disadvantage in this controversy because it is so rarely understood and so commonly misrepresented both by its critics and by its supposed defenders.

The widespread misrepresentation of Arminianism in the context of the continuing evangelical debate over predestination and free will is a travesty. People of good will involved in it ought to get both sides straight. Misrepresentation is what most often happens in the lively and sometimes vitriolic debates about Arminianism that take place on the Internet, in small groups and in evangelical publications. Arminianism is treated as a straw man all too easily chopped down or burned up because it is not fairly described. This book is centered around the most common myths surrounding and the corresponding truths about Arminian theology. Lovers of truth will want to be correctly informed about Arminianism before they engage in or are persuaded by polemical arguments for or against it.

Some Important Words About Words

The most common root of confusion in theology is misunderstanding terms. Theological discourse is fraught with such confusion. To avoid adding to it, some clarification of terminology is needed. Because some discussion of theological viewpoints and movements other than Arminianism is inevitable, and because self-description is usually preferred over descriptions by adherents of other theologies, I will make clear how theological terms are used when describing both Arminian and non-Arminian theologies. I hope that adherents of those theologies find their own viewpoints fairly represented.

Calvinism is used to denote the shared soteriological beliefs of persons who regard John Calvin (1509-1564) of Geneva as the greatest organizer and purveyor of biblical truth during the Protestant Reformation. Calvinism is that theology which emphasizes God's absolute sovereignty as the all-determining reality, especially with regard to salvation. Most classical or high Calvinists agree that human beings are totally depraved (helpless to do anything spiritually good, including exercising a good will toward God), unconditionally elected (predestined) to either salvation or damnation (although many Calvinists reject Calvin's "horrible decree" of reprobation), that Christ's atoning death on the cross was meant only for the elect (some Calvinists disagree), God's saving grace is irresistible (many Calvinists prefer the term *effectual*), and saved persons will persevere to final salvation (eternal security). Calvinism is the soteriological system stemming from Calvin, which is generally known under the rubric of TULIP (Total depravity, Unconditional election, Limited atonement, Irresistible grace, Perseverance of the saints).[2] *Reformed theology* will be used to designate something broader than Calvinism even though the two are often equated. Reformed theology stems not only from Calvin but also from a host of his contemporaries, including Ulrich Zwingli and Martin Bucer. It has broadened to include many thinkers and denominations represented by the World Alliance of Reformed Churches, not all of which are Calvinists in the high or classical sense.[3]

Throughout this book *Arminianism* will be used synonymously with Arminian theology. It describes not so much a movement as an outlook on salvation (and other theological subjects) shared by people who differ on other matters. Arminianism has no headquarters; it is not especially associated with any organization. In that it is similar to Calvinism. Both are theological points of view or even systems stemming from the writings of a seminal thinker. Neither is a movement or organization.

When *Arminianism* is used, it will connote that form of Protestant theology that rejects unconditional election (and especially unconditional reprobation), limited atonement, and irresistible grace because it affirms the character of God as compassionate, having universal love for the whole world and everyone in it, and extending grace-restored free will to accept or resist the grace of God, which leads to either eternal life or spiritual de-

---

[2]It should be noted that whether Calvin himself taught limited atonement is debatable. For a modern statement of Calvinism see Edwin H. Palmer, *The Five Points of Calvinism* (Grand Rapids: Baker, 1972). Of course, numerous other and perhaps more scholarly and detailed descriptions of Calvinism are available. Some important modern evangelical Calvinist authors who describe and defend high Calvinism include Anthony Hoekema and R. C. Sproul. For a more recent and more detailed account of high Calvinism and the five points of Calvinism see David Steele, Curtis Thomas and S. Lance Quinn, *The Five Points of Calvinism*, 2nd ed. (Phillipsburg, Penn.: Presbyterian & Reformed, 2004).

[3]One of the great ironies of this context of dispute between Calvinists and Arminians is that the contemporary Dutch denomination known as the Remonstrant Brotherhood, which stems from the work of Arminius and his followers, is a full member of the World Alliance of Reformed Churches! People who equate Calvinism and Reformed theology may be on shaky ground in light of the very broad sweep of Reformed thought in the modern world.

struction. The Arminianism under consideration is an Arminianism of the heart as opposed to Arminianism of the head—a distinction introduced by Reformed theologian Alan Sell in *The Great Debate: Calvinism, Arminianism, and Salvation.*[4] Arminianism of the head is an Enlightenment-based emphasis on free will that it is most often found in liberal Protestant circles (even among liberalized Reformed people).[5] Its hallmark is an optimistic anthropology that denies total depravity and the absolute necessity of supernatural grace for salvation. It is optimistic about the ability of autonomous human beings to exercise a good will toward God and their fellow creatures without supernatural prevenient (enabling, assisting) grace; that is, it is Pelagian or at least semi-Pelagian

Arminianism of the heart—the subject of this book—is the original Arminianism of Arminius, Wesley and their evangelical heirs. Arminians of the heart emphatically do not deny total depravity (even if they prefer another term to denote human spiritual helplessness) or the absolute necessity of supernatural grace for even the first exercise of a good will toward God. Arminians of the heart are the true Arminians because they are faithful to the basic impulses of Arminius and his first followers as opposed to the later Remonstrants (who wandered away from Arminius's teachings into early liberal theology) and modern Arminians of the head who glorify reason and freedom over divine revelation and supernatural grace.

Synergism and *monergism* are terms with many shades of meaning. Both are essential theological concepts in this discussion, but both apply to wider spheres than Arminianism and Calvinism. Synergism is any theological belief in free human participation in salvation. Its heretical forms in Christian theology are Pelagianism and semi-Pelagianism. The former denies original sin and elevates natural and moral human ability to live spiritually fulfilled lives. The latter embraces a modified version of original sin but believes that humans have the ability, even in their natural or fallen state, to initiate sal-

---

[4]Alan P. F. Sell, *The Great Debate: Calvinism, Arminianism, and Salvation* (Grand Rapids: Baker, 1983).

[5]Liberal theology is notoriously difficult to define, but here it means any theology that allows maximal acknowledgment of the claims of modernity within Christian theology, especially by affirming a positive view of humanity's condition and by a tendency to deny or seriously weaken the traditional supernaturalism of Christian thought. For a detailed account of liberal theology see chapter two in Stanley J. Grenz and Roger E. Olson, *20th-Century Theology* (Downers Grove, Ill.: InterVarsity Press, 1992).

vation by exercising a good will toward God.[6] When conservative theologians declare that synergism is a heresy, they are usually referring to these two Pelagian forms of synergism. Classical Arminians agree. This is a major theme of this book. Contrary to confused critics, classical Arminianism is neither Pelagian nor semi-Pelagian! But it *is* synergistic. Arminianism is *evangelical synergism* as opposed to heretical, humanistic synergism. The term *synergism* will be used throughout this book, and the context will make clear what type of synergism is meant. When Arminian synergism is referred to, I am referring to evangelical synergism, which affirms the prevenience of grace to every human exercise of a good will toward God, including simple nonresistance to the saving work of Christ.

Monergism is also a broad and sometimes confusing term. Its broadest sense points to God as the all-determining reality, which means that everything in nature and history is under the direct control of God. It does not necessarily imply that God causes all things directly, but it does necessarily imply that nothing can happen that is contrary to the will of God, and that God is intimately involved (even if working through secondary causes) in everything, so all of nature and history reflect God's primary will. Thus, monergism is often taken to mean that even the Fall of humanity in the primeval garden was planned and directed by God.[7] (Synergism of all varieties

---

[6]The whole history of Pelagianism and semi-Pelagianism is recounted in Rebecca Harden Weaver, *Divine Grace and Human Agency* (Macon, Ga.: Mercer University Press, 1996). I accept Weaver's treatment of these concepts because she is faithful to the original sources and consistent with most other authoritative contemporary sources on the history and development of these movements.

[7]Admittedly, some theologians who claim the label *monergist* nuance the claim that the Fall was foreordained by God. Calvinist theologian R. C. Sproul makes a point of this in (among other books) *Chosen by God* (Wheaton, Ill.: Tyndale House, 1988). That Sproul is a monergist few would deny. According to him and some other Calvinists God foreordained the Fall "in the sense that he chose to allow it, but not in the sense that he chose to coerce it" (p. 97). Many (if not most) Calvinists, however, would follow Calvin in saying that God foreordained the Fall in a sense greater than merely permitting or allowing it. (See Calvin's *Institutes of the Christian Religion* 3.23.8.) One does not have to say that God coerced the Fall to say that God foreordained it. As will be seen later in this book many Calvinists believe God willed the Fall and rendered it certain but did not cause it. The great American Calvinist theologian Charles Hodge affirmed the efficacious nature of all God's decrees (including God's decree to permit the Fall) in the first volume of his *Systematic Theology* (Grand Rapids: Eerdmans, 1973). There he emphasized that although God's eternal decree to permit the Fall does not make God the author of evil it does render it certain. Arminians wonder how that works; if God willed the Fall, decreed it and rendered it certain (even by "efficacious permission") how is God not the author of sin? Of the Fall and all events Hodge wrote, "All events embraced in the purpose of God are equally certain, whether He has determined to bring them to pass by his own power,

generally rejects this and traces the Fall to a risk God took in creation that resulted in the misuse of humanity's free will.) Monergism especially means that God is the sole determining agency in salvation. There is no coopera- tion between God and the person being saved that is not already deter- mined by God working in the person through, for example, regenerating grace. Monergism is larger than Calvinism; Martin Luther was a monergist (even if inconsistently). So was Augustine, in his later writings. Some Cath- olic thinkers have been monergists, although Catholic theology tends to fa- vor a form of synergism. In this book I use *monergism* to denote God's all- determining will and power to the exclusion of free human cooperation or resistance.

The debate between Calvinism and Arminianism is often said to be based on a disagreement about predestination and free will. That is the common, almost folkloric myth about this entire subject. At a more polemical level, some say the disagreement is more about grace (Calvinism) and good works (Arminianism). Arminians take umbrage at that! They affirm grace just as emphatically as any other branch of Christianity, and more so than some. But Arminians also affirm predestination, just as many Calvinists affirm free will in some sense. Throughout this book an attempt will be made to straighten out some of the misuses of concepts and terms that plague the conversations between Calvinists and Arminians. People who say that Cal- vinists teach predestination and deny free will, and that Arminians deny predestination and teach free will are simply wrong. Both teach both! They interpret them differently. Arminians believe in election and predestina- tion—because the Bible teaches them. These are good biblical truths that cannot be discarded. And Calvinists generally teach free will (although some are less comfortable with the term than others).

What Arminians deny is not predestination but *unconditional* predestina- tion; they embrace conditional predestination based on God's foreknowl- edge of who will freely respond positively to God's gracious offer of salvation and the prevenient enablement to accept it. Calvinists deny that free will en-

---

or simply to permit their occurrence through the agency of his creatures. . . . Some things He purposes to do, others He decrees to permit to be done" (p. 541). In any case, whether God foreordains the Fall in some greater sense than mere permission (as in Calvin) or foreordains to permit the Fall with efficacious permission, for monergists God plans and renders the Fall certain. The effect seems to be that Adam and Eve were predestined by God to sin and all of humanity with them. Arminians fear that a good and necessary consequence of that view is that God is the author of sin.

tails the ability of a person to do other than what he or she in fact does. Insofar as they use the term *free will* positively, Calvinists mean what philosophers call compatibilist free will—free will that is compatible with determination. Free will is simply doing what someone wants to do even if that is determined by some force internal or external to the person willing. Of course, Calvinists do not think the Arminian account of predestination is adequate, and Arminians do not think Calvinists' account of free will is adequate. But it is simply wrong to say that either group denies either concept! Here, then, when *free will* is used, it will be modified by either *compatibilist* or *noncompatibilist* (or *incompatibilist*), depending on the context. (Noncompatibilist free will is the free agency that allows persons to do otherwise than they do; it may also be called libertarian free will. For example, a person may choose freely between pizza or spaghetti for dinner [assuming both are available]. If he or she chooses spaghetti, the choice is free in the noncompatibilist sense that pizza could just as well have been chosen. Nothing determined the choice for spaghetti except the decision of the person. Arminians believe such libertarian free will in spiritual matters is a gift of God through prevenient grace—grace that precedes and enables the first stirrings of a good will toward God.) When *predestination* is used, it will be modified by either *conditional* (Arminian form) or *unconditional* (Calvinists form), depending on the context.

The Story of Arminian Theology

I will begin the story of Arminian theology with Arminius and his earliest followers, known as the Remonstrants, and continue with John Wesley and the leading evangelical Methodist theologians of the nineteenth century, and then survey a variety of conservative, classical Arminian Protestants of the twentieth and twenty-first centuries.

First, a reminder and an explanation. Because Arminianism has become such a term of reproach in evangelical theological circles, many Arminians do not use that label. I once informed a leading evangelical theologian that his newly published systematic theology is thoroughly Arminian even though he never uses the term. His response was, "Yes, but don't tell anyone!" Several (possibly many) twentieth- and twenty-first-century theological books are completely compatible with classical Arminianism, and some are even informed by Arminius's own theology without ever mentioning Arminianism. Two very influential evangelical Methodist theologians quite vehemently deny that they are Arminians even though historically it is widely said that all Methodists are Arminians! Why? Because they do not want to be thought of as somehow less than fully biblical and evangelical. Some critics have managed to convince some Arminians that Arminianism is heterodox—less than fully orthodox or biblical. They have so successfully equated it with semi-Pelagianism (if not outright Pelagianism) that even many Methodist, Holiness and Pentecostal evangelicals do not want to wear the Arminian label.

The point is that especially in the last half century, since the rise of post-fundamentalist evangelicalism (whose theology is largely dominated by Calvinism), Arminians have struggled for respectability within the wider evangelical scholarly and theological world, and some have simply given up on the term itself. It is not uncommon to hear Arminians describe themselves as "moderately Reformed" in order to ingratiate themselves to the movers and shakers of the evangelical movement. To declare oneself Arminian is to invite a barrage of questions (or merely quiet suspicions) about heresy. Many uninformed evangelical leaders simply take it for granted that Arminians do not believe in the absolute necessity of supernatural grace for salvation. Some evangelicals have openly declared that if evangelical Arminians are not already in heresy, they are headed there. One leading evangelical apologist publicly stated that Arminians are Christians, but "just barely." An influential evangelical theologian suggested that satanic deception may lie at the root of Arminianism. Therefore, even though some of my sources lack the explicit Arminian label, all are indeed Arminian.

Arminius. The root source of all Arminian theology is Jacob Arminius himself. The three volumes of his collected works have been in almost continuous publication in English for over a century.[8] They contain occasional speeches, commentaries and letters. These writings are not a systematic theology, although some of Arminius's lengthier treatises cover a great deal of theological ground. Almost all of his writings were composed in the heat of controversy; he often was under attack by critics and leaders of the Dutch state and church, who demanded that he explain himself. His famous debate with his Calvinist colleague Franciscus Gomarus at the University of

---

[8]James Arminius, *The Works of James Arminius,* London ed., trans. James Nichols and William Nichols, 3 vols. (Grand Rapids: Baker, 1996). This Baker edition is a republication, with an introduction by Arminius scholar Carl Bangs, of the London translation and edition published in 1825, 1828 and 1875. All Arminius quotations in this book are from this edition and will be designated simply as *Works* with volume and page numbers.

Leiden lies at the root of much of this controversy. Arminius was accused of all kinds of heresies, but charges of heresy never stuck to him at any official inquiry. Ludicrous charges of being a secret agent of the pope and the Spanish Jesuits, and even the Spanish government (the United Provinces had recently liberated themselves from Spanish Catholic domination), swirled around him. None were true. Arminius died at the height of the controversy in 1609, and his followers, the Remonstrants, picked up where he left off, attempting to broaden the theological norms of the state church of the United Provinces to allow for evangelical synergism.[9]

Arminius did not believe he was introducing anything new to Christian theology. Whether he in fact did is debatable. He explicitly appealed to the early church fathers, used medieval theological methods and conclusions, and pointed to Protestant synergists before himself. His followers made clear that Melanchthon, an orthodox Lutheran leader, and other Lutherans held similar if not identical views. Although he did not mention the Catholic reformer Erasmus by name, it is clear that Arminius's theology was similar to his. Also the sixteenth-century Anabaptist leaders Balthasar Hubmaier and Menno Simons presented synergistic theologies that foreshadowed Arminius's. Arminius's most important theological works include his "Declaration of Sentiments," "Modest Examination of Dr. Perkins's Pamphlet," "Examination of the Theses of Dr. F. Gomarus Respecting Predestination," "A Letter to Hippolytus A Collibus," and "Certain Articles to Be Diligently Examined and Weighed."

Arminius's relationship to Arminianism should be treated much as is Calvin's relationship to Calvinism. Not every Calvinist agrees entirely with everything found in Calvin, and Calvinists often debate Calvin's meaning. After Calvin's death, Calvinism broadened and now includes real diversity. Among Calvin's followers we find supralapsarians and infralapsarians (debating the order of the divine decrees in relation to predestination), and disagreements about the atonement and other weighty matters related to salvation. Nevertheless, all look back to Calvin as their common root and strive to be faithful to him in spirit if not every detail. So it is with Arminians and Arminius. He is the root, and they are the branches.

---

[9]The story of Arminius's life and career, including the struggle with Gomarus, may be found in Carl Bangs, *Arminius: A Study in the Dutch Reformation* (Grand Rapids: Zondervan, 1985). The story of the post-Arminius Remonstrant struggle up to the fallout from the Synod of Dort (1619) is recounted in A. W. Harrison, *The Beginnings of Arminianism to the Synod of Dort* (London: University of London Press, 1926).

The Remonstrants. After Arminius's untimely death in 1609 at the age of forty-nine and at the height of his career, about forty-five ministers and theologians of the United Provinces formed a front that has come to be called "the Remonstrants." They were given this name after the title of their theological statement known as the Remonstrance, which summarized in a few basic points what Arminius and they believed about salvation, including election and predestination. Among the leaders of this movement was Simon Episcopius (1583-1643), who became the acknowledged leader of the Arminians before and after they were exiled from the United Provinces from 1619 to 1625. Episcopius is probably the author of the main documents of the Remonstrants, and he eventually became the first professor of theology of the Remonstrant seminary founded after they were allowed to return from exile. (That seminary, known as the Remonstrants Seminarium, exists to this day in Holland.) Another important Remonstrant leader was Europe's most influential political scientist and statesman Hugo Grotius (1583-1645), who was imprisoned by the Dutch government after the Synod of Dort, which condemned Arminianism, but he escaped. A later Remonstrant named Philip Limborch (1633-1712) took Arminianism closer to the liberalism of later "Arminianism of the head." Unfortunately, many eighteenth-century critics of Arminianism knew only of Limborch's Arminianism, which was closer to semi-Pelagianism than to the teachings of Arminius himself.

The eighteenth century. From the time of Limborch many Arminians, especially those in the Church of England and in the Congregational churches, blended Arminianism with the new natural religion of the Enlightenment; they became early liberals within Protestantism. In New England John Taylor (1694-1761) and Charles Chauncy (1705-1787) of Boston represented the Arminianism of the head that often leaned perilously close to Pelagianism, universalism and even Arianism (denial of Christ's full deity). The great Puritan preacher and Calvinist theologian Jonathan Edwards (1703-1758) vehemently opposed these men and contributed to the habit of American Calvinists to equate Arminianism with this type of liberalizing modern theology. Without doubt many English and American Arminians (mainly Congregationalists and Baptists) converted to liberal theology and even unitarianism. Whether classical Arminianism is responsible for this is doubtful; these people made a radical departure from Arminius and the early Remonstrants, just as Friedrich Schleiermacher, the father of German liberal theology, departed from Calvin without ever coming under the influence of Arminianism. To his dying day Schleiermacher, who is credited with liberalizing Protestant theology on the European continent, remained a Calvinist of a different order. It is no fairer to blame Arminius or Arminianism for the later Remonstrants' defection than to blame Calvin or Calvinism for Schleiermacher's departure from orthodoxy.

One clear proof that not all Arminians became liberals is John Wesley (1703-1791), who called himself an Arminian and defended Arminianism against accusations that it led to heterodoxy if not outright heresy. He was stung by Calvinists' treatment of Arminianism, and his own response to Calvinism was often too harsh. Because he felt that most critics of Arminianism had little knowledge of it, he wrote in 1778: "Let no man bawl against Arminians til he knows what the term means."[10] In "The Question, 'What Is an Arminian?' Answered by a Lover of Free Grace," Wesley noted that "to say, 'This man is an Arminian,' has the same effect on many hearers, as to say 'This is a mad dog.'"[11] He continued to lay out the essentials of Arminianism and contradicted the popular notion that it is tantamount to Arianism or other heresies. In this and other writings Wesley defended evangelical synergism by emphasizing that the prevenient grace of God is absolutely necessary for salvation. Wesley is a major source of Arminianism of the heart; he never defected from classical, orthodox Protestant belief; in spite of rejecting Calvinism, he affirmed passionately and wholeheartedly justification by grace alone through faith alone because of what Christ has done on the cross. Calvinists often accuse Wesley of defecting from true Protestantism because he underscored sanctification, but even that, according to Wesley, is a work of God within a person that is received by faith alone.[12]

After Wesley's death, most of the leading Arminian theologians were

---

[10]John Wesley, *The Works of John Wesley*, ed. Thomas Jackson, 14 vols. (Grand Rapids: Baker, 1978), 10:360.

[11]Ibid., p. 358.

[12]Wesley's commitment to Protestant orthodoxy has long been a matter of dispute; Calvinists especially (perhaps only) have sometimes accused him of teaching salvation by works. This is based on a misreading of Wesley, whose sermons on "Free Grace," "Working Out Our Own Salvation," "Salvation by Faith" and "Justification by Faith" cannot have been read by them. These are found in the various editions of Wesley's collected works such as *The Works of John Wesley*, ed. Albert C. Outler (Nashville: Abingdon, 1986). The crucial ones may be found in many one-volume collections such as *John Wesley: The Best from All His Works*, ed. Stephen Rost (Nashville: Thomas Nelson, 1989).

his followers. The entire Methodist movement and its offshoots (e.g., the multiform Holiness movement) adopted Wesley's version of Arminian theology, which differed hardly at all from Arminius himself.[13] The first real systematic theologian of Methodism was Wesley's younger contemporary John Fletcher (1729-1785), whose written works fill nine volumes. He produced carefully crafted polemics against Calvinism and for Arminian theology. One of the most influential Arminian theologians of the nineteenth century was British Methodist Richard Watson (1781-1833), whose *Christian Institutes* (1823) provided Methodism with its first authoritative systematic theology text. Watson quoted Arminius freely and clearly considered himself and all Wesleyan Methodists Arminians. He carefully demonstrated the defection of later Remonstrants, such as Limborch, from the true Arminian heritage. Watson's Arminianism provides something of a gold standard for evangelical Arminians even though it is for the most part unavailable today.

The nineteenth century. Other important Methodist and Arminian theologians of the nineteenth century include Thomas Summers (1812-1882) and William Burton Pope (1822-1903). Summers produced *Systematic Theology: A Complete Body of Wesleyan Arminian Divinity,* which became a standard textbook for Arminians in the latter part of the nineteenth century; he was to that era what Watson was to the first half of the century. Like Watson he shows the departures of Limborch and other late Remonstrants from Arminius (and the early Remonstrants) into semi-Pelagianism and liberal theology. He was filled with indignation at evangelical Calvinist theologians of his time who misrepresented Arminianism as if it were heretical: "What ignorance or impudence have those men who charge Arminius with Pelagianism, or any leaning thereto!"[14] Pope contributed the three-volume system of theology *A Compendium of Christian Theology* (1874). He presents a thoroughly Protestant account of Arminian theology that leaves no doubt about his commitment to Reformation theology,

---

[13]It should be noted here that Wesley's fellow evangelist George Whitefield was instrumental in leading a Calvinist Methodist connection (network) in the eighteenth century; it survived into the twentieth century and may still have a few small churches scattered around Great Britain and North America. As a whole, however, Methodism is stamped with Wesley's Arminianism. Wesley taught the possibility of entire sanctification, which is not typical of all Arminians, but it is consistent with the teachings of Arminius himself, who interpreted Romans 7 as reflecting Paul's preconversion experience of war between the flesh and the spirit.

[14]Thomas O. Summers, *Systematic Theology: A Complete Body of Wesleyan Arminian Divinity* (Nashville: Publishing House of the Methodist Episcopal Church, South, 1888), 2:34.

including salvation by grace alone through faith alone. He explores the nature of prevenient grace more fully and deeply than any other Arminian theologian before him or during his lifetime.

One of the more controversial Arminian theologians of the nineteenth century was Methodist systematician John Miley (1813-1895), whose *Systematic Theology* (1893) provoked Princeton Calvinist theologian B. B. Warfield into publishing a lengthy attack. Miley introduced a somewhat liberalizing tendency into Wesleyan Arminian theology, although it is extremely mild by comparison with the Arminians of the head who often fell headlong into deism, unitarianism and outright liberal theology. Though he modified some traditional Arminian positions in a more modern direction, Miley remained an evangelical Arminian. In some ways he represents a bridge between conservative, evangelical Arminianism (Arminius, Wesley, Watson, Pope and Summers) and later mainline, liberalized Methodist theology in the twentieth century (L. Harold DeWolf). But Miley firmly held onto the supremacy of Scripture and always argued from the Bible in staking out his theological positions. He affirmed original sin, including "native depravity" (helplessness in spiritual matters), while rejecting "native demerit" (inherited guilt). He argued for the governmental theory of the atonement, harking back to Hugo Grotius (not all Arminians adopted this view). And Miley defined justification simply as forgiveness rather than as imputation of Christ's active and passive obedience (righteousness). Some of Warfield's criticisms of Miley were valid, but they were stated in such an extreme way as to raise questions about Warfield's own generosity of interpretation and treatment of fellow Christians. Many twentieth-century Calvinists know little about Arminianism except what they read in nineteenth-century Calvinist theologians Charles Hodge and B. B. Warfield. Both were vitriolic critics who could not bring themselves to see any good in Arminianism. And they blamed it for every possible evil consequence they could see it possibly having.

Before leaving the nineteenth century behind in this telling of Arminianism's story, it is essential to stop and briefly discuss the theology of revivalist, theologian and college president Charles Finney (1792-1875). Finney's career is one of the most fascinating in all of modern church history. He was an attorney who converted to evangelical Christianity, only to become the foremost revivalist of the so-called Second Great Awakening.[15]

---

[15]This depends a great deal on how we define the Second Great Awakening. A narrow definition limits it to the first couple decades of the nineteenth century and sees it as centering

Finney became president of Oberlin College in Ohio in 1835 and published a series of influential lectures on revival and on systematic theology. His *Lectures on Systematic Theology* was published first in 1846 with later enlarged editions following. Finney rejected high Calvinism in favor of a vulgarized version of Arminianism that is closer to semi-Pelagianism. His legacy in American popular religion is profound. He denied original sin, except as a misery that has fallen on the majority of humanity and is passed on through bad examples ("aggravated temptation"). He believed that every person has the ability and responsibility, apart from any special assistance of divine grace (prevenient grace) other than enlightenment and persuasion, to freely accepting the forgiving grace of God through repentance and obedience to the revealed moral government of God. He wrote that "There is no degree of spiritual attainment required of us, that may not be reached directly or indirectly by right willing," and "The moral government of God everywhere assumes and implies the liberty of the human will, and the natural ability of men to obey God."[16]

Finney vulgarized Arminian theology by denying something Arminius, Wesley and all the faithful Arminians before him had affirmed and protected as precious to the gospel itself—human moral inability in spiritual matters, and the absolute necessity of supernatural prevenient grace for any right response to God, including the first stirrings of a good will toward God. According to Finney, in distinction to classical Arminianism (but similar to Limborch's later Remonstrantism), the only work of God necessary for the exercise of a good will toward God and obedience to God's will is the Holy Spirit's illumination of human reason, which is clouded by self-interest and is in a state of misery due to the common selfishness of humanity: "The Spirit takes the things of Christ and shows them to the soul. The truth is employed, or it is truth which must be employed, as an instrument to induce a change of choice."[17] Arminius, Wesley and classical Arminians in general affirmed inherited total depravity as utter helplessness apart from a supernatural awakening called prevenient grace. But Finney denied the need for prevenient grace. For him, reason, developed by the Holy Spirit, turns the

---

solely around the revivals at Yale College and along the Virginia and Kentucky frontiers (e.g., the famous Cane Ridge Revival in Kentucky in 1801). A broader definition carries it up through Finney's revivals in New England and New York in the 1820s through the 1830s.

[16]Charles Finney, *Finney's Systematic Theology*, ed. J. H. Fairchild, abridg. ed. (Minneapolis: Bethany Fellowship, 1976), pp. 299, 261.

[17]Ibid., p. 224.

heart toward God. He labeled the classical Arminian doctrine of gracious ability (ability to exercise a good will toward God bestowed by the Holy Spirit through prevenient grace) an "absurdity."[18]

Unfortunately, Calvinists tend to look to Finney as either the model of a true Arminian or the end point of the Arminian theological trajectory. Both are wrong. Classical Arminians adore Finney for his revivalistic passion while deploring him for his bad theology. Finney himself said of Jonathan Edwards, "Edwards I revere; his blunders I deplore."[19] An evangelical classical Arminian might say "Finney I revere; his blunders I deplore."[20]

The twentieth century. The twentieth century witnessed the demise of evangelical synergism among the mainline denominations, including Methodism, as they fell into liberal theology. That Arminianism does not inexorably lead there, however, is proven by the rise of conservative forms of Arminianism among Nazarenes (an evangelical offshoot of Methodism), Pentecostals, Baptists, Churches of Christ and other evangelical groups. However, many of these twentieth-century Arminians neglect or even reject the label Arminian for a variety of reasons, not least of which is Calvinists' success in tarring it with the colors of Finney and Arminians of the head, such as the later Remonstrants. One twentieth-century theologian who held onto the label was Church of the Nazarene leader H. Orton Wiley (1877-1961), who produced the three-volume *Christian Theology* and a one-volume summary of Christian doctrine. Wiley's is a particularly pure form of classical Arminianism with the addition of Wesleyan perfectionism (which not all Arminians accept). Every good, including the first inclinations of the heart toward God, is attributed to God's grace alone. Like Watson, Summers, Pope and Miley, Wiley insists on a distinction between semi-Pelagianism and true Arminianism, and demonstrates the difference in his own doctrinal statements. Wiley's theology became the gold standard for theological education in the Church of the Nazarene and other Holiness denominations during the twentieth century.

---

[18]Ibid., p. 278.

[19]Ibid., p. 269.

[20]No doubt some admirers of Finney will find this account of his theology too severe while many Reformed critics will find it too generous. The problem is that Finney was not entirely consistent in his explanations of sin and salvation; on some occasions he verged closer to semi-Pelagianism and on other occasions he seemed more willing to affirm the divine initiative in salvation. Overall and in general, however, I find Finney's account of sin and salvation closer to semi-Pelagianism than to classical Arminianism for the reasons given here.

Another twentieth-century Arminian theologian whose work power-fully demonstrates the orthodoxy of classical Arminianism is evangelical Methodist Thomas Oden. Oden does not accept the label Arminian for himself or his theology because he prefers his own appellation *paleo-ortho-doxy*. He appeals to the consensus of the early church fathers. But so did Arminius and Wesley! Oden's *The Transforming Power of Grace* (1993) is a gem of Arminian soteriology; it is the first book I recommend to those wanting a systematic account of true Arminian theology. Unfortunately, Oden does not regard it as such! However, Oden's classical Arminianism is manifest in his enthusiastic endorsement of Arminius's theology as a res-toration of the early Christian consensus about salvation and in such state-ments as this:

> If God absolutely and pretemporally decrees that particular persons shall be saved and others damned, apart from any cooperation of human freedom, then God cannot in any sense intend that all shall be saved, as 1 Timothy 4:10 declares. The promise of glory is conditional on grace being received by faith active in love.[21]

Oden has also produced the massive three-volume *Systematic Theology*, which reconstructs the early Christian doctrinal consensus and is com-pletely consistent with Arminius's own theology. Oden's debt to Arminius and Wesley is beyond question.

Other twentieth-century Arminian theologians (some of whom do not wish to be called Arminian) include Baptists Dale Moody, Stanley Grenz, Clark Pinnock and H. Leroy Forlines; Church of Christ theologian Jack Cot-trell; and Methodists I. Howard Marshall and Jerry Walls. I consider it a great tragedy and travesty that a historical heritage such as Arminianism is routinely being denied by its own adherents out of political necessity. I have no doubt that some administrators of evangelical organizations not specifi-cally committed to Calvinism tend to look down on Arminianism and on Arminians as "theologically shallow" and on a heretical trajectory. Under the influence of a leading evangelical Calvinist statesman, an evangelical college president of the Holiness heritage declared himself a "recovering Arminian!" An influential evangelical Calvinist publication denied the very existence of "evangelical" Arminians and labeled that an oxymoron. Under this kind of blistering if ignorant calumny it is no wonder that the term

---

[21]Thomas C. Oden, *The Transforming Power of Grace* (Nashville: Abingdon, 1993), p. 135.

Arminianism is not used even by its most passionate proponents! Nevertheless, Arminianism lives on, and Arminian theology continues to be done in
a variety of denominational circles.

A Brief Overview of Arminian Theology

One of the most prevalent myths spread by some Calvinists about Arminianism is that it is the most popular type of theology in evangelical pulpits
and pews. My experience contradicts this belief. Much depends on how we
regard Arminian theology. The Calvinist critics would be correct if Arminianism were semi-Pelagianism. But it is not, as I hope to show. The gospel
preached and the doctrine of salvation taught in most evangelical pulpits
and lecterns, and believed in most evangelical pews, is not classical Arminianism but semi-Pelagianism if not outright Pelagianism. What's the difference? Nazarene theologian Wiley correctly defines semi-Pelagianism by
saying, "It held that there was sufficient power remaining in the depraved
will to initiate or set in motion the beginnings of salvation but not enough
to bring it to completion. This must be done by divine grace."[22] This ancient heresy stems from the teachings of the so-called Massilians, led especially by John Cassian (d. A.D. 433), who tried to build a bridge between
Pelagianism, which denied original sin, and Augustine, who argued for
unconditional election on the ground that all of Adam's descendants are
born spiritually dead and guilty of Adam's sin. Cassian believed that people are capable of exercising a good will toward God even apart from any
infusion of supernatural grace. This was condemned by the Second Council of Orange in 529 (without endorsement of Augustine's strong doctrine
of predestination).

Semi-Pelagianism became the popular theology of the Roman Catholic
church in the centuries leading up to the Protestant Reformation; it was
roundly rejected by all the Reformers except the so-called rationalists or an-
titrinitarians, such as Faustus Socinus. Some Calvinists adopted the practice
of referring to every theology that fell short of high Calvinism (TULIP) as
semi-Pelagian. This, however, is incorrect. Today, semi-Pelagianism is the
default theology of most American evangelical Christians.[23] This is revealed
in the popularity of clichés such as "If you'll take one step toward God, he'll

---

[22]H. Orton Wiley, *Christian Theology* (Kansas City, Mo.: Beacon Hill, 1941), 2:103.
[23]I cannot say the same of evangelical Christians in other countries, because I do not know
enough about them to make such a claim.

come the rest of the way toward you," and "God votes for you, Satan votes against you, and you get the deciding vote," coupled with the almost total neglect of human depravity and helplessness in spiritual matters.

Arminianism is almost totally unknown, let alone believed, in popular evangelical Christianity. One purpose of this book is to overcome this deficit. One overriding myth about Arminianism is that Arminian theology is tantamount to semi-Pelagianism. This will be refuted in the process of refuting several other myths that deal with the human condition and salvation. Here only the briefest overview of the Arminian point of view will be provided as a foretaste of what is to come.

First, it is important to understand that Arminianism does not have a distinctive doctrine or point of view about everything in Christianity. There is no special Arminian doctrine of Scripture. Arminians of the heart—evangelical Arminians—believe in Scripture and have the same range of opinions about its details as Calvinists do. Some Arminians believe in biblical inerrancy and some do not. All evangelical Arminians are committed to the Bible's supernatural inspiration and authority over all matters of faith and practice. Likewise, there is no distinctive Arminian ecclesiology or eschatology; Arminians reflect the same spectrum of interpretations as do other Christians. A popular myth promoted by some Calvinists is that all Arminian theologians accept the governmental theory of the atonement and reject the penal-substitution theory. That is simply false. Arminians believe in the Trinity, the deity and humanity of Jesus Christ, the depravity of humanity due to the primeval Fall, salvation by grace alone through faith alone, and all other essential Protestant beliefs. Justification as imputed righteousness is affirmed by classical Arminians following Arminius himself. The distinctive doctrines of Arminianism have to do with God's sovereignty over history and salvation; providence and predestination are the two key doctrines where Arminians part company with classical Calvinists

There's no better starting place to examine the issues of providence and predestination than the Remonstrance itself. It is the foundational document of classical Arminianism (beyond Arminius's writings). The Remonstrance was prepared by forty-three or so (the exact number is debated) Dutch Reformed pastors and theologians after Arminius's death in 1609. It was presented in 1610 to a conference of church and state leaders at Gouda, Holland, to explain Arminian doctrine. It focuses mainly on issues of salvation and especially predestination. Various versions of the Remonstrance (from which the Remonstrants got their name) exist. We will use an English translation of the Latin original provided in somewhat condensed form by English scholar of Arminianism A. W. Harrison:

1. That God, by an eternal and unchangeable decree in Christ before the world was, determined to elect from the fallen and sinning race to everlasting life those who through His grace believe in Jesus Christ and persevere in faith and obedience; and, on the contrary, had resolved to reject the unconverted and unbelievers to everlasting damnation (John iii, 36).

2. That, in consequence of this, Christ the Saviour of the world died for all and every man, so that He obtained, by the death on the cross, reconciliation and pardon for sin for all men; in such manner, however, that none but the faithful actually enjoyed the same (John iii, 16 ; I John ii, 2).

3. That man could not obtain saving faith of himself or by the strength of his own free will, but stood in need of God's grace through Christ to be renewed in thought and will (John xv, 5).

4. That this grace was the cause of the beginning, progress and completion of man's salvation; insomuch that none could believe nor persevere in faith without this co-operating grace, and consequently that all good works must be ascribed to the grace of God in Christ. As to the manner of the operation of that grace, however, it is not irresistible (Acts vii, 51).

5. That true believers had sufficient strength through the Divine grace to fight against Satan, sin, the world, their own flesh, and get the victory over them; but whether by negligence they might not apostatize from the true Faith, lose the happiness of a good conscience and forfeit that grace needed to be more fully inquired into according to Holy Writ.[24]

Notice that the Remonstrants, like Arminius before, did not take any stand on the question of the eternal security of believers. That is, they left open the question of whether a truly saved person could fall from grace or not. They also did not follow the pattern of TULIP. Though the fivefold pattern of expressing Calvinist belief was developed later, the denial of the three middle points is quite clear in the Remonstrance. However, contrary

---

[24]The Remonstrance, in Harrison *Beginnings of Arminianism*, pp. 150-51.

to popular thought about Arminianism (especially among Calvinists), neither Arminius nor the Remonstrants denied total depravity; they affirmed it. Of course the Remonstrance is not a complete statement of Arminian doctrine, but it addresses its essence well. Beyond what it says lies a realm of interpretation where Arminians sometimes disagree among themselves. Nevertheless, a general Arminian consensus exists, and that is what this brief overview will explain, drawing heavily on Nazarene theologian Wiley, who drew heavily on Arminius, Wesley and the leading nineteenth-century Methodist theologians mentioned earlier.

Arminianism teaches that all humans are born morally and spiritual depraved, and helpless to do anything good or worthy in God's sight without a special infusion of God's grace to overcome the affects of original sin. "Not only are all men born under the penalty of death, as a consequence of sin, but they are born with a depraved nature also, which in contradistinction to the legal aspect of penalty, is generally termed inbred sin or inherited depravity."[25] Classical Arminianism agrees with Protestant orthodoxy in general that the unity of the human race in sin results in all being born "children of wrath." However, Arminians believe that Christ's death on the cross provides a universal remedy for the guilt of inherited sin so that it is not imputed to infants for Christ's sake. This is how Arminians, in agreement with Anabaptists, such as Mennonites, interpret the universalistic passages of the New Testament such as Romans 5, where all are said to be included under sin just as all are included in redemption through Christ. It is also the Arminian interpretation of 1 Timothy 4:10, which indicates two salvations through Christ: one universal for all people and one especially for all who believe. Arminian belief in general redemption is not universal salvation; it is universal redemption from Adam's sin. Thus, in Arminian theology all children who die before reaching the age of awakening of conscience and falling into actual sin (as opposed to inbred sin) are considered innocent by God and are taken to paradise. Among those who commit actual sins only those who repent and believe have Christ as Savior.

Arminianism regards original sin primarily as a moral depravity that results from deprivation of the image of God; it is the loss of power to avoid actual sin. "Depravity is total in that it affects the entire being of man."[26] This means that all people are born with alienated affections, darkened in-

---

[25]Wiley, *Christian Theology*, 2:98.
[26]Ibid., p. 128.

tellect and perverted will.[27] There is both a universal cure and a more particular remedy for this condition; Christ's atoning death on the cross removed the penalty of original sin and released into humanity a new impulse that begins to reverse the depravity with which they all come into the world. Christ is the new Adam (Rom 5) who is a new head of the race; he came not only to save some but to provide a new start for all. A measure of prevenient grace extends through Christ to every person born (Jn 1).

> Thus the true Arminian position admits the full penalty of sin, and consequently neither minifies *[sic]* the exceeding sinfulness of sin, nor holds lightly the atoning work of our Lord Jesus Christ. It does so, however, not by denying the full force of the penalty, as do the semi-Pelagians, but by magnifying the sufficiency of the atonement, and the consequent communication of prevenient grace to all men through the headship of the last Adam.[28]

Christ's headship is coextensive with Adam's, but people must accept (by not resisting) this grace of Christ in order fully to benefit from it.

> Man is condemned solely for his own transgressions. The free gift removed the original condemnation and abounds unto many offenses. Man becomes amenable for the depravity of his own heart, only when rejecting the remedy for it, he consciously ratifies it as his own, with all its penal consequences.[29]

Inherited depravity includes bondage of the will to sin, which is only overcome by supernatural, prevenient grace. This grace begins to work in everyone through Christ's sacrifice (and the Holy Spirit sent into the world by Christ), but it comes in special power through the proclamation of the gospel. Wiley, following Pope and other Arminian theologians, calls the human condition—because of inherited sin—"impotence to the good," and he rejects any possibility of spiritual goodness apart from the special grace of Christ prevening.

Because God is love (Jn 3:16; 1 Jn 4:8) and does not want anyone to perish but all to come to repentance (1 Tim 2:4; 2 Pet 3:9), the atoning death of Christ is universal; some of its benefits are automatically extended to all (e.g., release from the condemnation of Adam's sin) and all of its benefits are for everyone who accepts them (e.g., forgiveness of actual sins and imputation of righteousness).

---

[27]Ibid., p. 129. In this belief, Wiley followed John Fletcher.
[28]Ibid., pp. 132-33.
[29]Ibid., p. 135.

The atonement is universal. This does not mean that all mankind will be unconditionally saved, but that the sacrificial offering of Christ so far satisfied the claims of the divine law as to make salvation a possibility for all. Redemption is therefore universal or general in the provisional sense, but special or conditional in its application to the individual.[30]

Only those will be saved, however, who are predestined by God to eternal salvation. They are the elect. Who is included in the elect? All who God foresees will accept his offer of salvation through Christ by not resisting the grace that extends to them through the cross and the gospel. Thus, predestination is conditional rather than unconditional; God's electing foreknowledge is caused by the faith of the elect.

> In opposition to this [Calvinist scheme] Arminianism holds that predestination is the gracious purpose of God to save mankind from utter ruin. It is not an arbitrary, indiscriminate act of God intended to secure the salvation of so many and no more. It includes provisionally, all men in its scope, and is conditioned solely on faith in Jesus Christ.[31]

The Holy Spirit works on the hearts and minds of all people to some extent, gives them some awareness of God's expectations and provision, and calls them to repentance and faith. Thus, "God's Word is in some sense universally uttered, even when not recorded in a written language." "Those who hear the proclamation and accept the call are known in the Scriptures as the elect."[32] The reprobate are those who resist the call of God.

A crucial Arminian doctrine is prevenient grace, which Calvinists also believe, but Arminians interpret it differently. Prevenient grace is simply the convicting, calling, enlightening and enabling grace of God that goes before conversion and makes repentance and faith possible. Calvinists interpret it as irresistible and effectual; the person in whom it works *will* repent and believe unto salvation. Arminians interpret it as resistible; people are always able to resist the grace of God, as Scripture warns (Acts 7:51). But without prevenient grace, they will inevitably and inexorably resist God's will because of their slavery to sin.

> Prevenient grace, as the term implies, is that grace which "goes before" or prepares the soul for entrance into the initial state of salvation. It is the prepara-

---

[30]Ibid., p. 295.
[31]Ibid., p. 337.
[32]Ibid., pp. 341, 343.

tory grace of the Holy Spirit exercised toward man helpless in sin. As it
respects the guilty, it may be considered mercy; as it respects the impotent, it
is enabling power. It may be defined, therefore, as that manifestation of the
divine influence which precedes the full regenerate life.[33]

In some sense then, Arminians, like Calvinists, believe that regeneration
precedes conversion; repentance and faith are only possible because the
old nature is being overcome by the Spirit of God. The person who receives
the full intensity of prevenient grace (i.e., through the proclamation of the
Word and the corresponding internal calling of God) is no longer dead in
trespasses and sins. However, such a person is not yet fully regenerated. The
bridge between partial regeneration by prevenient grace and full regeneration by the Holy Spirit is *conversion,* which includes repentance and faith.
These are made possible by the gift of God, but they are free responses on
the part of the individual. "The Scriptures represent the Spirit as working
[in conversion] through and with man's concurrence. Divine grace, however, is always given pre-eminence."[34]

The emphasis on the prevenience and preeminence of grace forms common ground between Arminianism and Calvinism. It is what makes Arminian synergism "evangelical." Arminians take with utmost seriousness the
New Testament's emphasis on salvation as a gift of grace that cannot be
earned (Eph 2:8). However, Arminian and Calvinist theologies—like all syn-
ergisms and monergisms—diverge over the role humans play in salvation.
As Wiley notes, prevenient grace does not interfere with the freedom of the
will. It does not bend the will or render the will's response certain. It only
enables the will to make the free choice to either cooperate with or resist
grace. Cooperation does not contribute to salvation, as if God does part and
humans do part; rather cooperation with grace in Arminian theology is simply nonresistance to grace. It is merely deciding to allow grace to do its work
by laying down all attempts at self-justification and self-purification, and admitting that only Christ can save. Nevertheless, God does not make this decision for the individual; it is a decision individuals, under the pressure of
prevenient grace, must make for themselves.

Arminianism holds that salvation is all of grace—every movement of the
soul toward God is initiated by divine grace—but Arminians recognize also
that the cooperation of the human will is necessary because in the last stage

[33]Ibid., p. 346.
[34]Ibid., p. 355.

the free agent decides whether the grace proffered is accepted or rejected.[35]

Classical Arminianism teaches that predestination is simply God's determination (decree) to save through Christ all who freely respond to God's offer of free grace by repenting of sin and believing (trusting) in Christ. It includes God's foreknowledge of who will so respond. It does not include a selection of certain people to salvation, let alone to damnation. Many Arminians make a distinction between election and predestination. Election is corporate—God's determination of Christ to be the Savior of that group of people who repent and believe (Eph 1); predestination is individual—God's foreknowledge of those who will repent and believe (Rom 8:29). Classical Arminianism also teaches that people who respond positively to the grace of God by not resisting it (which involves repenting and trusting in Christ) are born again by the Spirit of God (which is full regeneration), forgiven of all their sins and regarded by God as righteous because of Christ's atoning death for them. None of this is based on any human merit; it is a sheer gift, not imposed but freely received. "The sole ground of justification . . . is the propitiatory work of Christ received by faith," and "the one act of justification when viewed negatively is the forgiveness of sins; when viewed positively, is the acceptance of the believer as righteous [by God]."[36] The only significant difference between classical Arminianism and Calvinism in this doctrine, then, is the role of the individual in receiving the grace of regeneration and justification. As Wiley puts it, salvation "is a work wrought in the souls of men by the efficient operation of the Holy Ghost. The Holy Spirit exerts His regenerating power only on certain conditions, that is, on the conditions of repentance and faith."[37] Thus salvation is conditional, not unconditional; humans play a role and are not passive or controlled by any force, internal or external.

This is where many monergistic critics of Arminianism point the finger and declare Arminian theology to be a system of works salvation, or at least something less than Paul's strong doctrine of salvation as a sheer gift. If it must be freely accepted, they assert, it is earned. Because the act of acceptance is crucial, what is received is not a free gift. Arminians simply cannot understand this claim and its implied accusation. As we will see at several points throughout this book, Arminians have always asserted most emphat-

---

[35]Ibid., p. 356.
[36]Ibid., p. 395, 393.
[37]Ibid., p. 419.

ically that salvation is a free gift; even repentance and faith are only the instrumental causes of salvation and are impossible apart from an internal operation of grace! The only efficient cause of salvation is God's grace through Jesus Christ and the Holy Spirit. The logic of the argument that a gift freely received (in the sense that it could be rejected) is not a free gift boggles the Arminian's mind. But the main reason Arminians reject the Calvinist notion of monergistic salvation, in which God unconditionally elects some to salvation and bends their wills irresistibly, is that it violates the character of God and the nature of a personal relationship. If God saves unconditionally and irresistibly, why doesn't he save all? Appeal to mystery at this point does not satisfy the Arminian mind because the character of God as love showing itself in mercy is at stake. If the humans chosen by God cannot resist having a right relationship with God, what kind of relationship is it? Can a personal relationship be irresistible? Are such predestined persons really persons in such a relationship? These are bedrock questions that cause Arminians— like other synergists—to question every form of monergism, including high Calvinism. The issue is most emphatically not a humanistic vision of autonomous free will, as if Arminians were in love with free agency for its own sake. Any fair-minded reading of Arminius, Wesley or any other classical Arminian will reveal that this is not so. Rather, the issue is the character of God and the nature of personal relationship.

Earlier I noted that not only predestination but also providence provides a point of difference between Arminianism and Calvinism. In brief, Arminians believe in divine sovereignty and providence but interpret it differently from high Calvinists. Arminians regard God as self-limiting in relation to human history. Therefore, much that happens in history is contrary to the perfect antecedent will of God. Arminians affirm that God is in charge of nature and history but deny that God controls *every* event. Arminians deny that God "hides a smiling face" behind the horrors of history. The devil is not "God's devil" or even an instrument of God's providential self-glorification. The Fall was not foreordained by God for some secret purpose. Classical Arminians believe that God foreknows all things, including every evil event, but they reject any notion that God provides "secret impulses" that control even the actions of evil creatures (angelic or human).[38] God's gov-

---

[38]Calvin famously attributed even the sinful and evil acts of wicked people to the secret promptings of God. A careful reading of book 1, chap. 18—"God So Uses the Works of the Ungodly, and So Bends Their Minds to Carry out His Judgments, That He Remains Pure from Every

ernment is comprehensive, but because God limits himself to allow for human free agency (for the sake of genuine relationships that are not manipulated or controlled), it is exercised in different modes. Whatever happens is at least allowed by God, but not everything that happens is positively willed or even rendered certain by God. Thus synergism enters into the Arminian doctrine of providence as well as predestination. God foreknows but does not act alone in history. History is the product of both divine and human agencies. (We should not forget angelic and demonic agencies, either!) Sin especially is neither willed nor governed by God except in the sense that God allows it and limits it. Most importantly, God does not predestine it or render it certain. No better brief expression of the Arminian understanding of providence is possible than that provided by revisionist Reformed theologian Adrio König:

> There are distressingly many things that happen on earth that are not the will of God (Luke 7:30 and every other sin mentioned in the Bible), that are against his will, and that stem from the incomprehensible and senseless sin in which we are born, in which the greater part of mankind lives, and in which Israel persisted, and against which even the "holiest men" (Heid. Cat. q. 114) struggled all their days (David, Peter). God has only one course of action for this and that is to provide for its atonement by having it all crucified and buried with Christ. To try to interpret all these things by means of the concept of a plan of God, creates intolerable difficulties and gives rise to more exceptions than regularities. But the most important objection is that the idea of a plan is against the message of the Bible since God himself becomes incredible if that against which he has fought with power, and for which he sacrificed his only Son, was nevertheless somehow part and parcel of his eternal counsel. So it is better to proceed from the idea that God had a certain goal in mind (the covenant, or the kingdom of God, or the new earth—which are all the same thing viewed from different angles) that he will achieve with us, without us, or even against us.[39]

Stain"—of *Institutes of the Christian Religion* reveals this. There, among other things, Calvin says that "since God's will is said to be the cause of all things, I have made his providence the determinative principle for all human plans and works, not only in order to display its force in the elect, who are ruled by the Holy Spirit, but also to compel the reprobate to obedience" (*Institutes of the Christian Religion* 1.18.2, ed. John T. McNeill, trans. Ford Lewis Battles [Philadelphia: Westminster Press, 1960], p. 232). Arminians believe high Calvinism cannot escape making God the author of sin and evil, and thus impugning his character.

[39]Adrio König, *Here Am I! A Believer's Reflection on God* (Grand Rapids: Eerdmans, 1982), pp. 198-99.

Myths and Misconceptions About Arminianism

The thumbnail sketch of Arminian theology provided in this introduction is a bare beginning. It is just enough to contrast true evangelical Arminianism with its critics' caricatures. And the misinformation and distortion surrounding Arminianism in theological literature is nothing short of appalling. Reformed critics repeatedly misrepresents Arminius and Arminianism as semi-Pelagian. For example, the first edition of Shirley C. Guthrie's *Christian Doctrine*, a widely used textbook of Reformed theology, used Arminius as an example of semi-Pelagianism. After at least one Arminian pointed out the significant differences between his theology and semi-Pelagianism, a 1994 revision of Guthrie's text deleted Arminius's name. But even in the revised edition, the context and a footnote dealing with the Synod of Dort point toward Arminianism as the historical model of semi-Pelagianism. Twenty-five years of damage to Arminius's reputation was not completely undone by the revision. The book *The Five Points of Calvinism* also provides many examples of distorted images of Arminian theology. Calvinist pastor and theologian Edwin H. Palmer explicitly equates Arminianism with semi-Pelagianism, completely ignoring the Arminian doctrine of prevenient grace. He even went so far as to declare that "the Arminian denies the sovereignty of God." He added insult to injury by suggesting throughout that Arminianism is based on rationalism rather than on humble submission to the Word of God.[40] Anyone who reads evangelical Arminian literature sees immediately that Arminians are just as committed to the authority of Scripture as are any other Protestants.[41]

Other examples of misrepresentation of Arminianism abound in theological literature. One of the first issues of *Modern Reformation*, a journal devoted to monergistic theology and led primarily by Calvinists, was devoted to Arminianism. One author states that "Arminianism is not only a departure from historic orthodoxy, but a serious departure from the evangel [gospel] itself."[42] Throughout his vitriolic attack on Arminianism (focused pri-

---

[40]Edwin H. Palmer, *The Five Points of Calvinism* (Grand Rapids: Baker, 1972), pp. 59, 85, 107.

[41]Some Calvinists have accused Wesley of defecting from *sola scriptura*—"scripture alone"—as the norm for all doctrine. This arises from Methodist theologian Albert Outler's description of Wesley's theological method as a "quadrilateral" composed of Scripture, tradition, reason and experience. However, people who read Wesley rather than only his modern interpreters know that Wesley constantly affirmed the supremacy of Scripture over tradition, reason and experience, which were for him secondary authorities.

[42]Kim Riddlebarger, "Fire & Water," *Modern Reformation* 1 (1992): 10. I wonder whether the author even read Miley or only B. B. Warfield, his critic.

marily on Methodist theologian John Miley) the author blames all of Arminianism for the unfortunate wording of one Arminian theologian, ignoring the broad sweep of Arminian history and theology, and falsely attributing to Arminianism beliefs (e.g., the denial of original sin and substitutionary atonement) that he regards as good and necessary consequences of that one theologian's somewhat eccentric point of view.

Several authors in the Arminianism issue of *Modern Reformation* contrast Arminianism with evangelicalism and deny the possibility of evangelical Arminianism. At least one blatantly calls Arminianism a "natural, God-rejecting, self-exalting religion and heresy."[43] Throughout the issue these mostly Calvinist authors (one is a Lutheran) treat Arminianism as the heresy of semi-Pelagianism but never deal with the key doctrine of prevenient grace or quote Arminian theologians' many strong affirmations of the preeminence of grace. The common tendency is to impute to Arminianism every false belief that the authors see lying at the bottom of an imaginary slippery slope. If the same method were used on Calvinism (as some Arminians have), Calvinists would howl in protest. We could argue that the Calvinist God, who predestines some people unconditionally to hell (even if only by decreeing to pass over them in election), is not a God of love but an arbitrary, capricious supreme being concerned only with displaying his own glory—even at the cost of the eternal destruction of souls he created. One principle that ought to be observed by all parties to this debate is *Before you disagree make sure you understand.* In other words, we must make sure that we can describe another's theological position as he or she would describe it before we criticize or condemn. Another guiding principle should be *Do not impute to others beliefs you regard as logically entailed by their beliefs but that they explicitly deny.*

Even allegedly neutral church historians and historical theologians often get Arminianism wrong. One recent example is in the otherwise excellent *Theology in America* by church historian E. Brooks Holifield. He writes: "To the New England clergy, any suggestion that human beings might prepare their own hearts for salvation would have suggested the error of Arminius, who contended that the natural will, aided only by common grace, could accept or reject the divine offer of salvation."[44] This is

---

[43]Alan Maben, "Are You Sure You Like Spurgeon?" *Modern Reformation* 1 (1992): 21. Maben is quoting Charles Spurgeon approvingly.
[44]E. Brooks Holifield, *Theology in America* (New Haven: Yale University Press, 2003), p. 44.

manifestly mistaken; Arminius affirmed the necessity of supernatural assisting (prevenient) grace to unbind the will of the fallen person before
he or she could respond to the gospel. Apart from that (not common
grace, as Holifield says) every child of Adam would automatically reject
the gospel. Listen to Arminius:

> In his lapsed and sinful state, man is not capable, of and by himself, either to
> think, to will, or to do that which is really good; but it is necessary for him to
> be regenerated and renewed in his intellect, affections or will, and in all his
> powers, by God in Christ through the Holy Spirit, that he may be qualified
> rightly to understand, esteem, consider, will, and perform whatever is truly
> good. When he is made a partaker of this regeneration or renovation, I con-
> sider that, since he is delivered from sin, he is capable of thinking, willing, and
> doing that which is good, but yet not without the continued aids of Divine
> grace.[45]

Clearly Arminius (like all classical Arminians afterward) did not believe
common grace alone was sufficient for willing the good. (Common grace is
the universal grace of God that enables civil justice in society in spite of human depravity.) A special infusion of supernatural, regenerating or renovating grace is required for even the first exercise of a good will toward God.
This is so basic to Arminius's theology and to Arminianism that claims such
as Holifield makes, which are very common in theological literature, boggle
the mind.

Perhaps the most egregious example of the very common distortion of
Arminianism in theological literature is found in an Arminian! Henry C.
Thiessen taught theology at Wheaton College for many years and produced the materials for a theological textbook published after his death
under the title *Lectures in Systematic Theology* (1949). Some may wish to attribute the confusion about Arminianism to the book's editor, who ar-
ranged the unpublished materials for publication, but the editor (Thiessen's son) makes that excuse impossible in his preface. Thiessen's account
of election is clearly and unequivocally Arminian: "The Scriptures teach
that election is based on foreknowledge."[46] According to him, God produces salvation in those who respond positively to God's prevenient
grace.[47] These are the elect. Thiessen teaches the classical Arminian posi-

---

[45]Arminius, "A Declaration of the Sentiments of Arminius," *Works*, 1:659-60.
[46]Henry C. Thiessen, *Lectures in Systematic Theology* (Grand Rapids: Eerdmans, 1949), p. 156.
[47]Ibid., p. 157.

tion throughout the volume in every subject touching on soteriology. However, surprisingly, in his chapter on original sin he writes about the "Arminian Theory" and calls it "semi-Pelagianism!"[48] He attributes to it the belief that "man is sick," but not so spiritually damaged as to be unable on his or her own to initiate salvation. In contradiction to this supposed Arminian theory, he lays out as his own what is actually the classical Arminian position![49] Nowhere does he attach the name Arminius or the label Arminianism to his own view—even though it is thoroughly Arminian. Thiessen's book was used as the introductory text in numerous theology courses throughout the evangelical world for many years. As late as 1982 when I first took a full-time teaching position, I inherited Thiessen's book (as course textbook) from the teacher I succeeded, who for years had been using it on beginning theology students in the university. No wonder most evangelicals, including students of theology, pastors and even theologians, are confused about Arminianism!

This Book's Purpose

The purpose of this book is simple and straightforward: to correctly delineate true Arminian theology and to begin to undo the damage that has been done to this theological heritage by both its critics and friends. Because what most people know, or think they know, about Arminianism is largely composed of myths, this book is organized around these misconceptions. However, the thrust of the book is not negative but positive. The affirmations of Arminianism (provided on the first page of each chapter) form the backbone of this book. Even though reasons why Arminians are not Calvinists will be provided, *Arminian Theology* is not a polemic against Calvinism. Nor is it intended so much as a defense of Arminianism as a statement of true Arminian theology. That is why the book is not replete with exegesis. Finally, I am not attempting to convert anyone to Arminianism. The purpose of the book is not persuasion (except to a fair understanding of Arminian theology) but information. I hope that in the future critics of Arminianism will describe Arminianism as its adherents describe it and strictly avoid caricature or misrepresentation, just as they would want others to treat their own theology.

---

[48]Ibid., p. 261.
[49]Ibid., pp. 261-62.

MYTH 1:

Arminian Theology Is the Opposite of Calvinist/Reformed Theology

Jacob Arminius and most of his faithful followers fall into the broad understanding of the Reformed tradition; the common ground between Arminianism and Calvinism is significant.

LIKE ARMINIANISM, *REFORMED* IS A CONTESTED TERM. An extremely narrow definition limits *Reformed* to persons and movements that swear allegiance to the three "symbols of unity"—the Heidelberg Catechism, the Belgic Confession and the Canons of the Synod of Dort. That would exclude, however, the many Presbyterians throughout the world who believe they too are Reformed! It would also exclude Congregationalists, Baptists and many other churches and organizations that claim to be and generally have been thought of as Reformed in their theology. The broadest definition of Reformed theology includes everyone who claims to be Reformed and can demonstrate some historical connection with the Swiss and French wing of the Protestant Reformation—even if his or her theology is a radical revision of Calvin's, Zwingli's and Bucer's theology. The World Alliance of Reformed Churches (WARC) includes many such revisionist groups, including the Remonstrant Brotherhood of the Netherlands (the original Arminian denomination)! Between the narrowest and broadest definitions lie a variety of descriptions of Reformed theology, including any Protestant theologies that stress God's sovereignty, that emphasize Word and Spirit as the twin sources and norms of theology, and that appreciate Calvin as the purest Reformer of the sixteenth century. Lutheran church historians and historical theologians tend to lump virtually all Protestants outside of the Lutheran tradition into the Reformed category. To many Lutherans even the Church of England (Episcopal churches in the United States) and Methodist churches are Reformed. Surely this is stretching the term uncomfortably thin.

Defining categories such as this is notoriously difficult, and there is no central headquarters or agency with the power to make any definition stick for everyone. One example of the problem is the difficulty of locating Arminianism in relation to the Reformed tradition. As should be obvious from this book's introduction, most conservative Calvinists (who tend to view the Reformed tradition as their own to define), tend to reject Arminianism from their heritage. To them Arminianism is to Reformed theology and tradition much as Protestantism is to Roman Catholicism—a departure rather than a branch. This is the approach taken by Reformed historical theologian Richard A. Muller, who is considered an expert on post-Reformation Protestant orthodoxy. In his magisterial work *God, Creation, and Providence in the Thought of Jacob Arminius,* he distances Arminianism from Reformed theology while acknowledging Arminius's education at Geneva under Calvin's successor Theodore Beza, and Arminius's intention of merely broadening the Reformed faith to allow for inclusion of evangelical synergism. Muller's description of Arminius's theology emphasizes its "paradigm shift" from standard Reformed thought to something more akin to Catholic theology.[1] According to Muller, "Arminius's system . . . can only be interpreted as a full-scale alternative to Reformed theology."[2] Muller's reasons will be given and discussed more fully in chapter two, which points to the relative incommensurability of Arminianism and high Calvinism. Suffice it to say here that Muller represents many Reformed scholars who regard God's all-determining and controlling power over history (to the exclusion of any divine self-limitation) as crucial to Reformed thought.

However, I think it is a myth or misconception that Arminianism and Reformed theology, including moderate if not high Calvinism, are at opposite poles from each other on the Christian theological spectrum. Even if Arminianism should not be included under the rubric "Reformed" in the taxonomy of Protestant types, it is not totally incommensurate with the Reformed tradition. Common roots and themes abound; shared emphases are more numerous than most people think. It is unfortunate that so many peo-

---

[1]Richard A. Muller, *God, Creation, and Providence in the Thought of Jacob Arminius* (Grand Rapids: Baker, 1991), p. 271.
[2]Ibid., p. 281.

ple, including pastors and theologians, pit Arminianism and Reformed theology against each other as if they are necessarily at war, portraying them in such a way that only one can be orthodox. One popular Reformed apologist remarked to an audience that in his opinion only one of the two can "honor scripture." I am not implying that both are true at every point. In fact, I reject any hybrid of Arminianism and Calvinism on crucial points of soteriology. Nevertheless, to say that only one honors Scripture is wrong. Neither tradition is the gospel itself; both are fallible attempts to interpret the gospel and Scripture, and both can honor them even if one or the other is wrong at certain points.

Many moderate Reformed theologians now acknowledge Arminianism and Reformed theology as closely related, though not partners. Some Arminian theologians share this perspective even as they disagree with high Calvinism. One example of a Reformed theologian who nods to Arminianism's validity vis-à-vis Reformed faith is Alasdair Heron, who teaches Reformed theology at the University of Erlangen in Germany. In his article "Arminianism" in *The Encyclopedia of Christianity* (1999) Heron concludes that

> the concern of Arminius to look afresh at a doctrine of predestination that had become much too abstract, viewing it in light of Christ and faith, was less well represented by such movements [as the Remonstrants] than by modern Reformed theology itself, though with considerable course corrections.[3]

Reformed theologians to whom Heron is referring (as adjusting the doctrine of predestination along the lines pointed by Arminius) are Karl Barth, whom Heron explicitly mentions, Hendrikus Berkhof and Adrio König. Because they belong to Dutch Reformed denominations, the latter two are most definitely members of the worldwide fraternity of Reformed thinkers. However they have adopted stances with regard to God's sovereignty and human free will that are more consistent with Arminianism than with high Calvinism. The same can be said of Alan P. F. Sell, former theological secretary of the WARC, and the late Lewis B. Smedes of Fuller Theological Seminary. All of these men appeal to God's self-limitation in relation to creation—and especially to human free agency—to explain the covenant relationship between God and his people, and the rise of sin and evil in the

---

[3]Alasdair I. C. Heron, "Arminianism," in *The Encyclopedia of Christianity*, trans. Geoffrey W. Bromiley (Grand Rapids: Eerdmans, 1999), 1:128-29.

world. This certainly represents a different account of Reformed theology than given by Muller. So much depends on how we define Reformed theology! Overall it seems valid to include Arminianism within the broad category of the Reformed family of faith.

Arminius and Reformed Theology

Certainly some Calvinists consider Arminianism a heresy. The Internet is replete with them. All we need do to confirm this is to type *Arminianism* into any search engine and observe all the Calvinist websites that condemn Arminianism as heretical. However, many moderate Calvinists or Reformed thinkers and leaders have opened up to Arminianism and embraced it as a valid expression of Reformed theology. Where do Arminians stand on this issue? Do Arminians consider their theology Reformed? Did Arminius himself consider his theology Reformed? Here we wade into a quagmire of diverse opinions. One famous televangelist declared Calvinism the worst heresy in the history of Christianity. That opinion can certainly be found among some Arminians. Others simply wish to put distance between themselves and all varieties of Calvinism. Others call themselves "moderately Reformed" or even "Calminians"—pointing to a mythical hybrid of Calvinism and Arminianism!

One of the most reliable twentieth-century scholars of Arminianism was Methodist Carl Bangs, who wrote a magisterial theological biography of Arminius titled *Arminius: A Study in the Dutch Reformation* (1985). Bangs grew up in the thick of the Holiness movement. (His sister wrote books on Arminian theology for the Nazarenes.) Nevertheless, in *Arminius* Bangs departed from the popular belief that the Dutch theologian was opposed to everything of Calvinism or Reformed theology, and pointed out his repeated attempts to underscore their common ground. One popular story about Arminius is that he was a committed high Calvinist until he was asked to examine and refute the teachings of a radical Reformer who rejected Calvinist teachings about predestination. According to this account Arminius became persuaded of the truth of Dirk Coornhert's synergistic theology and shook the Calvinist dust off his feet. Bangs dispels that legend as myth or at least as unproven and unprovable. Rather, Arminius never did fully adopt Beza's or Calvin's monergism: "All [the] evidence points to one conclusion: namely, that Arminius was not in agreement with Beza's doctrine of predestination when he undertook his ministry at

Amsterdam; indeed, he probably never had agreed with it."[4] Nevertheless, according to Bangs, Arminius always considered himself Reformed and in the line of the great Swiss and French Reformers Zwingli, Calvin and Bucer. He studied under Calvin's successor Beza in Geneva and was given a letter of recommendation by him to the Reformed church of Amsterdam. It seems highly unlikely that the chief pastor of Geneva and principle of its Reformed academy would not know the theological inclinations of one of his star pupils.

What is the explanation for all this? According to Bangs and some other historians, the Reformed churches of the United Provinces in Arminius's time were generically Protestant rather than rigidly Calvinistic.[5] While they accepted the Heidelberg Catechism as their primary statement of faith, they did not require ministers or theologians to adhere to the tenets of the high Calvinism being developed in Geneva under Beza. Arminius genuinely seems to have been shocked and surprised by the opposition mounted by Calvinists against his evangelical synergism; he was used to a type of Reformed theology that allowed for diverse opinions with regard to the details of salvation. According to Bangs the "older reformers" of the United Provinces were not Calvinists any more than they were Lutherans. Their theology was a generic and perhaps unique blend of the two main wings of Protestantism, and they allowed people to lean one direction (including Melanchthon's synergistic flavor of Lutheranism) or the other (including Beza's fairly extreme Calvinism, known as supralapsarianism). But Franciscus Gomarus, Arminius's colleague at the University of Leiden, claimed that high Calvinism was implied by the doctrinal standards of the Dutch churches and universities, so he launched an attack on the moderates, including Arminius.

At first this campaign to impose high Calvinism was unsuccessful; church and state conferences inquiring into Arminius's theology routinely exonerated him of heterodoxy, until politics began to intrude. Somehow or other Gomarus and other high Calvinists managed to convince the rulers of the United Provinces, and especially the prince Maurice of Nassau, that only their theology provided sure protection against the encroachments of Spanish Catholic influence. (The United Provinces were still involved in a protracted war of liberation against Spain and Catholic domination during

---

[4]Carl Bangs, *Arminius* (Grand Rapids: Zondervan, 1985), p. 141.
[5]Ibid., p. 198.

Arminius's lifetime.)[6] After Arminius's death the government began to interfere more and more in the theological controversy over predestination in the United Provinces and eventually Prince Maurice purged Arminians from governmental positions; one was executed and others were imprisoned. When the national church synod was held at Dort in 1618-1619, the high Calvinist party had the backing of the government. The Remonstrants were excluded from participating, except as defendants; they were condemned as heretics and expelled from their positions; their property was taken away, and they were exiled from the country. As soon as Prince Maurice died in 1625, the high Calvinist party lost its iron grip and the Remonstrants found their way back into the country, where they founded churches and a seminary. The point is that the earlier Dutch Protestant church contained theological diversity; both monergists and synergists were represented in it. Only the power of the prince allowed the monergist party to control the church, and with the power of the state to persecute synergists.

Arminius always thought of himself as Reformed in a broad sense. To his way of thinking high Calvinism was just one branch of Reformed theology; he belonged to another. That did not make him less Reformed. Bangs disagrees with Richard Muller, who argues that Arminius and his theology represent a radical departure from Reformed thought. For Bangs, Arminius and his theology represent a variety of Reformed thought, even if it is outside the mainstream. Arminianism is a correction of Reformed theology rather than a departure from it. "Arminius stands firmly in the tradition of Reformed theology in insisting that salvation is by grace alone and that human ability or merit must be excluded as a cause of salvation. It is faith in Christ alone that places a sinner in the company of the elect."[7] The correction lies in Arminius's rejection of strict monergism, which many have come to equate with Reformed theology itself. In Arminius's mind monergism was not necessary to Reformed theology; he preferred to focus on the common ground he shared with other Reformed thinkers rather than on their points of disagreement. (Although, he was often forced to state his dissenting opinions from the more extreme versions of Calvinism.)

The opinion that Arminius and classical Arminianism are part of the

---

[6]The complicated story of this controversy surrounding Arminius and his followers in the years leading up to the Synod of Dort is masterfully recounted in A. W. Harrison, *The Beginnings of Arminianism to the Synod of Dort* (London: University of London Press, 1926).

[7]Bangs, *Arminius,* p. 198.

greater Reformed tradition and not opposite of Calvinism is shared by many
scholars. Dutch theologian Gerrit Jan Hoenderdal says, "Much Calvinism
can be found in the theology of Arminius; but he tried to be a Calvinist in a
rather independent way."[8] He confirms Bangs's assertion that this was commonly accepted in the Dutch churches and universities before Arminius's
time, but that a certain rigidity had set in to Calvinism during Arminius's career at the University of Leiden.[9] James Luther Adams concurs. According
to him, Arminius retained fundamental features of Calvinism.[10] These include emphasis on the sovereignty of grace as necessary for even the first
stirrings of the heart toward God and stress on salvation as a free gift that
cannot be earned or merited. Donald Lake agrees and says that Arminius
was "in most points a mild Calvinist."[11] Howard Slaatte also agrees. According to him Arminius brought adjustments into Reformed theology; he did
not break away from it. Later Remonstrants, which Slaatte calls "quasi-
Arminians" (almost certainly Philip Limborch), departed from true Arminianism, that held by Arminius and his first generation of followers (Episcopius and the other early Remonstrants). He calls Arminius a "left wing
Calvinist" and asserts that whereas Pelagius was a moralist, Arminius was a
confirmed product of the Protestant reformation.[12] Arminius, Slaatte
rightly avers, only sought to modify the stream of Calvinism:

> True Arminian theology [that is faithful to Arminius] always shows a profound
> respect for the primacy of the faith-related grace of God and the doctrine of
> the sinfulness of man, while at the same time pleading for man's consistent re-
> sponsibility in the saving relationship.[13]

Slaatte puts his finger on the concrete point at which Arminius remained
faithful to the Reformed cause:

> Hence, the responsive factor [in the human person according to Arminius]

---

[8]Gerrit Jan Hoenderdaal, "The Life and Struggle of Arminius in the Dutch Republic," in
Man's Faith and Freedom: The Theological Influence of Jacobus Arminius, ed. Gerald O. McCulloh
(Nashville: Abingdon, 1962), p. 25.
[9]Ibid.
[10]James Luther Adams, "Arminius and the Structure of Society," in *Man's Faith and Freedom,* ed.
Gerald O. McCulloh (Nashville: Abingdon, 1962), p. 94.
[11]Donald M. Lake, "Jacob Arminius's Contribution to a Theology of Grace," in *Grace Unlimited,*
ed. Clark Pinnock (Minneapolis: Bethany House, 1975), p. 232.
[12]Howard A. Slaatte, *The Arminian Arm of Theology* (Washington, D.C.: University Press of America, 1979), pp. 19, 23.
[13]Ibid., p. 24.

may be described as a grace-qualified, grace-inspired and grace-guided free-dom. The sinner may sin freely in capitulating to temptations and evil con-straints within his existence, but he can respond to grace freely only as grace touches him through the Spirit-illuminated Word.[14]

Even such a conservative and venerable Arminian theologian as H. Or-ton Wiley regarded Arminius and Arminianism as a correction of Reformed theology rather than a total departure from it: "In its purest and best forms, Arminianism preserves the truth found in the Reformed teachings without accepting its errors."[15]

Two Links Between Arminius's Theology and Reformed Theology

Two areas where Arminius's theology stayed close to Reformed theology and the standard Calvinism of his day are its emphasis on God's glory and its use of covenant or federal theology. These will no doubt come as some-thing of a surprise to many anti-Arminian Calvinists. First, Arminius asserted that the supreme purpose of God in creation and redemption is his own glory, and that the creature's greatest happiness lies precisely in enjoying God. This is, of course, a major tenet of Calvinism and Reformed thought in general. The first question and answer in the Westminster Shorter Cate-chism, a Reformed confessional statement, is "What is the chief end [pur-pose] of man? To glorify God and enjoy him forever." In his second oration Arminius concurs: "In this act of the mind and the will,—in seeing a present God, in loving him, and therefore in the enjoyment of him,—the salvation of man and his perfect happiness consist."[16] Furthermore, the chief pur-pose of all God's actions is his own glory:

> Let us reflect, for what cause God has brought us out of darkness into this mar-velous light; has furnished us with a mind, understanding, and reason; and has adorned us with his image. Let this question be revolved [sic] in our minds,—"For what purpose or END has God restored the fallen to their pris-tine state of integrity, reconciled sinners to himself, and received enemies into favour?"—and we shall plainly discover all this to have been done, that we might be made partakers of eternal salvation, and might sing praises to him forever.[17]

---

[14]Ibid., p. 66.
[15]H. Orton Wiley, *Christian Theology* (Kansas City, Mo.: Beacon Hill, 1941), 2:107.
[16]Arminius, "Oration II," *Works*, 1:363.
[17]Ibid., pp. 371-72.

Arminius extols the glory of God as God's supreme end in everything:

> That End [purpose, goal] is entirely divine,—being nothing less than the
> glory of God and man's eternal salvation. What can be more equitable than
> that all things should be referred to him from whom they have derived their
> origin? What can be more consonant to the wisdom, goodness, and power of
> God, than that he should restore, to his original integrity, man who had been
> created by him, but who had by his own fault destroyed himself; and that he
> should make him a partaker of his own Divine blessedness? . . . In such a con-
> summation as this, the glory of God most abundantly shines forth and displays
> itself.[18]

In sum, Arminius was at one with Reformed theology in his vision of
God's glory as the end or purpose of everything in creation and redemption. Of course, he and all later Arminians added to the Reformed emphasis
on God's glory an equal stress on God's love shown in universal compassion
and will to show mercy; for them the two—God's glory and God's love—cannot be divided.

Another important area where Arminius's theology stayed close to Reformed theology is federal or two-covenants theology. During Arminius's
own lifetime many Calvinist scholars were developing the idea that God
binds himself to humans through covenants, and they used the covenant
motif as the hermeneutical key to unlock the mysteries of Scripture and salvation history. Anyone who reads Arminius's "Orations" cannot miss this
theme. Arminius's account of God's relationship with humanity in redemption is at one with basic Calvinist covenant theology, which regards that
divine-human relationship as governed by two covenants: one based on
works and the other based on grace. According to Arminius, all the ways of
God with people in history begin with the covenant of works that God established with Adam and his posterity. Adam broke this covenant by disobedience, to the great misery of the whole of humanity:

> He did not fall alone; All whose persons he at that time represented and
> whose cause he pleaded, (although they had not then come into existence,)
> were with him cast down from the elevated summit of such a high dignity. Nei-
> ther did they fall from the priesthood only, but likewise from the covenant.[19]

Arminius affirmed a second covenant as a remedy for Adam's infidelity

---

[18]Ibid., pp. 384-85.
[19]Arminius, "Oration IV," *Works,* 1:409.

to the first; this second covenant centers around Jesus Christ as the mediator and grace as the means of redemption. This is a "better covenant established on better promises."[20] Its only condition is faith.

Arminius scholar William Gene Witt explains this covenant theology in terms of Arminius's distinction between two "theologies," which are really two ways of interpreting God's redemptive purpose and relationship with human beings. For Arminius, "legal theology" correlates with the covenant of the law with Adam as head of the race, whereas "evangelical theology" correlates with the covenant of grace with Christ as the head of the race—insofar as people accept him by faith.[21] For Arminius, according to Witt, evangelical theology reveals more fully than legal theology the nature and will of God, and yet both covenants are established by God according to grace. Evangelical theology and the covenant of grace transcend and fulfill legal theology and the covenant of works; the change is not a change in God's nature or purpose but a change in God's response to human actions. The same God is the author of both covenants for the same purpose—union of humanity with himself for his own glory and humanity's happiness.[22] God's grace is the basis of both covenants. Grace keeps coming back as a major motif of Arminius's theology, which shows in his account of the new covenant God established with humanity through Jesus Christ. It is what South African Reformed theologian Adrio König calls a "monopluristic covenant"—established by God but requiring a free human response. It is solely based on God's grace, which is not forced by human decisions or actions. William Witt is right that "Arminius has a very high theology of grace. He insists emphatically that grace is gratuitous because it is obtained through God's redemption in Christ, not through human effort."[23] The difference between Arminius's federal theology and that of the continental Calvinists (and the British Puritans) is the former's conditionality and the latter's absoluteness. That is, for Arminius, inclusion in the covenant of grace is not determined solely by God but by the free response of the human person to God's initiative in Christ and through the Holy Spirit. The Calvinist version regards inclusion as absolute and unconditional; the elect

---

[20]Arminius, "Oration I," *Works,* 1:337.
[21]William Gene Witt, *Creation, Redemption and Grace in the Theology of Jacob Arminius* (Ph.D. diss., University of Notre Dame, 1993), pp. 215-49.
[22]Interestingly, this motif in Arminius's theology is not far off from Calvinist John Piper's "Christian hedonism" even though Piper does not think highly of Arminianism.
[23]Witt, *Creation, Redemption and Grace,* pp. 259-60.

may feel that faith is their own acquisition, but in truth it is a gift of God they
are not able to reject.

It seems safe to conclude then that Arminius himself held no absolute an-
tipathy to Reformed theology and even considered himself an exponent of
it in some fashion. He was a "reformer of the Reformed." He was not con-
sciously breaking away from or attempting to overturn it. Certainly Muller's
claim that Arminius's theology represented a "full scale alternative to Reformed theology" is too extreme. At many points Arminius retained fundamental distinctives of the Reformed version of Protestantism, and this will
be seen even more clearly in later chapters where his views on providence
and grace are examined more fully. Contrary to popular (and some scholarly) opinion, then, Arminius may fairly be considered part of the story of
Reformed theology. Of course, if one decides quite arbitrarily that the Canons of Dort are definitive of Reformed theology, then Arminius's theology
cannot be considered Reformed. But that definition of Reformed theology
is anachronistic when applied to Arminius's own historical setting and too
narrow and brittle even by contemporary Reformed standards.

Arminian-Calvinist Common Ground

Do later Arminians share common ground with Reformed theology and especially Calvinism? This depends, of course, on how we define those terms
or which versions of them we work with. Less common ground will be found
between Arminianism and high Calvinism, of the TULIP variety (see p. 16),
than between Arminianism and revisionist Reformed thought represented
by many mainline Reformed thinkers. The common ground, for example,
between Arminianism and the theology of Reformed theologian Alan P. F.
Sell, the former theological secretary of the WARC, is vast.[24] However, common ground is harder to find or is smaller between committed Arminians
and strict Calvinists such as Edwin Palmer, author of *The Five Points of Calvinism*. Nevertheless, I believe enlightened, intelligent and thoughtful Christians in both camps need to see the areas of agreement and underscore
them for the sake of the cause of the gospel. Both are firmly planted within
the evangelical movement. Within the National Association of Evangelicals,

---

[24]See Sell's three-volume systematic theology, *Doctrine and Devotion* (Shippensburg, Penn.:
Ragged Edge, 2000), where he repeatedly affirms human freedom and denies absolute divine
control over human choices and actions. "God's omnipotence . . . is not sheer, unconditioned
might. Nor is it such as to violate the freedom he has given us" (1:108). Sell's Reformed theology embraces synergism while combining it paradoxically with Calvinist monergism.

member denominations include the Presbyterian Church in America, a conservative Calvinist organization, and the thoroughly Arminian Church of the Nazarene (to say nothing of many Pentecostal and Holiness organizations). Surely these and other similar groups share much in common. Their theologies cannot be opposites, even though they disagree at points. I will attempt to uncover and highlight that common ground in order to overcome the myth that Arminians and Calvinists are warring parties and that only one can be God-honoring and biblically faithful.

One place to begin is with John Wesley, who did not hesitate to affirm that Calvinists, though mistaken about several important theological matters, were fellow evangelicals in the work of revival. Wesley claimed that his own theology was "within a hair's breadth" of Calvin's teachings. He asked "Wherein may we come to the very edge of Calvinism?" and answered in three points: "(1) In ascribing all good to the free grace of God. (2) In denying all natural free will, and all power antecedent to grace. And (3) In excluding all merit from man; even for what he has or does by the grace of God."[25] This undoubtedly will come as something of a surprise and relief to Calvinists who have been told that Wesley believed in a works-based salvation. One noted evangelical Calvinist, noting Wesley's agreement with Calvinism (and Protestant theology in general) declared him a "confused Calvinist" rather than Arminian. Of course, this mistake arises from a misconception of Arminius's own theology or from mistakenly equating Arminianism with the late Remonstrant Arminianism of the head. Wesley wrote an essay titled "Thoughts upon God's Sovereignty" (1777) in which he asserted that God may "in the most absolute sense, do what he will with his own."[26] He placed no limits on God's right or power to dispose of creatures as he wills, but he appealed to God's character of love and justice to balance God's omnipotence and sovereignty.

Common ground between Calvinism and Arminianism may be found in other Arminian theologians.[27] Arminians together with Calvinists affirm total depravity because of the fall of humanity in Adam and its inherited consequence of a corrupted nature in bondage to sin. A common myth about

---

[25]John Wesley, quoted in Arthur Skevington Wood, "The Contribution of John Wesley to the Theology of Grace," in *Grace Unlimited*, ed. Clark Pinnock (Minneapolis: Bethany House, 1975), p. 211.

[26]Ibid.

[27]Common ground can also be found by examining Calvinist theologians, of course, but here focus will remain on Arminian writings.

Arminianism is that it promotes an optimistic anthropology. And yet even some Reformed critics of Arminianism admit that they share significant common ground with it. "Arminians and Calvinists alike believe in total depravity: because of the fall, every aspect of human nature is tainted by sin."[28] Classical Arminians are relieved to find some Calvinists finally understanding and admitting this Arminian commitment to total depravity![29] Arminius's own account of human fallenness could hardly be stronger if he had been a full-blown Calvinist! In his "Public Disputations" the founder of Arminianism declared unequivocally that because of Adam's fall all humanity has come under the dominion of sin and that

> In this state, the Free Will of man towards the True Good is not only wounded, maimed, infirm, bent and weakened *[attenuatum]*; but it is also imprisoned *[captivatum]*, destroyed, and lost: And its powers are not only debilitated and useless unless they be assisted by grace, but it has no powers whatever except such as are excited by Divine grace.[30]

This Arminian statement alone should put to rest the all-too-common misconception that Arminius and Arminians believe human free will survived the Fall intact. Leading Reformed scholar Robert Letham perpetuates this myth in his article "Arminianism" in *The Westminster Handbook to Reformed Theology*. Describing Arminius's theology he writes, "Moreover, [for him] the fallen will remains free."[31] This is, of course, simply not true.

Arminius continued his description of the result of the Fall by extending it beyond the will to the mind of the human person ("dark, destitute of the saving knowledge of God, and . . . incapable of those things which belong to the Spirit of God"), to the heart ("it hates and has an aversion to that which is truly good and pleasing to God; but it loves to pursue what is evil"), and to any power to perform the good ("utter weakness *[impotentia]* to perform that which is truly good"). Finally he declared that "nothing can be

---

[28]Robert A. Peterson and Michael D. Williams, *Why I Am Not an Arminian* (Downers Grove, Ill.: InterVarsity Press, 2004), p. 163.

[29]This common ground in pessimistic anthropology is overlooked or denied in most standard Calvinist accounts of Arminianism. This is clearly illustrated in Palmer's *Five Points of Calvinism*, where Arminianism is frequently distorted as semi-Pelagian, and in the *Modern Reformation* 1 (1992) issue on Arminianism, where the distance between Arminian anthropology and Calvinist anthropology is exaggerated.

[30]Arminius, "Public Disputations," *Works*, 2:192.

[31]Robert Letham, "Arminianism," in *The Westminster Handbook to Reformed Theology*, ed. Donald K. McKim (Louisville: Westminster John Knox Press, 2001), p. 4.

spoken more truly concerning man in this state, than that he is altogether dead in sin."[32] Later Arminians, including John Wesley and the main Methodist Arminian theologians of the nineteenth century, agreed completely with Arminius.[33] Not even Calvin believed that fallen human beings are as bad as they can possibly be!

It is only fair to acknowledge, however, that later Remonstrants and Arminians of the head did move away from Arminius's strong teaching on human depravity. In his excellent dissertation about Remonstrant theology, John Mark Hicks demonstrates this defection, focusing especially on late-seventeenth-century Remonstrant leader Philip Limborch. He quotes Reformed theologian Moses Stuart as saying of Arminius that "the most thorough advocate of total depravity will scarcely venture to go farther in regard to unregenerate man than Arminius does."[34] Limborch, however, diverged radically from Arminius and from true Arminianism:

> Both believe that original sin is fundamentally a deprivation, but their definition of deprivation is radically different. For Arminius man is deprived of the actual ability to will the good, but for Limborch man is only deprived of the knowledge which informs the intellect, but the will is fully capable within itself, if it is informed by the intellect, to will and perform anything good.[35]

Limborch's interpretation of the effects of original sin is very similar to Charles Finney's, although a direct line of influence of the former on the latter, who lived over a century later, is difficult to establish. Both, and many pseudo-Arminians between them, are theologically closer to semi-Pelagianism than to true Arminianism. Unfortunately, so it seems, many Calvinist critics of Arminianism know only of Limborch's and Finney's ideas and are totally unaware of Arminius's own affirmation of total depravity.

Did Limborch's theology replace Arminius's own theology as true Arminianism? Hardly. Wesley harked back to Arminius in affirming original sin, including human depravity and the bondage of the will to sin apart from supernatural prevenient grace. So did the leading nineteenth-century Arminian theologians Richard Watson, Thomas O. Summers, Wil-

---

[32]Arminius, "Public Disputations," *Works,* 2:194.

[33]Some Methodists, though, came to prefer the term *deprivation* to *depravity* because of the common misunderstanding of the latter term as denoting absolute evil.

[34]John Mark Hicks, *The Theology of Grace in the Thought of Jacobus Arminius and Philip van Limborch: A Study in the Development of Seventeenth-Century Dutch Arminianism* (Ph.D. diss., Westminster Theological Seminary, 1985), p. 34.

[35]Ibid., p. 286.

liam Burton Pope and John Miley (see chap. 6). For example, Wiley said, "The Scriptures as we have shown, represent human nature as being totally depraved," and "Depravity is total in that it affects the entire being of man."[36] Wiley made clear that he included the bondage of the will within the doctrine of total depravity. Later Nazarene theologian H. Ray Dunning agrees: "Humanity is wrong, all wrong, before God, and therefore everything that is done is wrong. It is in this way that actual sin is always an expression of original sin."[37] Any fair-minded person who reads serious Arminian theology (as opposed to popular literature that reflects folk religion) cannot help but see the overwhelming Arminian insistence on inherited total depravity; it is simply a myth that Arminianism rejects or denies this point of the high Calvinism. This agreement between true Arminianism, as opposed to the pseudo-Arminianism of Limborch and his heirs, and Reformed theology should not be overlooked by either Calvinists or Arminians.

Anthropology, and especially human depravity resulting from the Fall and caused by original sin, is just one small piece of the common theological ground shared by Arminianism and Reformed theology. I could go on to show common ground on divine sovereignty (Arminians too believe in providence!) and humanity's absolute dependence on grace for any spiritual good, including the first inclination of the will toward God. Evangelical Arminians, including Arminius and Wesley, affirm the inspiration of the Bible and its sole supreme authority in all matters pertaining to faith and practice, the deity and humanity of Jesus Christ as God incarnate, the Trinity, justification through Christ's death on the cross alone by grace alone through faith alone. (Some classical Arminians want to make clear that true faith is never "alone" but results in works of love, but they do not attribute any merit to good works.) Thus, traditional Arminians are fully orthodox even though some Calvinists and Lutherans object on the ground that only those who adhere to monergism are orthodox. Such a narrow standard of orthodoxy, however, rules out all of the early Greek church fathers, including Athanasius, who set the gold standard of orthodoxy!

Common Ground with Real Differences

Arminianism and Calvinism share significant common ground, including

---

[36]Wiley, *Christian Theology*, 2:128.
[37]H. Ray Dunning, *Grace, Faith, and Holiness* (Kansas City, Mo.: Beacon Hill, 1988), p. 301.

Arminianism's views on God's sovereignty and grace.[38] In fact, on the full spectrum of Christian theologies these two huddle fairly close together near the middle. At times Wesley himself could see only a hair's breadth of difference between them. Prevenient grace that frees the human will to respond to the gospel in repentance and faith comes quite apart from any freely determined reception on the part of the person. It is a sheer gift of God through Christ to all humanity (to some degree) and to those who hear the gospel proclaimed (to a greater degree). Wesley and some other Arminians have even affirmed a sense in which grace is irresistible!

None of this is meant to minimize the real differences between classical Arminianism and especially high Calvinism. (Again, though, the differences between Arminianism and some types of modern revisionist Calvinism or Reformed theology is slighter.) But advocates of both viewpoints should not magnify their differences out of proportion as some on both sides are want to do.[39] No advantage to truth is gained by Calvinists and Arminians treating each other as pariahs or creating straw men out of each others' theologies. Much of the harsh polemics of traditional Calvinist-Arminian debate could and should be overcome simply by understanding each others' real theological positions. The good of the entire evangelical movement would be enhanced by evangelicals of both camps acknowledging each other as genuine evangelicals rather than treating each other as second-class evangelicals if not *false brethren* (a term used in the Reformation for heretics who pretended to be part of the Protestant movement). As a classical Arminian, I consider faithful Calvinists (as opposed to pseudo-Calvinists among the liberalized, revisionist Reformed) evangelical brothers and sisters, and I believe they make a singularly important contribution to the overall theological balance in Christian theology. Calvinism's stress on God's sovereignty, human depravity and the gratuity of grace in salvation, though not absent from Arminian thought, provides a positive reminder of truths modern culture too easily brushes aside. Similarly, Arminian theol-

---

[38]A fuller examination of Arminianism's conventional views on God's sovereignty and grace is found in chaps. 5 and 7.

[39]Two opposite examples come to mind from the Calvinist side. Most of the authors in the *Modern Reformation* 1 (1992) issue exaggerate their differences with Arminianism. On the other hand, Calvinists Robert A. Peterson and Michael D. Williams of Covenant Theological Seminary in St. Louis, Missouri (authors of *Why I Am Not an Arminian*) irenically stress their agreements with classical Arminian theology while clearly explaining their reasons for not accepting its distinctive points of difference from Calvinism.

ogy underscores and highlights God's love and mercy, which is often lacking (though not totally absent) in other Protestant theologies. To a very great extent the differences between Arminianism and Calvinism (insofar as they remain firmly rooted in their native soils) are more a matter of emphasis than radical difference. Each can be enriched by the other through dialogue. On the other hand, they do have points of real difference, though these differences are secondary in importance compared to the agreed-on doctrines of God's Word and classical orthodoxy. Nevertheless, chapter two will show no reasonable hybrid of the two is possible; they can peacefully coexist but they cannot be combined.

MYTH 2:

A Hybrid of Calvinism and Arminianism Is Possible

In spite of common ground, Calvinism and Arminianism are incommensurable systems of Christian theology; on issues crucial to both there is no stable middle ground between them.

IN CHAPTER ONE WE SAW THAT THERE'S MUCH common ground beneath evangelical Arminianism (Arminianism of the heart) and evangelical (even high) Calvinism. In it I attempted to show that in fact Calvinism and Arminianism are expressions of one faith, and that in their classical expressions both affirm human dependency on God's grace for everything good. For example, contrary to what many Calvinists seem to believe, classical Arminians share with classical Calvinists a firm belief in human depravity and the necessity of divine initiative for salvation. They agree that fallen humans cannot exercise a good will toward God apart from the initiative of grace. In this both honor Scripture and are equally evangelical.

This chapter addresses a different myth: that because of their common ground, Arminianism and Calvinism can be combined, creating a hybrid. It is not unusual in evangelical circles to hear sincere and well-intentioned Christians declare themselves "Calminians," a combination of Calvinist and Arminian. I have encountered this claim numerous times when presenting Calvinism and Arminianism to classes in colleges, seminaries or churches. Often students ask, Why can't there be a middle ground between Calvinism and Arminianism? To which someone replies, There is—it's called Calminianism! A sincere desire to bridge the gulf that has caused so much conflict underlies this misconception. By no means should the desire for unity be belittled; it is admirable even though its fulfillment is, in this case, impossible.

Before plunging into an explanation of why they are incompatible, it would be helpful (especially for those who have skipped the introduction) to review what is meant by Calvinism and Arminianism. If unity is the overriding concern, their stark particularities can be artificially softened. When they are defined in ways that diverge from their classical definitions, combining them is simple. Thus their so-called unity is determined by how we define and describe them. However, when Arminianism and Calvinism are understood in their historical, classical senses, no such combination is possible; they will always remain alternatives, especially in soteriological matters. *Calvinism* is the system of Protestant Christian belief that stems from the sixteenth-century teachings of John Calvin. It is the most familiar form of the Reformed branch of Protestantism, and its most systematic and logically stringent expression is found in two doctrinal statements of the seventeenth century: the Canons of the Synod of Dort (1618) and the Westminster Confession of Faith (1648). The heart and soul of Calvinism (beyond Protestant orthodoxy) is a distinctive emphasis on the sovereignty of God, especially in salvation. God is the all-determining reality who foreordains and renders certain everything that happens, especially and most importantly the salvation of sinners.[1] This extends to individuals so that they are predestined by God unconditionally to eternal salvation. According to high Calvinism, God also determines to pass over others (the decree of reprobation), leaving them to their deserved eternal condemnation. God's grace for salvation is irresistible and effectual, and for most traditional Calvinists Christ's atoning death on the cross was intended by God only for the elect.

Arminianism stems from the teachings of Jacob Arminius of Holland, who reacted against high Calvinism and rejected many of its distinctive tenets.

---

[1]This claim of meticulous providence is denied by some Calvinists, but strongly affirmed by most Calvinist scholars, including Calvin himself. Calvinist theologian Edwin Palmer expresses Calvin's own belief about God's sovereignty faithfully when he writes that "Foreordination means God's sovereign plan, whereby He decides all that is to happen in the entire universe. Nothing in this world happens by chance. God is in back of everything. He decides and causes all things to happen that do happen" (*The Five Points of Calvinism* [Grand Rapids: Baker, 1972], pp. 24-25). Some Calvinists want to limit God's determining foreordination to matters of salvation so that God is not responsible for every calamity—including the fall of humanity—that befalls the world. Whether this is consistent with classical Calvinism or whether classical Calvinism includes meticulous providence as expressed by Palmer is something for Calvinists to decide.

He and his followers, known as the Remonstrants, denied Calvin's moner-gism (salvation determinism) and opted instead for a self-limiting God who grants free will to people by means of the gift of prevenient grace. God al-lows his grace for salvation to be resisted and rejected, and determines to save all who do not reject it but instead embrace it as their only hope for eternal life. Christ's atonement is universal in scope; God sent Christ to die for the sins of every person. But the atonement's saving efficacy extends only to those who embrace the cross by faith. Arminianism confronts mon-ergism with an evangelical synergism that affirms a necessary cooperation between divine and human agencies in salvation (though it places them on entirely different planes). In salvation, God's grace is the superior partner; human free will (nonresistance) is the lesser partner. Arminius and his faithful followers reacted against high Calvinism without propagating any new doctrines; they pointed back to the Greek church fathers and to certain Lutherans. They were also influenced by Catholic reformer Erasmus.

When Calvinism and Arminianism are so described, their incommensu-rability should be fairly obvious. The gap between them at several points is wide and deep. It centers around the middle three points of the famous TULIP scheme: total depravity, unconditional election, limited atone-ment, irresistible grace, and perseverance of the saints. While Arminians accept divine election, they believe it is conditional. While they accept a form of limited atonement, they reject the idea that God sent Christ to die only for a portion of humanity. The atonement's limited nature is grounded not in God's intention but in human response. Only those who accept the grace of the cross are saved by God; those who reject it and seek salvation elsewhere fail to be included in it by their own choice, much to God's dismay. While Arminians embrace the necessity of supernatural grace for salvation (as for any spiritual good, including the first stirring of the will toward God), they deny that God irresistibly bends human wills so that they are effectually saved apart from their own spontaneous (not au-tonomous) response.

Arminianism and Calvinism Contrasted

At the beginning of chapter one I admitted that Arminianism and Calvin-ism are essentially contested concepts. No one speaks for all Calvinists on everything just as no one speaks for all Arminians about every subject. Thus to back up my thumbnail sketches I appeal to Reformed minister and theologian Edwin Palmer and Arminian (Nazarene) theologian H. Orton Wiley. Describing classical Calvinism, Palmer wrote: "The Arminian teaches conditional election; whereas the Calvinist teaches unconditional election," and "This, then, is unconditional election: God's choice does not rest on anything that man does."[2] Regarding election Wiley said:

> Arminianism holds that predestination is the gracious purpose of God to save mankind from utter ruin. It is not an arbitrary, indiscriminate act of God intended to secure the salvation of so many and no more. It includes provisionally, all men in its scope, and is conditioned solely on faith in Jesus Christ.[3]

According to Palmer, and classical Calvinism in general, Christ's atoning death was sufficient for the whole world, including every individual who has ever lived or who will ever live, but intended by God only for the elect: "The Bible teaches again and again that God does not love all people with the same love," and "the atonement of Christ is limited in its scope, that Christ intended to and actually did remove the guilt of the sins of a limited number of people—namely, those whom God has loved with a special love from eternity. The atonement of unlimited value is limited to certain people."[4] Wiley, speaking for all Arminians, wrote:

> The atonement is universal. This does not mean that all mankind will be unconditionally saved, but that the sacrificial offering of Christ so far satisfied the claims of the divine law as to make salvation a possibility for all. Redemption is therefore universal or general in the provisional sense, but special or conditional in its application to the individual.[5]

The contrast may not be as crystal clear as we might hope, because both Calvinists and Arminians believe that the atonement is *both* universal *and* limited, but in different senses. According to Calvinism the atonement is

---

[2]Palmer, *Five Points of Calvinism,* p. 27. Palmer's presentation of Calvinism is pithy and sometimes stated in a rather stark manner. Nevertheless, he was not only a pastor of Reformed churches but also served as instructor at Westminster Theological Seminary, which is a widely respected Calvinist institution. His presentation of Calvinism is consistent with the earlier presentations given by the Princeton theologians Archibald Alexander, Charles Hodge, A. A. Hodge and B. B. Warfield.

[3]H. Orton Wiley, *Christian Theology* (Kansas City, Mo.: Beacon Hill, 1941), 2:337. Wiley relied heavily on the major nineteenth-century Arminians Richard Watson, William Burton Pope, Thomas Summers and John Miley. Wiley's theology is entirely consistent with theirs and with Arminius's own thought.

[4]Palmer, *Five Points of Calvinism,* p. 44, 42.

[5]Wiley, *Christian Theology,* 2:295.

universal in value; it is sufficient to save everyone. According to Arminianism it is universal in intent; it is meant to save everyone. According to Calvinism it is limited in scope; it is intended to save only the elect and does save them. According to Arminianism it is limited in efficacy; it actually saves only those who accept it by faith.

Arminians believe that the Calvinist account of the scope of the atonement is flawed; it cannot avoid limiting the love of God, which contradicts Scripture passages such as John 3:16, which Calvinists must interpret as referring not to the whole world (that is, all individuals) but to persons out of every tribe and nation.[6] Calvinists fear that Arminians' emphasis on the universality of the atonement results inexorably in universalism; if Christ actually bore the sins of every person, why would any person go to hell? Wouldn't all be saved by Christ's atoning death? Wouldn't hell be redundant punishment? Arminians respond that this is indeed what makes hell so tragic—it is absolutely unnecessary. People go there not because their punishment was not suffered by Christ but because they reject the amnesty provided by God through Christ's substitutionary death.

This is how Palmer explained irresistible grace:

> God sends His Holy Spirit to work in the lives of people so that they will definitely and certainly be changed from evil to good people. It means that the Holy Spirit will certainly—without any and's, if's or but's—cause everyone whom God has chosen from eternity and for whom Christ died to believe on Jesus.[7]

Calvinists typically describe this process as "bending the will." In other words, God does not coerce anyone spiritually but causes the elect to desire the grace of God and respond joyfully to God's initiative with faith. Arminians fear that this violates the God-human relationship so that humans become pawns in God's hands. They reject this not because they value human

---

[6]Palmer, *Five Points of Calvinism*, p. 45. Arminians typically find this limitation of the atonement's scope to the elect astounding in light of Scripture's emphasis on God's love for the whole world and Christ's death on behalf of humanity. Baptist theologian Vernon Grounds, long-time president of Denver Seminary, says, "A mere *catena* of passages discloses the fact, for fact it is, that the divine purpose in Jesus Christ embraces not a segment of the human family but the race *en toto*," and "It takes an exegetical ingenuity which is something other than a learned virtuosity to evacuate these texts of their obvious meaning; it takes an exegetical ingenuity verging on sophistry to deny their explicit universality" (*Grace Unlimited*, ed. Clark H. Pinnock [Minneapolis: Bethany House, 1975], pp. 26, 28).

[7]Palmer, *Five Points of Calvinism*, p. 58.

autonomy (as many Calvinists think) but because they value the genuinely
personal nature of the God-human relationship. Love that is not freely chosen does not seem to be genuine love. Furthermore, if God selects some to
be saved unconditionally and irresistibly, why doesn't he choose all? On
what basis and for what reason does God pass over some sinners and bend
the wills of others to respond with faith? The unconditional and irresistible
nature of grace in the Calvinist scheme seems arbitrary if not capricious. In
contrast Arminians contend that God's grace is resistible:

> Arminianism holds that salvation is all of grace, in that every movement of the
> soul toward God is initiated by divine grace; but it recognizes also in a true
> sense, the co-operation of the human will, because in the last stage, it remains
> with the free agent as to whether the grace thus proffered is accepted or re-
> jected.[8]

And with all Arminians Wiley argued that grace can always be resisted,
even prevenient grace—the enabling grace that God provides before salvation—which comes quite apart from human asking or willing. Once it appears, it can be and often is rejected.

It is extremely important that the real issues between Calvinism and
Arminianism are uncovered, and that people are not charmed by illusory
similarities. Just as both Calvinists and Arminians believe in universal and
limited atonement, but in different senses, so both believe that grace is irresistible and resistible, but in different senses. Calvinists believe that the reprobate, those God has chosen to pass over in salvation, naturally resist the
grace of God. And the elect, those chosen for salvation and who are spiritually regenerated prior to salvation, find God's grace irresistible and therefore accept the gospel. Similarly, Arminians believe people have no choice
with regard to prevenient grace; it is irresistible in the sense that it is a gift
of God that is bestowed on everyone. But prevenient grace does not bend
the will or set aside free agency; in spiritual matters it creates the free will
and free agency, and thus humans can freely resist it once they receive it.
Again, both common ground and a deep divide lie beneath Calvinist and
Arminian feet.

By now it should be clear why real Calvinism and real Arminianism cannot be combined. No hybrid is possible in spite of the fact that they do not
disagree about everything. On these three crucial issues no bridge is possi-

[8]Wiley, *Christian Theology*, 2:356.

ble between them. Once the terms are properly elucidated, it becomes apparent that the scope of election, atonement and grace differ appreciably between Arminianism and Calvinism.

The Impossibility of Calminianism

Nevertheless, in spite of the stark contrast between Calvinism and Arminianism on certain fundamental points of doctrine, many people try to force them into a hybrid: Calminianism. Classical Calvinists and classical Arminians agree that this is not possible. Calvinist author W. Robert Godfrey, president of Westminster Theological Seminary California, rejects it:

> Some try to split the difference between Arminianism and Calvinism. They say something like "I want to be 75% Calvinist and 25% Arminian." If they mean that literally, then they are 100% Arminian since giving any determinative place to human will is Arminian. Usually they mean that they want to stress the grace of God and human responsibility. If that is what they mean, then they can be 100% Calvinist for Calvinism does teach both that God's grace is entirely the cause of salvation and that man is responsible before God to hear and heed the call to repentance and faith.[9]

Consistent classical Arminians agree with Godfrey that their system of belief is incompatible with Calvinism and would argue that most people who declare themselves Calminians or 75 percent Calvinist and 25 percent Arminian are actually Arminian! Some are simply inconsistent and willing to embrace contradictory propositions.

Some who seek a hybrid of Calvinism and Arminianism do so by appealing to a higher unity of truth that transcends our time-bound and finite perspectives. They notice that the Bible seems to affirm both absolute divine sovereignty and human cooperation with God in history and salvation. The classical passage that seems to teach the paradox of grace is Philippians 2:12-13: "work out your own salvation with fear and trembling; for God is at work in you, both to will and to work for his good pleasure" (RSV). A common illustration used to support the argument that both monergism and synergism are true (and not only contain some aspect of truth) is two parallel train tracks that seem to converge beyond the horizon. The problem with this illustration, of course, is that they do not converge! Another common illustration is the imaginary sign over the entry gate to heaven that

---

[9]W. Robert Godfrey, "Who Was Arminius?" *Modern Reformation* 1 (1992): 24.

reads "Whosoever will may enter here freely." On the heaven side the same sign reads "For you were chosen from before the foundation of the world." Both truths are clearly taught in Scripture. But British Baptist preacher Charles Spurgeon, who was probably the author of this illustration, meant it to illustrate Calvinism! And so it does. Placing "For you were chosen from before the foundation of the world" inside heaven's gate implies that proposition's greater truth.

The plain fact of the matter is that *on certain points* classical Calvinism and classical Arminianism simply disagree, and no bridge uniting them can be found; no hybrid of the two can be created. Calvinism can be seen as the middle ground between fatalism and synergism; Arminianism can be seen as the middle ground between semi-Pelagianism and Calvinism. But between Calvinism and Arminianism there is no mutual compatibility. Logic will always force a person to go one way or the other. Of course, if we do not care about logic, then we inhabit an artificially constructed Calminian house built on sand. But it will be ravaged by the harsh questions of logic and common sense. Is election of individuals to salvation conditional or unconditional? If we answer "I don't know," no Calminian hybrid exists. But if we respond "Both," where is the middle ground? How do we logically combine conditional and unconditional? The same questions could be posed to the Calminian view of atonement and grace. Does God intend Christ's atoning death to save everyone or only some? If we answer that God intends to save all but knows only some will be saved, we are Arminians! If we answer that God intends to save only some even though it is sufficient to save all, we are Calvinists! Almost all the clever responses of Calminianism to such questions end up being Calvinistic or Arminian. Is saving grace resistible or irresistible? Is it always effectual, or can it be rejected? Where is the middle ground? Once the Calminian begins clarifying and qualifying, he or she inevitably reveals either Calvinist or Arminian colors.

One very popular attempt to transcend Calvinism and Arminianism is to appeal to God's alleged timelessness (or God's eternity as above and beyond time). Some say that from God's perspective there is no conflict between predestination and free will. (Of course, Arminians have always argued that there is no conflict between them because predestination is conditional!) However, assuming that those who appeal to God's timelessness mean that election and predestination are both conditional and unconditional, how does divine timelessness help relieve the contradiction? The same could be asked about atonement and grace. Timelessness does not help, because even from a timeless God's perspective the decree to save some persons must be based either on an unconditional election or on something God sees (timelessly) in them, such as their nonresistance to grace. Both the early followers of classic Calvinism and Arminianism assumed divine timelessness, yet neither side appealed to God's timelessness as the solution, because they saw that the other side could also appeal to divine timelessness. Even if all moments of time are simultaneously before the eyes of God, God's timeless choice of some to be saved is based either on something he sees in them or it is not. Either God's intention and purpose in and through the atonement is to save every fallen child of Adam's race or it is to save only some. Either God's saving grace can be resisted or it can't. Appealing to the time-eternity dichotomy does not solve the problem or create a hybrid.

As harsh as it sounds to people who highly value unity (especially among Christians), we need to shoulder the responsibility of choosing between Calvinism and Arminianism. That does not mean choosing between Christianity and something else. It means choosing between two respectable interpretations of Scripture that have both existed within evangelical Christianity for centuries. For many persons this choice poses very little risk because their church allows both perspectives to coexist peacefully side by side.[10] However, many denominations do require a certain confessional position vis-à-vis monergism and synergism for leadership if not for membership.[11]

The Continental Divide Between Calvinism and Arminianism

Can Calvinism or Arminianism prove itself by appeal to Scripture alone? We can only wish it to be so. However, many astute and convinced Calvinists and Arminians agree it is not so simple. Both monergism and synergism can pile up impressive lists of supporting Scripture passages and scholarly exegesis that undergird their conclusions. After twenty-five years of studying this sub-

---

[10]This is true of many Baptist churches as well as other churches rooted in the pietist tradition, such as the Evangelical Free Church of America, whose motto is "In essentials unity, in nonessentials liberty, in all things charity." Such churches usually relegate beliefs about monergism and synergism to the realm of nonessentials. This does not mean that these doctrinal issues are unimportant but that they are not of the essence of Christianity.

[11]The Christian Reformed Church and the Presbyterian Church in America are decidedly Calvinistic whereas the Church of the Nazarene and most of the Methodist churches (including their offshoots) are Arminian.

ject, I have concluded that appealing to Scripture alone cannot prove one side right and the other side wrong. Equally reasonable and spiritually mature Christians have scoured Scripture and come to radically different conclusions about the relationship of election and free will, and the resistibility of atonement and grace. In fact, this has been happening for centuries. Does one side alone honor Scripture? No. Similarly, while Democrats and Republicans interpret the United States Constitution differently, both honor it as they seek to interpret it responsibly.

If appeal to Scripture alone will not solve our problem, what will? I doubt it can be solved by argument or dialogue. It is largely a matter of that mystery called perspective. Philosophers have called it "blik." It is a basic way of seeing reality. We see the world as such-and-such even when proof is lacking. Think of the famous drawing that can be seen as either a duck or a rabbit. Some people instantly see a rabbit but not the duck, but others see the duck without being able to see rabbit. One does not see both simultaneously and seeing the other (than one first saw) is a matter of changed perspective and not of selling "something else." So it is with Calvinism and Arminianism. In spite of all the huffing and puffing of extremists on both sides who seem to believe adherents of the other theology are exercising bad faith, people of equally good faith come down on different sides. Why? Because when they read the Bible, they find God identified one way or another. At the bottom of these doctrinal differences lies a different perspective on the identity of God, based on God's self-revelation in Jesus Christ and Scripture, that colors the rest of Scripture. All of Scripture wears the aspect of monergism because the whole of Scripture reveals God as primarily sovereign ruler, or all of Scripture wears the aspect of synergism because the whole of Scripture reveals God as primarily loving and compassionate heavenly father. This epistemology of "seeing as" (perspective) does not circumvent Scripture but reveals perceived patterns in it.[12] Even though biblical exegesis alone cannot prove either Calvinism or Arminianism, biblically correct exegesis undergirds each system of theology. Scripture is the material that provides the pattern (gestalt) that forms the perspective (blik) that controls interpre-

---

[12]I am not suggesting a relativism of revelation such that Scripture does not mean anything in particular. My own view is that monergism is not the right interpretation of Scripture's revelation of God, but I can see how monergists arrive at their misunderstanding. But that is only by "crawling inside" their perspective to the best of my ability and seeing Scripture as they do, which reveals a different pattern. However, I still believe that my perspective is nearer the truth.

tation of individual passages. This explains why people are Calvinists or Arminians when clear and unequivocal exegetical proof for either system is lacking. Both see God as identified by the whole of Scripture (synthetic vision) in a certain way.

Another issue that complicates the choice between Calvinism and Arminianism is that both systems contain very difficult if not insurmountable problems. Both struggle mightily to explain large chunks of Scripture; both have to admit mysteries that border on contradictions within their systems. Edwin Palmer expressed more strongly than most Calvinists a problem in his belief system. God, he admitted, foreordains everything and therefore foreordains even sin and evil, yet humans alone are to blame for doing what they cannot avoid doing.[13] "He [the Calvinist] realizes that what he advocates is ridiculous. . . . The Calvinist freely admits that his position is illogical, ridiculous, nonsensical, and foolish." And yet, with most Calvinists, Palmer claimed that "this secret matter belongs to the Lord our God, and we should leave it there. We ought not to probe into that secret counsel of God."[14]

Many Calvinists would cringe at Palmer's admission of the mystery embedded in Calvinist belief. It is a bit extreme, especially for Calvinists who care about logic. But nearly all Calvinists agree that there are points such as this one where Calvinism comes up against mystery and cannot provide a rationally satisfying solution. Reflective Arminians similarly acknowledge logical difficulties and problems within their own system of belief. Who can explain how free agency is the ability to do other than what one in fact does? Free will is not a problem in Calvinism, because it is either denied or explained in such a way as to remove all mystery from it. But all classical Arminians believe in libertarian free will, which is self-determining choice; it is incompatible with determination of any kind. That seems to amount to belief in an uncaused effect—the free choice of the self to be or do something without antecedent. Buridan, a medieval cynic, scoffed at such free will, suggesting that a mule who possessed it would starve to death even though two identical bowls of food were put before it, because nothing would incline it to eat out of one or the other! Arminians are not swayed by such arguments; they know that a starving mule would freely choose to eat out of one or the other. But all caviling aside, Arminians know that their be-

---

[13]Palmer, *Five Points of Calvinism*, p. 85.
[14]Ibid., pp. 85, 87.

lief in libertarian freedom is a mystery (not a contradiction).

The point here is that both sides (and perhaps all significant theological systems) involve mystery, and in making their theological systems perfectly intelligible, mystery is a problem. Ironically, both sides tend to point out the other's weakness in appealing to mystery without acknowledging their own. Both point to the speck in the other's eye while ignoring the equally large speck (beam?) in their own! Thus it appears that people are not Calvinists or Arminians because one side has proven itself right, but because these people can find one set of mysteries (or problems) easier to live with than the other. Of course, adherents of both also point to supporting Scriptures and experiences (such as being grasped by God apart from an awareness of choice). But in the end neither side can completely defeat the other or conclusively prove its own system. Philosopher Jerry Walls expertly points this out:

> Notice that both Calvinists and free will theologians [Arminians] ultimately arrive at a point where further explanations are impossible. Both reach the limit of finally inexplicable choice. The free will theologian cannot fully explain why some choose Christ while others do not. The Calvinist cannot tell us why or on what basis God chooses some for salvation and passes others by.[15]

Both, then, face insuperable difficulties in explaining certain features of their system and should admit it. Nevertheless, the two systems stand within Protestant Christianity with equal sincerity toward Scripture, equal exegetical prowess, equal historical appeal and equal commitment to basic Christian orthodoxy.

So what is the solution? Why be either a Calvinist or an Arminian? At rock bottom some Christians are Calvinists because when they read Scripture (and perhaps examine their own experience) they see God as almighty, supremely glorious, absolutely sovereign and the all-determining reality. This is their "blik," the synthetic vision that guides the hermeneutics of individual passages. The great Puritan theologian Jonathan Edwards was obsessed with this vision of God, and it guided his theology throughout. Other Christians are Arminians because when they read Scripture (and perhaps examine their own experience) they see God as supremely good, loving, merciful, compassionate and the benevolent Father of all creation, who desires

---

[15]Jerry Walls, "The Free Will Defense, Calvinism, Wesley, and the Goodness of God," *Christian Scholar's Review* 13, no. 1 (1983): 25.

the best for everyone. This vision of God guided the theology of the great revivalist John Wesley, who was Edwards's contemporary. Of course, both sides recognize some truth in the other perspective; Calvinists acknowledge God as loving and merciful (especially toward the elect), and Arminians acknowledge God as almighty and sovereign. Both believe God is supremely great and good. But one side starts with God's greatness and conditions God's goodness in that light; the other side starts with God's goodness and conditions God's greatness in that light. Each side has its "blik," which largely determines how it interprets Scripture. Arminian theologian Fritz Guy expresses the Arminian controlling "blik" bluntly: "In the character of God love is more fundamental than control."[16] This basic perspective on God is echoed throughout Arminian literature. When writing of the Calvinist belief in unconditional reprobation (that God passes over some and choosing others for salvation unconditionally), John Wesley was brutally honest: "Whatever that scripture proves, it never can prove this."[17] Note that Wesley did not say this because he was charmed by some extrabiblical norm that trumps Scripture itself. Rather, he was guided by a vision imposed by Scripture itself that makes certain interpretations of the text impossible.

Contrary to popular belief, then, the true divide at the heart of the Calvinist-Arminian split is not predestination versus free will but the guiding picture of God: he is primarily viewed as either (1) majestic, powerful, and controlling or (2) loving, good, and merciful. Once the picture (blik) is established, seemingly contrary aspects fade into the background, are set aside as "obscure" or are artificially made to fit the system. Neither side absolutely denies the truth of the other's perspective, but each qualifies the attributes of God that are preeminent in the other's perspective. God's goodness is qualified by his greatness in Calvinism, and God's greatness is qualified by his goodness in Arminianism.

Arminians can live with the problems of Arminianism more comfortably than with the problems of Calvinism. Determinism and indeterminism cannot be combined; we must choose one or the other. In the ultimate and final reality of things, people either have some degree of self-determination or they don't. Calvinism is a form of determinism. Arminians choose indeterminism largely because determinism seems incompatible with God's

---

[16]Fritz Guy, "The Universality of God's Love," in *The Grace of God, the Will of Man,* ed. Clark H. Pinnock (Grand Rapids: Zondervan, 1989), p. 33.

[17]John Wesley, quoted in ibid., p. 266. This is from Wesley's sermon "Free Grace."

goodness and with the nature of personal relationships, which includes the very nature of salvation itself. Arminians agree with Arminius, who stressed that "the grace of God is not 'a certain irresistible force . . . it is a Person, the Holy Spirit, and in personal relationships there cannot be the sheer over-powering of one person by another.' "[18] And Wesley asked of unconditional election (and unconditional reprobation): "Now what can possibly be a more flat contradiction than this, not only to the whole scope and tenor of Scripture, but also to all those particular texts which expressly declare, 'God is love'?"[19] Contemporary Wesleyan philosopher Jerry Walls argues that it is simply impossible to reconcile God's goodness with divine determinism in any form, including Calvinism. He points out that for Wesley (and all Arminians) "it is unthinkable that so much evil would abound if God has determined all human choices."[20] Walls argues that moral intuition as well as Scripture informs us that the amount and intensity of evil in the world is simply incompatible with the goodness of God *if* God is the all-determining reality. But most importantly, if God solely determines salvation and does not save everyone or regard free human choices in saving, God's goodness is simply inexplicable and therefore debatable. God then becomes morally ambiguous. That is the Arminian problem with Calvinism; it is a problem Arminians cannot live with.

The continental divide between Calvinism and Arminianism, then, lies with different perspectives about God's identity in revelation. Divine determinism creates problems in God's character and in the God-human relationship that Arminians simply cannot live with. Because of their controlling vision of God as good, they are unable to affirm unconditional reprobation (which inexorably follows from unconditional election) because it makes God morally ambiguous at best.[21] Denying divine determinism in salvation leads to Arminianism.

---

[18]Charles M. Cameron, "Arminius—Hero or Heretic?" *Evangelical Quarterly* 64, no. 3 (1992): 225.

[19]John Wesley, "Free Grace," *The Works of John Wesley* 3.3, ed. Albert C. Outler (Nashville: Abingdon, 1986), p. 552.

[20]Walls, *Free Will Defense*, p. 28.

[21]I fully realize that many Calvinists claim to believe in only "single predestination." That is, they say predestination is only to salvation and that no one is predestined by God to reprobation. However, if a Calvinist denies universalism, as most do, how is it possible to deny a divine decree of reprobation and thus double predestination? Even if God only "passes by" or "passes over" some, that is tantamount to predetermining their damnation. Calvinist author R. C. Sproul makes this point very clearly in *Chosen by God* (Wheaton, Ill.: Tyndale House, 1986), pp. 139-60.

The nature of free will is another point where Calvinism and Arminianism diverge and where no middle ground seems possible. Because of their vision of God as good (loving, benevolent, merciful), Arminians affirm libertarian free will. (Philosophers call it incompatibilist free will because it is not compatible with determinism.) When an agent (a human or God) acts freely in the libertarian sense, nothing outside the self (including physical realities within the body) is causing it; the intellect or character alone rules over the will and turns it one way or another. Deliberation and then choice are the only determining factors, although factors such as nature and nurture, and divine influence come into play. Arminians do not believe in absolute free will; the will is always influenced and situated in a context. Even God is guided by his nature and character when making decisions. But Arminians deny that creaturely decisions and actions are controlled by God or any force outside the self.

Calvinists, on the other hand, believe in compatibilist free will (insofar as they talk about free will at all). Free will, they believe, is compatible with determinism. This is the only sense of free will that is consistent with Calvinism's vision of God as the all-determining reality. In compatibilist free will, persons are free so long as they do what they want to do—even if God is determining their desires. This is why Calvinists can affirm that people sin voluntarily and are therefore responsible for their sins even though they could not do otherwise. According to Calvinism God foreordained the Fall of Adam and Eve, and rendered it certain (even if only by an efficacious permission) by withdrawing the grace necessary to keep them from sinning. And yet they sinned voluntarily. They did what they wanted to do even if they were unable to do otherwise. This is a typical Calvinist account of free will.[22]

Once again it is difficult to see how a hybrid of these two views of free will could be created. Could people have freely chosen to do something different than they actually did? Some Calvinists (such as Jonathan Edwards) agree with Arminians that people have the *natural* ability to do otherwise (e.g., avoid sinning). But what about the moral ability? Arminians agree with Calvinists that apart from the grace of God all fallen humans choose to sin; their will is bound to sin by original sin manifesting itself as total depravity. However, Arminians do not call this free will because these people can-

---

[22]See Robert A. Peterson and Michael D. Williams, *Why I Am Not An Arminian* (Downers Grove, Ill.: InterVarsity Press, 1992), pp. 136-61. This is not to say it is the only Calvinist account of free will; many Calvinists follow Calvin himself in simply denying free will.

not do otherwise (except in terms of deciding which sins to commit!). From the Arminian perspective prevenient grace restores free will so that humans, for the first time, have the ability to do otherwise—namely, respond in faith to the grace of God or resist it in unrepentance and disbelief. At the point of God's call, sinners under the influence of prevenient grace have genuine free will as a gift of God; for the first time they can freely say yes or no to God. Nothing outside the self determines how they will respond. Calvinists say that humans never have that ability in spiritual matters (and possibly in any matters). People always do what they want to do, and God is the ultimate decider of human wants even though when it comes to sin, God works through secondary causes and never directly causes anyone to sin. These two views are incommensurable. To the Arminian, compatibilist free will is no free will at all. To the Calvinist, incompatibilist free will is a myth; it simply cannot exist because it would amount to an uncaused effect, which is absurd.[23] When it comes to deciding to resist or accept the saving grace offered by God, people's decisions and choices are either determined or not determined. To say they are not determined but merely influenced does not produce a hybrid; it is classical Arminianism.[24] To say they are determined but free begs further explanation. To say they are under such powerful influence of grace that they could not do otherwise than comply with God's will is no middle ground; it is classical Calvinism.

No Hybrid, but Common Ground

On several crucial issues related to soteriology, then, no middle ground or hybrid between Calvinism and Arminianism is logically possible. Calminian-

---

[23]The classic Calvinist critique of libertarian free will is found in Jonathan Edwards's treatise "Freedom of the Will." Just in case a reader is wondering whether so-called middle knowledge provides a middle ground, something needs to be said about it here. Middle knowledge would be God's knowledge of what free creatures would do freely in any given set of circumstances. But believers in middle knowledge normally affirm libertarian free will. The question of whether they could do otherwise is still open even in the case of middle knowledge, which is said by those who believe in it not to be determinative.

[24]For a very thorough and detailed examination of Arminius's own concept of free will see William Gene Witt, *Creation, Redemption and Grace in the Theology of Jacob Arminius* (Ph.D. diss., University of Notre Dame, 1993), pp. 418-30. According to Witt, Arminius's concept of free will was the same as Thomas Aquinas's. It is not the same as Enlightenment autonomous free will because it has a supernatural foundation and is always oriented toward the good even though, because of sin's corruption, it has a fallen perception of the good and thus turns away from the true good until God's prevenient grace intervenes. Thus it is not absolute, autonomous free agency but situated and teleological free will.

ism can only be held in defiance of reason; ultimately every Calminianism turns out either to be a disguised form of Calvinism or Arminianism, or it slides inexorably into one or the other. Many people claim to be "four-point Calvinists," by which they usually mean they agree with total depravity, unconditional election, irresistible grace and perseverance of the saints but reject limited atonement. When pressed, however, such four-point Calvinists often turn out to have misunderstood the Calvinist idea of limited atonement, and when it is explained to them correctly (i.e., universal in sufficiency but limited in scope to the elect), they embrace it. Some doubt exists whether Calvin himself believed in limited atonement, but it does seem to be part and parcel of the Calvinist system. Why would God intend Christ's suffering to atone for the guilt of those God had already determined would not be saved? Some Arminians call themselves "two-point Calvinists," especially if they live, work or worship in contexts where Reformed theology is considered the norm for evangelicalism. By this they usually mean that they affirm total depravity and perseverance of the saints. (This is especially common among Baptists.) However, by rejecting unconditional election, limited atonement and irresistible grace, they show that they are really Arminians and not Calvinists at all. They may correctly consider themselves part of the larger Reformed tradition, however.

Having argued here that Calvinism and Arminianism are incompatible systems not amenable to hybridization, I do not want readers to forget that the two systems have much in common. Both affirm divine sovereignty, even if in different ways and to different degrees; both embrace the absolute necessity of grace for anything truly good in human life. Both believe salvation is a free gift that can only be received by faith apart from meritorious works of righteousness. Both deny any human ability to initiate a relationship with God by exercising a good will toward God. Both affirm the divine initiative of faith (a technical term for the first step in salvation). In a word, both are Protestant. This is hotly contested by some hostile Calvinist critics of Arminianism, but throughout the rest of this book I will demonstrate that classical Arminian theology is a legitimate form of Protestant orthodoxy, and thus Arminianism shares vast common ground with classical Calvinism.

MYTH 3:

Arminianism Is Not an Orthodox Evangelical Option

*Classical Arminian theology heartily affirms the funda-
mentals of Christian orthodoxy and promotes the hallmarks of evangelical Protestant faith; it is neither Arian
nor liberal.*

MANY CALVINIST CRITICS OF ARMINIAN theology accept true Arminianism
(and especially Arminianism of the heart) as compatible with evangelical
Christian faith even though they reject its distinctive doctrines as less than
fully biblical. One example of such a generous Calvinist treatment of Arminianism is the volume *Why I Am Not an Arminian* by Calvinist authors Robert
A. Peterson and Michael D. Williams. It stands out as a model of irenic polemics—something of an oxymoron, judging by the harshness of most theological polemics, including most Calvinist treatments of Arminianism.
Peterson and Williams, both professors of theology at Covenant Theological Seminary in St. Louis, Missouri, go out of their way to identify Arminians
as true evangelicals.

> Calvinism and Arminianism do disagree regarding significant issues having to
> do with salvation, issues that we believe Calvinism rightly addresses and
> Arminianism does not. . . . Yet we do not think of Arminianism as a heresy or
> Arminian Christians as unregenerate. . . . Whatever issues relevant to salva-
> tion we disagree upon, let us agree on this: the Calvinist and the Arminian are
> brothers in Christ. Both belong to the household of faith. The issue of debate
> is not between belief and unbelief but rather which of two Christian perspec-
> tives better represents the biblical portrayal of the divine-human relationship
> in salvation and the contributions of both God and man in human history.[1]

Unfortunately, such generosity toward Arminians and Arminian theology is often lacking in Calvinist treatments of the subject. Typical is the claim by Kim Riddlebarger: "Arminianism is not only a departure from historic orthodoxy, but [also] a serious departure from the evangel itself."[2] For centuries both Reformed and Lutheran theologians identified Arminianism with Arianism, Socinianism, Pelagianism, semi-Pelagianism, humanism or liberal theology. The charge of Arianism is the most serious of all and totally without foundation. But it is so common, especially among Lutherans, that I heard a Lutheran theologian repeatedly slip into saying "Arianism" when he meant "Arminianism" at a conference of Wesleyan-Arminian scholars celebrating John Wesley's three hundredth birthday! (Needless to say, the many Arminians in the auditorium at a leading Wesleyan seminary were more than a little shocked—even though they recognized the Lutheran theologian's inadvertency.) Arianism denies the full deity of Jesus Christ. In its most narrow sense it adheres to fourth-century Christian leader Arius's belief that Jesus Christ was the incarnation of God's first and greatest creature—a heavenly being godlike in glory but not fully sharing the Father's divine nature. In its broader sense it has come to serve as shorthand for any denial of Jesus' full and true deity. The root of the accusation that Arminianism is Arian lies in a misunderstanding of Arminius's own Christology. He

---

[1]Robert A. Peterson and Michael D. Williams, *Why I Am Not an Arminian* (Downers Grove, Ill.: InterVarsity Press, 2004), p. 13. In spite of their irenic tone and generosity of judgment about Arminians' salvation, Peterson and Williams occasionally fall into offensive language (the rhetoric of exclusion) about Arminianism. This is, unfortunately, all too common if not nearly universal in Calvinist treatments of Arminian theology. For example, they wrongly describe "commitment to the freedom of the will" as the "highest value and first principle of doctrinal construction" for Arminians (p. 157). This is simply false. True Arminianism, as all Arminians have declared repeatedly, is primarily committed to the authority of Scripture and God's loving character as revealed in Jesus Christ. Belief in free will follows as a secondary principle of doctrine. They do Arminius a grave injustice when they say, "The integrity of the autonomous creature is the one irreducible theological principle of Arminius's thought" (p. 111). Anyone who has read Arminius's own writings cannot say this in all fairness. Arminius's first principle was God's love shown in Jesus Christ; his theology was thoroughly Christocentric and not humanistic. The most egregious example of Peterson and Williams's slip from their normally irenic approach is their claim that Arminianism "enshrines an almost idolatrous doctrine of the autonomous human being that is in fact closer to a biblical description of sin than true humanity" (p. 117). How these statements can be correlated with their generous embrace of Arminians as brothers and sisters is unclear. Arminians shake their heads in grief and consternation over these slips into misrepresentation of true Arminian thought; they are all too common in Calvinists' descriptions of Arminianism and betray a lack of honesty or familiarity with Arminian theology.

[2]Kim Riddlebarger, "Fire and Water," *Modern Reformation* 1 (1992): 10.

did not even implicitly deny the ontological deity of Jesus Christ, as many suppose. He fully affirmed it. Though the accusation that Arminianism is Arian in nature persists among those who have little or no genuine acquaintance with real Arminianism, it is simply false.

The charge that Arminianism is Socinian is hardly different from the first accusation. Faustus Socinus (1539-1604) was a radical reformer from Italy who lived in Poland. He founded the first unitarian churches in Europe and is often considered the true reformer by modern Unitarians. Socinus denied the ontological deity of Jesus Christ, reducing him to a man elevated to a special relationship with God; he also denied the ontological Trinity, the substitutionary atonement and original sin as inherited total depravity. He was the arch-heretic of Protestant Europe in the sixteenth century. Arminius's opponents in the United Provinces (Netherlands) and elsewhere tried to identify him with Socinianism, but they were never able to make the charge stick. And Arminius adamantly denied it, going to great lengths to prove his orthodoxy on these points of doctrine. Some later Remonstrants departed from authentic Arminian theology and became, for all intents and purposes, unitarians and universalists. So did some Reformed Protestants! And classical Arminians, like John Wesley, who remained faithful to Arminius's own theology, remained firmly orthodox in spite of continuing false charges of heresy by their Calvinist counterparts.[3] The only thing that classical Arminians have in common with Socinians and unitarians is belief in freedom of the will. If orthodoxy is arbitrarily defined as necessarily including belief in monergism and excluding every form of synergism, then Arminianism is not orthodox. But that would also make all of the early Greek church fathers, most of the medieval Catholic theologians, all Anabaptists and many Lutherans (including Melanchthon) heretics! Arminianism would then be in very good company.

The accusation that Arminianism is tantamount to Pelagianism, or at least semi-Pelagianism, is common in Calvinist literature. Examples have already been cited. I invited the director of a university Calvinist student group to speak to my seminary theology class. The seminary-trained Calvinist declared flatly that "Arminianism is just Pelagianism." The same charge can be found at many anti-Arminian Internet sites that promote moner-

---

[3]Theologian and hymn writer Augustus Toplady, who wrote the hymn "Rock of Ages," declared Wesley a non-Christian. So did other eighteenth-century evangelical Calvinists.

gism. More cautious critics qualify the accusation, proclaiming Arminianism semi-Pelagian rather than Pelagian. A leading Calvinist theologian and Christian apologist spoke at a conference at a major Christian college and used *semi-Pelagian* and *Arminian* as synonyms. In A.D. 431 Pelagianism was condemned in Ephesus by the third ecumenical council of Christianity because it affirmed natural and moral human ability to do God's will apart from the special operation of divine grace. Arminius rejected this teaching, and so do all of his faithful followers. Semi-Pelagianism was condemned by the Second Council of Orange in A.D. 529 because it affirmed human ability to exercise a good will toward God apart from special assistance of divine grace; it places the initiative in salvation on the human side, but Scripture places it on the divine side. Arminius also rejected semi-Pelagianism, as have all of his faithful followers. Arminians consider both Pelagianism and semi-Pelagianism heresies.

Why do so many Calvinists insist on identifying Arminianism as Pelagian or semi-Pelagian? This puzzles Arminians because of the great lengths they have gone to distance their theology from those heresies. Perhaps critics believe that Arminianism leads to Pelagianism or semi-Pelagianism as its good and necessary consequence. But if that is the case, it should be stated clearly. Fairness and honesty demand that critics of Arminianism at least admit that classical Arminians, including Arminius himself, do not teach what Pelagius taught or what the semi-Pelagians (e.g., John Cassian) taught.

Closely connected with the charge that Arminianism is semi-Pelagian if not Pelagian is the accusation that it departs from Protestant orthodoxy by abandoning or rejecting monergism. This was the line taken by Calvinist theologian and author Michael Horton in early issues of the magazine *Modern Reformation*, which he edits. In an infamous article attacking "evangelical Arminianism" as an oxymoron, Horton declares that "an evangelical cannot be an Arminian any more than an evangelical can be a Roman Catholic."[4] He claims that Arminius revived semi-Pelagianism and that "Arminians denied the Reformation belief that faith was a gift and that justification was a purely forensic (legal) declaration. For them, it included a moral change in the believer's life and faith itself, a work of humans, was the basis for God's declaration."[5] According to Horton, the Arminian (including Wesley's) doc-

---

[4]Michael Horton, "Evangelical Arminians?" *Modern Reformation* 1 (1992): 18.
[5]Ibid., p. 16.

trine of salvation renders "faith a work which achieves righteousness before God."[6] Clearly, for Horton, as for many Calvinist critics, Arminianism cannot be considered orthodox Protestantism because it (allegedly) denies salvation by grace through faith alone.[7]

Finally, some have called Arminianism humanistic and have attempted to link it to liberal theology. My favorite seminary theology professor once told me to be careful of Arminian theology because it always leads to liberal theology. The example cited was mainline Methodist theology, which during the twentieth century largely adopted a liberal perspective. Of course, I knew of numerous conservative Arminians, such as Nazarenes, and tried to point this out to my professor. (He later changed his mind about the slippery slope.) Later, a Calvinist friend who taught seminary asked me if I ever considered the possibility that my Arminianism might be evidence of latent humanism. These attempts to link Arminian theology with humanism (or a human-centered philosophy) and liberal theology often pop up in Calvinist rhetoric, and is found at numerous Calvinist-inspired websites and in books by Calvinist authors.

Chapter six will show that there is no inexorable slippery slope from true Arminianism to liberal theology. I have already said enough about Arminian belief in total depravity to dispel the myth that Arminianism is humanistic (see pp. 33-34)! Here I will focus on doctrines not central to the Calvinist-Arminian debate. Do real Arminians affirm fundamental tenets of classical Christian orthodoxy, such as the authority of Scripture, the transcendence of God, the deity of Jesus Christ and the Trinity?

Arminianism and Divine Revelation

Classical Arminianism includes belief in the supernatural inspiration of Scripture and its supreme authority for Christian faith and practice; it does not base its claims on philosophy or reason apart from divine revelation. Arminianism flatly contradicts the charge often leveled against it that it is based more on philosophy than on Scripture. I have engaged in lengthy dialogues (which usually devolve into debates) with Calvinist critics of Arminianism on Internet discussion groups, by e-mail and sometimes face to face.

---

[6]Ibid., p. 18.
[7]Horton, who teaches theology at Westminster Theological Seminary California, has changed his mind about Arminians since 1992. He now considers them evangelicals, although he still does not consider Arminianism consistent with Reformation theology. He communicated this change of mind to me in personal conversations and through correspondence.

At some point the Calvinist interlocutor usually charges that fundamental Arminian doctrines (e.g., free will) are based on a philosophical a priori rather than on God's Word. A careful examination of classical Arminian literature proves that real Arminians have always held a high view of Scripture. As with all orthodox Protestants, Arminians believe in and follow the principle of *sola scriptura* (Scripture above every other source and norm) in theology.

Arminius. In his third oration Arminius carefully explained the role of divine revelation and Scripture in his theology. According to him, humanity's only hope for true knowledge of God lies in divine revelation: "All our hope . . . for attaining to this [theological] knowledge is placed in Divine revelation" for "God cannot be known except through himself, to whom also there can be no approach but through himself."[8] And where has God revealed himself? First and foremost in Jesus Christ, who is revealed through Scripture. Scripture, in turn, is the unique production of the Holy Spirit:

> We declare, therefore, and we continue to repeat the declaration till the gates of hell re-echo the sound—"that the Holy Spirit, by whose inspiration holy men of God have spoken this word, and by whose impulse and guidance they have, as his amanuenses, consigned it to writing,—that this Holy Spirit is the Author of that light by the aid of which we obtain a perception and an understanding of the divine meanings of the word, and is the Effector of that certainty by which we believe those meanings to be truly divine; and that He is *the necessary Author, the all-sufficient Effector.*[9]

Clearly Arminius believed in the divine authorship (if not dictation!) of Scripture. In the pages that follow this declaration in the oration, Arminius debated the Roman Catholic idea of two equal sources of truth, affirming the sole supremacy of Scripture's authority over tradition and the church's interpretation. In his "Declaration of Sentiments," delivered to the States of Holland (government leaders) a year before his death, Arminius testified to his devotion to the authority of Scripture by declaring that if anything he taught is contrary to Scripture he should be punished severely.[10]

Two more quotes from Arminius should sufficiently establish his trust in the sole and supreme authority of Scripture in all theological matters: "we render to *the word of God alone* such due and suitable honour, as to de-

---

[8]Arminius, "Oration III," *Works,* 1:374.
[9]Ibid., pp. 397-98.
[10]Ibid., p. 609.

termine it to be *beyond* (or rather *above*) *all disputes,* too great to be the subject of any exception, and worthy of all acceptance," and "the Church always has Moses and the Prophets, the Evangelists and the Apostles,—that is, the Scriptures of the Old and New Testaments; and these scriptures fully and clearly comprehend whatever is necessary to salvation."[11] Throughout all of his writings the father of Arminianism left no doubt where he stood with regard to the authority of Scripture; he places it above every tradition—including the Reformed confessions—as well as above his own thinking: "The rule of Theological Verity is not two-fold, one Primary and the other Secondary; but is one and simple, the Sacred Scriptures."[12] He argued that even creeds and confessions of faith must be held more lightly than Scripture and should be subject to revision if and when they are found to be incorrect when compared to Scripture's message. For this he was sometimes criticized by his Calvinist opponents, who desired to hold the creeds and confessional statements (e.g., the Heidelberg Catechism and the Belgic Confession) incorrigibly true and authoritative. Against them Arminius wrote:

> The doctrine once received in the Church should be subjected to examination, however great the fear may be [for] this is one of God's commands, "Search and try the spirits whether they be of God." (1 John iv. 1) If cogitation [fearful hesitation of thought?] . . . had operated as hindrances on the minds of Luther, Zwingli, and others, they would never have pried into the doctrine of the Papists, or have subjected it to a scrutinizing examination.[13]

Simon Episcopius. So, Arminius was committed to the supreme authority of God's Word over every tradition and philosophy. What about later Arminians? One of the earliest works of Arminian theology after Arminius was produced by Simon Episcopius, the leader of the first-generation Remonstrants (he became the head of the Remonstrant seminary in the Netherlands when Arminianism was once again tolerated in 1625). The short title of this seminal Arminian theological statement is *Confession of Faith of Those Called Arminians.* This confession is a very orthodox statement of Protestant doctrine with a strongly synergistic flavoring. Episcopius affirmed Scripture's superiority to all human confessions and statements of faith, and argued that they are secondary to Scripture and must always be challenged by Scrip-

---

[11]Ibid., pp. 701, 723.
[12]Arminius, *Works,* 2:706.
[13]Ibid., 1:722-23.

ture.[14] He confessed the infallibility of Scripture and its sufficiency and perspicuity.[15] Episcopius said, "In these very books [of the Bible] is perfectly contained a full and more than sufficient revelation of all the mysteries of faith."[16] Even the later Remonstrant leader Philip Limborch, who was most responsible for vulgarizing Arminianism with a strong dose of rationalism and semi-Pelagianism, affirmed Scripture's supreme authority and inerrancy.[17]

John Wesley. Some Calvinists have suggested that John Wesley defected from the true Protestant faith by using what later Methodists have called the "Wesleyan Quadrilateral" of sources and norms: Scripture, tradition, reason and experience. This is nowhere explicitly stated by Wesley as his theological method; it is a method discerned by Albert Outler and other Wesley scholars. However, one thing is crystal clear in Wesley's own writings—Scripture stands over and above every other source and norm as the supreme touchstone of truth in all matters related to religion and ethics. No less an authority on Wesley than evangelical Methodist theologian Thomas Oden has discounted claims against Wesley's Protestant credentials with regard to the authority of Scripture. To demonstrate this, Oden quotes Wesley extensively:

> It is "the faith of Protestants" to "believe neither more nor less than what is manifestly contained in, and provable by, the Holy Scriptures." "The written word is the whole and sole rule of their faith, as well as practice." "We believe the Scripture to be of God." We are asked to "be not wise above what is written. Enjoin nothing that the Bible does not clearly enjoin. Forbid nothing that it does not clearly forbid." "I allow no other rule, whether of faith or practice, than the Holy Scriptures." There is no hidden or screened canon within the canon, due to the plenary extent of scriptural inspiration.[18]

Clearly Wesley did not deny the Protestant principle of *sola scriptura*, and

---

[14]Simon Episcopius, *Confession of Faith of Those Called Arminians* (London: Heart & Bible, 1684), pp. 18-25.
[15]Ibid., pp. 61-75.
[16]Ibid., p. 71.
[17]Philip Limborch, *A Complete System, or, Body of Divinity*, trans. William Jones (London: John Darby, 1713), p. 10.
[18]Thomas Oden, *John Wesley's Scriptural Christianity* (Grand Rapids: Zondervan, 1994), p. 56. The quotes are from Wesley's sermons "On Faith" and "Justification by Faith" and from letters to John Dickins and James Hervey. Oden also quotes Wesley's "The Character of a Methodist" that "the written word of God [is] the only and sufficient rule both of Christian faith and practice" (ibid.).

if he violated it, this has yet to be shown by anyone. Of course, many Christians disagree with Wesley's interpretation of Scripture, but the claim that he did not believe in Scripture's sole, supreme and sufficient authority for all matters of faith and Christian practice is simply false.

Nineteenth-century Methodists. The main Arminian theologians of the nineteenth century were Methodists Richard Watson, William Burton Pope, Thomas O. Summers and John Miley. What do they have to say about the authority of divine revelation and especially Scripture in relation to other sources and norms of theology? All four most heartily affirmed *sola scriptura* and based all of their theological conclusions on Scripture rather than on extrabiblical sources or norms. This does not mean they made no use of tradition or reason, but they used these as tools for interpreting Scripture and not as primary sources or criteria for truth in theological critique or construction. Watson clearly affirmed the supremacy of inspired Scripture as a supernatural revelation of God over every other source or norm of doctrine, theology and conduct: "When a doctrine is clearly revealed to us, standing as it does upon an infallible authority [Scripture], no contrary doctrine can be true; for this is in fact no more than saying, that human opinions must be tried by Divine authority, and that revelation must be consistent with itself."[19] He made crystal clear that both reason and tradition (to say nothing of experience) are to be judged by Scripture, which is alone the written supernatural revelation of God and judge of all truth in doctrine and conduct. Pope also expounded and promoted the doctrine of *sola scriptura*— Scripture as sole supreme authority in all matters of faith and Christian practice. He described the divine inspiration of Scripture as a supernatural influence of the Holy Spirit and then declared:

> Its plenary inspiration makes Holy Scripture the absolute and final authority, all-sufficient as the supreme Standard of Faith, Directory of Morals, and Charter of Privileges to the Church of God. . . . [I]n the domain of religious truth, and the kingdom of God among men, its claim to authority and sufficiency is absolute.[20]

Miley called the Scriptures "a supernatural revelation of truth from God" and argued that every person ought to be "submissive to their authority in

---

[19]Richard Watson, *Theological Institutes, Or, a View of the Evidences, Doctrines, Morals, and Institutions of Christianity* (New York: Lane & Scott, 1851), 1:99.
[20]William Burton Pope, *A Compendium of Christian Theology* (New York: Phillips & Hunt, n.d.), 1:174-75.

questions of faith and practice."[21] He rejected the elevation of any source or norm above or alongside Scripture in terms of authority, and stated that all doctrines must be constructed solely out of Scripture. Have those who question Arminianism's view of Scripture read these seminal nineteenth-century Arminian theologians? Or are they thinking only of twentieth-century defectors from true Arminianism, especially certain post-World War II liberal Methodist thinkers?

Twentieth-century Arminians. Twentieth-century Arminian theologians also affirmed *sola scriptura*. Of course, we must distinguish between liberalized Arminians (Arminians of the head) and classical Arminians (Arminians of the heart). The former may be found especially in the mainline Methodist churches (particularly the United Methodist Church) and occasionally among Baptists, Episcopalians and Congregationalists. Few if any of them actually consider themselves Arminians; their belief in freedom of the will is derived not from the Bible or Arminian tradition (including Wesley) but from Enlightenment humanism and thought based on the process philosophy of Alfred North Whitehead. Classical Arminians work primarily within the wider evangelical movement and may be found especially in the various Holiness denominations, such as the Church of the Nazarene, the Free Methodist Church and the Wesleyan Church. Some work within the Restorationist movement and teach in institutions associated with the Churches of Christ or the Independent Christian Churches. Others are Free Will Baptists or Pentecostals. Nazarene theologian H. Ray Dunning speaks especially for Wesley's (Holiness) heirs:

> Following John Wesley, Wesleyan theology has always built its doctrinal work upon four foundation stones commonly referred to as the Wesleyan quadrilateral. In addition to the Scripture, they are tradition, reason, and experience. These are not of equal authority, however. In fact, properly understood, the three auxiliary sources directly support the priority of the biblical authority.[22]

Similar assertions of the supremacy and normativity of the Bible for theology can be found in virtually every conservative Arminian system of theology into the twenty-first century. One example, though perhaps more conservative than many, is Free Will Baptist and Arminian theologian F. Leroy Forlines, who holds a doctrine of Scripture that would make almost any fun-

---

[21]John Miley, *Systematic Theology* (Peabody, Mass.: Hendrickson, 1989), 1:46-47.
[22]H. Ray Dunning, *Grace, Faith, and Holiness* (Kansas City, Mo.: Beacon Hill, 1988), p. 77.

damentalist proud! And yet He advocates and defends belief in the plenary, verbal inspiration of the Bible as well as its inerrancy and absolute authority in every subject it communicates.[23] Critics who charge that Arminianism does not hold fast to the Protestant principle of *sola scriptura* need to set forth their case with quotations denying it or otherwise undermining it from classical Arminian sources. That they will be unable to do. They may claim that Arminian belief undermines biblical authority by conflicting with what the Bible teaches, but that is something quite different from its having a low view of the Bible. The plain fact is that all classical Arminians have always held a high view of Scripture. Not all believe in the Bible's inerrancy, but neither do all Calvinists. Dunning expertly explains Wesleyans' reasons for rejecting biblical inerrancy (along with a rationalist view of Scripture) while demonstrating their confession of the Bible's inspiration and supreme authority.[24]

Arminianism on God and Christ

Throughout its history Arminianism has suffered much calumny at the hands of conservative Protestant critics and especially Calvinists. Among the worst accusations are that it denies or undermines the glory and sovereignty of God and that it amounts to the heresy of Arianism—denial of the deity of Jesus Christ and of the Trinity. Neither of these accusations can be made to stick, however, because classical Arminians, beginning with Arminius himself, have always confessed God's transcendent glory and majesty as well God's sovereignty. They have also always affirmed the ontological (as opposed to merely functional) deity of Jesus Christ and the Trinity. William Witt expresses well Arminians' frustration at the misconceptions and false charges surrounding Arminianism: "One wonders at this tendency to want to find heresy where none is visibly present. It seems to indicate a desire to expect the worst."[25]

Arminius. In his massive Notre Dame dissertation on Arminius's theology, Witt demonstrates conclusively the Dutch Reformer's own commitment to classical Christian theism and his agreement with Augustine and Thomas Aquinas on all matters essential to the traditional Christian doctrine of God.

---

[23]F. Leroy Forlines, *The Quest for Truth* (Nashville: Randall House, 2001), pp. 50-55.
[24]Dunning, *Grace, Faith, and Holiness*, pp. 60-62.
[25]William Gene Witt, *Creation, Redemption and Grace in the Theology of Jacob Arminius* (Ph.D. diss., University of Notre Dame, 1993), p. 540.

According to Arminius, God is self-sufficient simple substance whose essence and existence are identical.[26] God is immutable and eternal (even timeless), sovereign and omnipotent.[27] Witt argues cogently that the single major difference between Arminius's doctrine of God and Calvin's lies in Arminius's rejection of nominalistic voluntarism, which (to Arminius) makes God's freedom in relation to creation arbitrary. (Norminalistic voluntarism views God as absolutely free to use his power in any way; it is not constrained or limited by God's character.) Arminius based his whole theology on metaphysical realism in which "God is not 'freely' good because God is good by nature."[28] This may seem to Calvinists to limit God, but for Arminius and his followers it only means that God's goodness is as fundamental to this nature as his power. In fact, Witt avers, Arminius thought that Calvinism tended to limit God by making the world necessary for God's self-glorification: "The transcendent God of voluntarism 'needs' a creation over which to be sovereign every bit as much as the God of immanentism 'needs' a creation in which to be present."[29] In any case, Witt conclusively shows that Arminius's basic theological underpinnings in his doctrine of God were classically theistic; nowhere did he deny anything crucial to the Christian doctrine of God. Sprinkled throughout Arminius's corpus of writings are statements like this: "The Life of God is his Essence itself, and his very Being; because the Divine Essence is in every respect simple, as well as infinite, and therefore eternal and immutable."[30] What more could he say to convince critics that his theology is in line with the orthodox doctrine of God?

Arminius's stand on the Trinity was also unequivocally orthodox. This shows in his explanation of his Christology in his "Declaration of Sentiments." He had been falsely accused of denying the deity of Jesus Christ because he rejected the formula that the Son of God was *autotheos*—God in his own right, or in and of himself. Arminius called the accusation that he denied the deity of the Son Jesus Christ a notorious calumny, and he adamantly affirmed the equality of essence between the Father, Son and Holy Spirit.[31] However, he denied the idea, implied by the formula *autotheos*, when applied to the Son, that the Son has his deity in and of himself and

---

[26]Ibid., pp. 267-85.
[27]Ibid., pp. 491-505.
[28]Ibid., p. 300.
[29]Ibid., p. 292.
[30]Arminius, *Works*, 2:119.
[31]Ibid., 1:691-95.

from no other. This is almost certainly the source of the longstanding charge of Arianism, but it is based on a misunderstanding that Arminius himself cleared up. Arminius was simply defending the ancient doctrine of the monarchy of the Father found in Athanasius and the Cappadocian Fathers (as well as in Origen and other earlier fathers of the church). According to this the Son's deity is derived from the Father eternally. The Father is the "fount of divinity" within the Godhead. Arminius confessed Jesus Christ as God, but said:

> The word "God" therefore signifies, that He has the true Divine Essence; but the word "Son" signifies, that he has the Divine Essence from the Father: On this account, he is correctly denominated both God and Son of God. But since He cannot be styled the Father, he cannot possibly be said *to have the Divine Essence from himself or from no one.*[32]

The context of this explanation of Arminius's denial of the Son's *autotheos* makes clear his belief in the ontological Trinity. The Son derives his essence from the Father (as does the Holy Spirit) but is equal with the Father in essence and is God. Arminius defended himself by saying, "In all this proceeding [i.e., the debate over his Christology] I am far from being liable to any blame; for I have defended the truth and the sentiments of the Catholic and Orthodox Church."[33] Critics may continue to debate whether Arminius was right about the monarchy of the Father, but if they declare him Arian or say that he denied the deity, on that account they will have to say the same of the early Greek church fathers and the entire Eastern Orthodox tradition as well as much of Western theology. Witt concludes that "the position Arminius defended is, of course, the orthodox Catholic position. It was not Arminius, but his critics . . . who were at least confused, if not heterodox in this matter."[34]

Episcopius. Later Arminian theologians have not echoed Arminius's own defense of the monarchy of the Father or engaged in debate about the source of the Son's deity, but they have embraced classical theism as well as orthodox Christology and trinitarianism. Episcopius devoted an entire chapter of his *Confession of Faith* to the essence of God and the divine nature, and another chapter to the Trinity. His Christology echoes clearly and with-

---

[32]Ibid., p. 694.
[33]Ibid., p. 693.
[34]Witt, *Creation, Redemption and Grace*, p. 544.

out qualification the hypostatic union doctrine of the Chalcedonian Definition (one person, two natures); his doctrine of the Trinity contains no hint
of Arianism or Socinianism (unitarianism). His account of God's nature is
entirely consistent with classical theism. God is one, eternal, immutable, infinite, omniscient, omnipotent, self-sufficient, just, true, faithful, righteous
and constant.[35] Above all God is good and does not cause or will evil or sin.[36]
God is the "ever inexhaustible fountain of all things that are good" such that
every creature is totally dependent on God for everything.[37]

The same orthodox confession of God's being as well as of the Trinity
and the deity of Christ can readily be found in virtually every classical
Arminian theologian from Arminianism's beginnings to the present. The
only deviations come among those pseudo-Arminians who departed from
Arminius, Episcopius and Wesley into Enlightenment and liberal Protestant
thought. These Arminians of the head are revisionists. Calvinism also has its
revisionists. Arminianism itself is no more to blame for pseudo-Arminian
heterodoxy than Calvinism is to be blamed for Schleiermacher's and his followers' heresies.

John Wesley. Wesley provides a clear example of a doctrinally orthodox
Arminian. Tom Oden provides another. Many others could be mentioned.
However, if critics declare that Arminianism is inherently heretical or heterodox and point to its doctrines of God and Jesus Christ to prove it, only
one counterexample is necessary to disprove the charge. Sometimes anti-
Arminian critics make special exceptions for Wesley and admit that he, unlike other Arminians, was orthodox. Some pit Wesley against Arminianism
and say that Wesley was really a confused and inconsistent Calvinist! Wesley
called himself an Arminian, and anyone would be hard-pressed to show any
significant differences between his theology and Arminius's or that of later
evangelical Arminians. With regard to Jesus Christ "Wesley effortlessly employed the language of Chalcedon in phrases like 'Real God, as real man,'
'perfect, as God and as man,' 'the Son of God and the Son of Man' whereby
one phrase is 'taken from his divine, and the other from his human
nature.'"[38] Oden shows conclusively that Wesley held firmly to classical
Christian theism, including God's attributes of eternity, omnipresence, wis-

---

[35]Episcopius, *Confession of Those Called Arminians,* pp. 82-88.
[36]Ibid., p. 84.
[37]Ibid., p. 87.
[38]Oden, *Wesley's Scriptural Christianity,* p. 177. These and similar quotations are taken from Wesley's sermons, such as "On Knowing Christ After the Flesh."

dom and so forth. According to Oden:

> Wesley summarized key points of his doctrine of God in his renowned "Letter
> to a Roman Catholic": "As I am assured that there is an infinite and indepen-
> dent Being and that it is impossible there should be more than one, so I be-
> lieve that this one God is the Father of all things," especially of self-
> determining rational creatures, and this One "is in a peculiar manner the Fa-
> ther of those whom he regenerates by his Spirit, whom he adopts in his Son
> as co-heirs with him."[39]

Finally, Wesley's trinitarianism is above reproach from an orthodox perspective.[40] He even confessed the Athanasian Creed, which contains one of
the strongest statements of trinitarian orthodoxy.

So what? If Wesley was Arminian, as he surely was, and orthodox on all
these essential points of Christian teaching, then the claim that Arminianism itself is heretical or heterodox is at least undermined if not given the lie.
To attempt to separate Wesley from Arminianism as an exception is impossible; he knew Arminianism well and embraced it, and his entire pattern of
soteriological thinking is at one with Arminius's and the entire tradition of
faithful Arminianism.

Nineteenth- and twentieth-century Arminians. We find the same ringing endorsement of classical Christian orthodoxy on these essential points in
nineteenth- and twentieth-century Arminian thinkers. Pope speaks for all
nineteenth-century Arminians by confessing the classical, orthodox Chalcedonian doctrine of the person of Christ: one person of two natures:

> The Divine-human Person is the union, the result of the union, of the two na-
> tures; or rather the personality that unites the conditions of Divine and hu-
> man existence. This personality is one and undivided. . . . The two natures of
> the one Person are not confounded or fused together.[41]

Pope and the others (Watson, Summers and Miley) affirmed the incarnation of God in Jesus Christ with no diminution of either his humanity or
divinity. As for the Trinity, Miley speaks for all; he affirmed the classical, orthodox doctrine of the Trinity as expressed at Nicea (A.D. 325) and Constan-
tinople (A.D. 381) and said, "There is in the doctrine no distinct nature for
each person of the Trinity. The distinction is of three personal subsistences

---

[39]Ibid., p. 29.
[40]Ibid., pp. 46-53.
[41]Pope, *Compendium of Christian Theology,* 2:118.

in the unitary being of God."[42] The twentieth century saw no deviation from orthodoxy among classical Arminians. Leading Nazarene theologian H. Orton Wiley endorsed the Athanasian Creed as the most complete statement of orthodoxy.[43] Like Pope and the nineteenth-century evangelical Methodist theologians, Wiley affirmed the doctrine of the hypostatic union in Christ and the ontological (immanent) Trinity in eternity.[44]

We could not ask for a more thoroughly orthodox Christology or doctrine of the Trinity than is found in all the classical Arminian theologians throughout these two centuries. When we worship with contemporary Nazarenes, Free Methodists, Wesleyans and other evangelical churches of the Wesleyan tradition or with Free Will Baptists or classical Pentecostals, we discover that they thoroughly embrace the orthodox Christian faith; all of them have statements of faith that echo the great themes and hallmarks of Protestant orthodoxy. Wiley's commitment to bedrock Christian orthodoxy is held also by theologians of all these Arminian churches and denominations.

Arminianism and Protestantism

Some might agree that classical Arminianism is orthodox with regard to the fundamental elements of ecumenical Christianity and still argue that it is heterodox vis-à-vis classical Protestantism. This is the approach apparently taken by some of Arminianism's harshest Calvinist critics who know that Arminius's and Wesley's theologies conform to the creedal standards of ecumenical Christianity on the doctrines of God (especially the Trinity) and Christ. But such critics often chide Arminians for falling short of complete Protestant orthodoxy when it comes to beliefs about God's providence and salvation. In other words, the basic conflict about God's sovereignty (see chap. 2) remains a stumbling block to fully accepting Arminians as orthodox in the minds of many Calvinists. For them, Protestant orthodoxy includes God as the all-determining reality and salvation as monergistically decreed and delivered by God.

One leading Calvinist theologian and apologist who publicly describes Arminians as "Christians, just barely," says that the only alternative to Calvinism (divine determinism) is atheism! The Alliance of Confessing Evangeli-

---

[42]Miley, *Systematic Theology,* 1:230.
[43]H. Orton Wiley, *Christian Theology* (Kansas City, Mo.: Beacon Hill, 1941), 2:169.
[44]Ibid., pp. 180, 181.

cals, which publishes *Modern Reformation,* does not allow Arminians to join even though it is supposed to be inclusive of many Protestant denominations and traditions. Why? Because its leaders consider monergism part and parcel of the true and full Protestant (evangelical) faith. I was told by a reviewer of my earlier book *The Mosaic of Christian Belief* (IVP, 2003) that synergism is simply heresy; he suggested that saying there will always be monergists and synergists within evangelicalism is like saying it will always include truth and error. Many of these critics of Arminianism know that evangelical Arminians of the heart are orthodox in their doctrines of God and Christology, and that they are trinitarian. But they regard "true" Protestantism as an essential addition to early ecumenical Christian orthodoxy. For them this includes God's absolute, meticulous sovereignty and soteriological monergism.

The question then becomes whether this is too narrow a definition of Protestantism and the evangelical faith. It excludes Luther's right-hand man, Philip Melanchthon, who, after Luther's death, sided with Erasmus's position on free will and embraced synergism. It excludes all of the Anabaptists as well as many Anglicans and Episcopalians. The great formulator of Anglican theology Richard Hooker (1554-1600) was no monergist; his theology leaned closer to later Arminianism. Why enshrine monergism as a touchstone of Protestant orthodoxy? Some would say because it is necessary to protect justification by grace alone through faith alone. Some critics of Arminianism even go so far as to claim that Arminians do not believe in that fundamental principle of Protestantism. (This will be proved false in chap. 9.) This is most certainly because these Calvinists imagine such close connection between justification by grace through faith alone and monergism that they jump from Arminianism's denial of the latter to an imagined denial of the former. But what if a person (e.g., John Wesley) heartily and warmly teaches the former while denying the latter? This is the case with most Arminians; they disconnect the two doctrines that Calvinists insist are intrinsic to each other. This is why some Calvinists say that Arminians are "Christians, just barely"—due to this "felicitous inconsistency," that is, between justification by grace alone through faith alone and synergism. In "Who Saves Who?" Michael Horton implies that Arminianism is not orthodox Protestantism because "if one does not believe in the doctrine of unconditional election, it is impossible to have a high doctrine of grace."[45] Of

---

[45]Michael S. Horton, "Who Saves Who?" *Modern Reformation* 1 (1992): 1.

course, Arminians deny this and point to their own doctrine of prevenient grace as proof. Salvation is all of grace, and merit is excluded. In fact, the charge that Arminianism is Pelagian or semi-Pelagian—that it undermines human dependence on grace for absolutely everything spiritually good—is false.

Can this monergistic definition of Protestant orthodoxy be sustained? Certainly the earliest and most influential Protestant voices—Luther, Zwingli and Calvin, to say nothing of Bucer, Cranmer and Knox—were monergists. Does this mean all Protestants must forever be monergists? All of these also practiced infant baptism. What if someone argued that only infant baptizers are true Protestants? They were also strong believers in union between church and state. Does authentic Protestantism necessarily include that too? The historical argument breaks down. Besides, beginning in 1525 the Anabaptists arose within the bosom of the Protestant Reformation (in Zwingli's Zurich) and spread throughout Europe. To declare them not Protestants would seem somewhat silly from a historical perspective. Later Wesley formed the Methodist movement; is Methodism not part of the Protestant story?

Some will argue that a distinction must be recognized and maintained between historical and sociological description, on the one hand, and normative theological judgment, on the other. Not everyone included historically and sociologically under the umbrella of Protestantism deserves to be judged theologically Protestant. Why? Because, they argue, Protestantism is synonymous with belief in *sola gratia* and *sola fides*—salvation by grace alone and through faith alone—and only monergism is consistent with these. But does synergism contradict *sola gratia* and *sola fides*? Arminians do not think so; they hold a form of evangelical synergism that sees grace as the efficient cause of salvation and calls faith the sole instrumental cause of salvation, to the exclusion of human merits. Even if this were inconsistent, why exclude Arminians from the Protestant fold when they affirm (even if inconsistently) the essential principle? Simply because powerful evangelical administrators and some influential scholars and leaders believe that Arminianism is defectively Protestant at best and possibly heterodox? Arminians do not get a fair and equal hearing in some evangelical (and also nonevangelical) Protestant boardrooms and classrooms. If they wear the Arminian label too proudly, they often find themselves marginalized within—if not excluded from—some transdenominational and multiconfessional evangelical Protestant organizations.

The rest of this book is devoted to demonstrating that classical Armini-anism is a form of Protestant orthodoxy. I will show that Arminianism is not devoted to free will out of any humanistic or Enlightenment motive or op-timistic anthropology. Classical Arminianism is a theology of grace that af-firms justification by grace alone through faith alone. Finally, the case will be made that it does not lead ineluctably to liberal theology, universalism or open theism.[46]

---

[46]This is not to suggest that open theism is on the same level with liberal theology or universal-ism! Some Calvinist and other critics of Arminianism, however, treat it as such and attempt to show that Arminian theology leads necessarily to it. Most classical Arminians—even those who do not consider open theism heretical—disagree with these critics. Open theism will be discussed in chap. 8.

MYTH 4

The Heart of Arminianism
Is Belief in Free Will

The true heart of Arminian theology is God's loving and just character; the formal principle of Arminianism is the universal will of God for salvation.

ASK MOST KNOWLEDGEABLE CHRISTIANS ABOUT Calvinism and Arminianism and they will say that the former believes in predestination and the latter believes in free will. Like much popular religious opinion this is incorrect as it stands. At the very least it is misleading. Many Calvinists claim to believe in free will. Of course, they mean free will that is compatible with divine determination (compatibilist free will). All real Arminians believe in predestination. Of course, they mean conditional election based on God's foreknowledge of faith. Nevertheless, in spite of these qualifications, the claim that all Calvinists believe in predestination and not free will is false, just as the claim that all Arminians believe in free will and not predestination is false.

Perhaps the most damaging calumny spread by critics against Arminianism is that it begins with and is controlled by belief in freedom of the will. Even some Arminians have come to believe this! But it is simply wrong. It is no more true that Arminianism is controlled by a priori belief in free agency than it is true that Calvinism is controlled by a priori denial of free will. Each theology's view of free will arises from and is based on more fundamental commitments. And yet, even astute theologians who should know better often claim that free will holds just such a powerful and controlling position in Arminian theology. According to Lutheran theologian Rick Ritchie: "The

guiding motif in Arminianism is the free will of man."[1] Calvinist Kim Riddlebarger calls human freedom a "first principle" of Arminianism.[2] For all their
research into and irenic rhetoric about Arminianism Calvinist theologians
Robert Peterson and Michael Williams get it wrong when they write: "The
incompatibilist commitment to the freedom of the will as the highest value
and first principle of doctrinal construction moves Arminianism to argue
that human choices and actions have no meaning if God directs them by his
ordaining power."[3]

   With all due respect to these two authors, and others who aim the same
criticism at Arminianism, this Arminian must object strenuously. All real
Arminians would chime in with this objection. First, commitment to the
freedom of the will is not the highest value or first principle of Arminian
doctrinal construction. That pride of place belongs to the Arminian vision
of the character of God as discerned from a synoptic reading of Scripture
using the revelation of God in Jesus Christ as the hermeneutical control.
Arminians believe in free will because they see it everywhere assumed in the
Bible, and because it is necessary to protect God's reputation. Second,
Arminians do not argue that human choices and actions have no meaning
if God directs them by his ordaining power. In fact, Arminians do not object
to the idea that God "directs" human choices and actions. All Arminians object to is belief that God controls human choices—especially evil and sinful
ones! And Arminians do not see any way to embrace divine determinism
(monergism) and avoid making God the author of sin and evil. Some Calvinists (like some Arminians) slip too easily into softer language than their
theology demands when making a point that may be offensive to others.
What Peterson and Williams should have written is that Arminians believe
human choices and actions have no meaning if they are absolutely controlled by God's ordaining power. Arminianism does not object to the idea
that God directs human choices and actions through the power of persuasion. Arminianism embraces the idea that God directs human choices and
actions by making them fit into his master plan for history. The only thing
Arminianism rejects, in this specific area, is that God controls all human
choices and actions. Arminians wish their critics would use clearer language

---

[1]Rick Ritchie, "A Lutheran Response to Arminianism," *Modern Reformation* 1 (1992): 12.
[2]Kim Riddlebarger, "Fire and Water," *Modern Reformation* 1 (1992): 9.
[3]Robert A. Peterson and Michael D. Williams, *Why I Am Not an Arminian* (Downers Grove, Ill.:
   InterVarsity Press, 2004), p. 157

that truly brings out the real differences and does not confuse the issues.

Why do Arminians object to belief that God controls human decisions and actions by his ordaining power? First, let's be clear about the reasons Arminians do *not* use in objecting to this deterministic belief. It is not because they are charmed by some modern commitment to humanistic freedom; there were Arminians before the rise of modernity (and the Enlightenment), and there were believers in incompatibilist free will long before Arminius! The early Greek church fathers believed in freedom of the will and rejected determinism of any kind. Second, it is not because they do not believe in God's ordaining power. Real Arminians have always believed God ordains and even controls many things in history; they affirm God's freedom and omnipotence. If God chose to control every human decision and action, he could do it. Rather, the real reason Arminians reject divine control of every human choice and action is that this would make God the author of sin and evil. For Arminians this makes God at least morally ambiguous and at worst the *only* sinner. Arminians acknowledge that Calvinists do not claim that God is morally ambiguous or evil! Some, however, do believe that God is the author of sin and evil. Calvinist theologian Edwin Palmer argued that God does foreordain sin: "The Bible is clear: God ordains sin." "Although all things—unbelief and sin included—proceed from God's eternal decree, man is still to blame for his sins."[4] This is why Arminians object to belief in exhaustive divine determinism in any form; it cannot avoid making God the author of sin and evil, and the logical conclusion must be that God is not wholly good even though Calvinists and other monergists disagree.[5]

Arminianism begins with God's goodness and ends by affirming free will. The latter follows from the former, and the former is based on divine revelation; God reveals himself as unconditionally and unequivocally good, which does not exclude justice and wrathful retribution. It only excludes the possibility of God sinning, willing others to sin or causing sin. If God's

---

[4]Edwin H. Palmer, *The Five Points of Calvinism* (Grand Rapids: Baker, 1972), pp. 85, 103, 106.

[5]I am well aware that Calvinists (and other divine determinists) say that God is wholly good, and they appeal to some higher good that justifies God's foreordination of sin and evil. But Arminians want to know what higher good can possibly justify the Holocaust? What higher good can possibly justify some significant portion of humanity suffering in hell eternally apart from any genuinely free choices they or their federal head Adam made? Appeal to God's glory to justify unconditional reprobation to hell, as Wesley said, makes our blood run cold. What kind of God is it who is glorified by foreordaining and unconditionally reprobating persons to hell? If appeal is made to the necessity of hell for the manifestation of God's attribute of justice, Arminians ask whether the cross was insufficient.

goodness is so mysterious that it is compatible with willing and actively rendering certain the Fall and every other evil (even if only by withdrawing the power necessary to avoid sinning) of human history, it is meaningless. A concept that is compatible with anything and everything is empty. There is no example within humanity where goodness is compatible with willing someone to do evil or sin and suffer eternally for it. Arminians are well aware of Calvinist arguments based on the Genesis narrative where Joseph's brothers meant his captivity for evil but God meant it for good (Gen 50:20). They simply do not believe this proves that God *ordains* evil that good may come of it. Arminians believe God *permits* evil and brings good out of it. Otherwise, who is the real sinner?

Arminianism is all about protecting the reputation of God by protecting his character as revealed in Jesus Christ and Scripture. Arminians are not concerned about some humanly derived fascination with fairness; God does not have to be fair. Fairness is not necessary to goodness. But love and justice are necessary to goodness, and both exclude willing determination of sin, evil or eternal suffering. At this point some critics of Arminianism object that protecting God's character in this way, by denying divine determinism, reveals an a priori commitment to reason over Scripture.[6] That is because, according to at least some Calvinists, Scripture teaches both exhaustive divine determinism, including foreordination of sin, and God's absolute, unconditional goodness, including no hint of injustice or lack of holiness. "All things, including sin, are brought to pass by God—without God violating His holiness." And "When God speaks—as He has clearly done in Romans 9—then we are simply to follow and believe, even if we cannot understand, and even if it seems contradictory to our puny minds."[7] Palmer, like many Calvinists, claimed to embrace antinomy—a kind of paradox—without trying to use reason to relieve it. Like many critics of Arminianism, he accused Arminians of using reason against the Bible to relieve the paradox. However, Palmer himself, like many Calvinists, also used reason to try to relieve the paradox and neglected to note that Arminians do not reject paradox; they simply think this one—that God is unconditionally good and yet foreordains sin and evil—is not taught in Scripture, making it an outright logical contradiction! Palmer averred that the Bible teaches that God ordains sin, and yet he still tried to get God off the hook by arguing

---

[6]Palmer, *Five Points of Calvinism*, p. 85.
[7]Ibid., pp. 101, 109.

that God does not cause sin but renders it certain by an "efficacious permission."[8] In other words, he could not bring himself to say that God actually causes sin or is the author of sin. Rather, humans alone are responsible for sin. God merely allowed humans to sin (even though he actually foreordained it). The mind begins to boggle.

Other Calvinists fill in the gaps for Palmer. God, the typical Calvinist explanation says, withdrew the moral power necessary for Adam and Eve to avoid sinning so that their rebellion was inevitable without God actually causing them to sin. Is this not a distinction without a difference? Palmer asserted that God wills sin and unbelief unwillingly; God takes no delight in them even though he wills them and effectuates them.[9] Realizing the logical difficulties with these claims, Palmer said, "Objections to the teaching of [divinely determined] reprobation are usually based on scholastic rationalism rather than on humble submission to the Word of God."[10] Not only is this insulting to Arminians but it also turns back against Palmer himself insofar as he is not content simply to say (with Swiss Reformer Ulrich Zwingli, who bit the bullet on this) that God is the author of sin and evil, and this raises serious questions about God's goodness. Instead, Palmer used reason to attempt to guard God's goodness by saying something the Bible does not say—that God effectuates sin and unbelief in a different way than he effectuates good deeds and faith (by merely withholding the grace necessary for creatures to avoid sin and unbelief).[11]

---

[8]Ibid., p. 98.

[9]Ibid., pp. 106-7.

[10]Ibid., p. 107.

[11]Ibid., p. 106. Because fairness is a major concern here, it is only right to acknowledge that some Calvinists affirm monergism of salvation without going so far as absolute divine determinism of all things. Peterson and Williams, for example, seem to say that God is not morally stained by the sin and unbelief of the reprobate or for passing over them in election because they inherit the sin of Adam and are born condemned as well as corrupt. Thus, they deserve hell; God is merciful in that he chooses some out of the mass of damnation to save. "Man himself causes unbelief. The Arminian depiction of Calvinists as believing that God creates people to be sinners and then damns them for being what he has made them is a gross misrepresentation. . . . Yes, God is the cause of belief. . . . But he does not need to cause unbelief. Our fall in Adam has already done that" (*Why I Am Not an Arminian*, pp. 132-33). However, not only does this seem to contradict Calvin and Palmer (both of whom affirm exhaustive divine determinism), it also raises serious questions about why Adam and Eve sinned. What was God's involvement there? And if God saves some out of the mass of perdition unconditionally, why does he not save all? Peterson and Williams write, "While God commands all to repent and takes no delight in the death of the sinner, all are not saved because it is not God's intention to give his redeeming grace to all" and "we do not know why God has chosen to save one but not another" (ibid., pp. 128, 130). The Arminian has the same problem with this as

Arminians are sometimes shocked by some Calvinists' apparent willing ignorance of Arminianism and their blindness to the double standards used in their criticisms of Arminianism. They are often eager to point out the flaws in Arminianism and blow them out of proportion while ignoring the flaws in their own system or excusing them by appeal to antinomy, yet they do their best to relieve the paradox—something they criticize Arminians for doing. But Arminians would be pleased if their Calvinist critics would simply acknowledge that the driving motif of Arminianism is not belief in free will but commitment to a certain vision of God's goodness. Any fair reading of Arminius or any of his faithful followers will show this to be the case.

Arminius and the Early Arminians on God's Goodness

Arminius. Contrary to popular opinion, Arminius did not begin with free will and work his way to conditional election or resistible grace. Rather, his basic theological impulse is absolute: commitment to God's goodness. His theology is Christocentric; Jesus Christ is our best clue to the character of God, and in him God is revealed as compassionate, merciful, loving and just. Arminius's theology is embedded in his arguments against Calvinism of all kinds—supralapsarian and infralapsarian. Therefore it is often impossible to illustrate his views with direct quotations without including some of his harsher statements against it. That is regrettable since the rhetoric of that time was ordinarily more pointed than most people today are comfortable with. Readers should remember that Arminius was under tremendous assault and was extremely frustrated; during his career as a theologian virtually all of his time was devoted to responding to accusations and charges of heresy. And the rhetoric of the Calvinists (including Calvin himself!) was no less harsh.

---

with the more extreme (but perhaps historically normative) Calvinist view that God foreordained the Fall of Adam and Eve and every individual's eternal destiny unconditionally. In effect it amounts to the same thing. Once Adam and Eve fell (which cannot be of their own libertarian free will as if they could do otherwise since Peterson and Williams reject incompatibilist freedom as incoherent), God chooses to save some regardless of their own libertarian free choices. If God is good in any sense analogous to the best of human goodness (as God commands it and says to imitate him in it!), why does he relegate some to eternal suffering unconditionally? The issue is not fairness but goodness and love. To appeal to ignorance solves nothing; God's character is still besmirched because whatever the reason may be it has nothing to do with goodness or badness or free choices. The only alternative is divine arbitrariness! However, I acknowledge that most Calvinists *do not* consider God arbitrary or the author of sin and evil even if Arminians cannot see how they avoid these conclusions.

Arminius's commitment to divine goodness appears especially in his responses to Calvinists William Perkins and Franciscus Gomarus. Arminius's most basic guiding principle in these debates is that God is necessarily and by nature good; God's goodness controls God's power. And God's goodness and glory are inseparable; God is glorified precisely in revealing his goodness in creation and redemption.[12] "God is good by a natural and internal necessity, not, *freely*."[13] This is one way that Arminius expressed his metaphysical realism, which opposed nominalist voluntarism (that is, God is good because he chooses to be good and is not good by nature). Clearly, Arminius feared that the Calvinism of his time was based, like Luther's theology, on nominalism, which denies any intrinsic, eternal divine nature that controls the exercise of God's power. According to Arminius, in Calvinism "the divine nature threatens to be swallowed up in the darkness of the hidden God of the secret decree [of unconditional election and reprobation]."[14] Arminius could abide no hint of arbitrariness or injustice in God because of God's revelation of his character in Jesus Christ, and this revelation does not hide a dark, hidden God who secretly wills the destruction of the wicked—except when they voluntarily choose their wickedness in free resistance to the grace of God. Arminius scholar William Witt is correct that Arminius's main concern was not free will but God's relation to rational creatures, and especially God's grace abounding toward them because of his nature, which is love.[15] "Arminius's main concern was to avoid making God the author of sin."[16] To put it bluntly, for Arminius, God could not foreordain or directly or indirectly cause sin and evil even if he wanted to (which he would not), because that would make God the author of sin. And God's good and just nature requires that he desires the salvation of every human being.[17] This is completely consistent with Scripture (1 Tim 2:4; 2 Pet 3:9).

When Arminius tackled the theologies of William Perkins and Franciscus Gomarus, he appealed not to free will as his critical principle but to divine

---

[12]Arminius, "Oration II," *Works,* 1:364.

[13]Arminius, "Certain Articles to Be Diligently Examined and Weighed," *Works,* 2:707.

[14]James Arminius, quoted in William Witt, *Creation, Redemption and Grace in the Theology of Jacob Arminius* (Ph.D. diss., University of Notre Dame, 1993), p. 312.

[15]William Witt, *Creation, Redemption and Grace in the Theology of Jacob Arminius* (Ph.D. diss., University of Notre Dame, 1993), p. 419.

[16]Ibid., p. 690.

[17]Ibid., p. 622.

goodness. First, he argued that even mild Calvinism (as opposed to supra-lapsarianism) cannot avoid making God the author of sin by making the Fall unavoidable insofar as it holds to divine determinism. Perkins was typi-cal of the Calvinists of that day in that he attributed the Fall to voluntary hu-man desertion of God and yet also claimed that the Fall was foreordained and rendered certain by God, who withdrew sufficient grace from Adam and Eve. To Perkins Arminius wrote:

> But you say that "the will of man intervened in this desertion [from God]," be-cause "man was not deserted, unless willing to be deserted." I reply, If it is so, then truly man deserved to be forsaken. But I ask whether man could have willed not to be forsaken. But if you say he could, then he did not sin necessarily, but freely. But if you say he could not, then the blame redounds to God.[18]

This is crucial to Arminius's argument against those who say that the Fall happened necessarily by God's decree and that God willed it and rendered it certain. Then God is not as he is revealed to be in Jesus Christ, nor is God perfectly good. Then the blame redounds to God. There is a dark side to God. To supralapsarianism (in which God decrees who will be saved and damned before creation and the Fall), Arminius declared, "no rational creatures have been created by God with this intention, that they might be damned . . . for this would be unjust."[19] Such a doctrine attributes to God a plan "worse than which not even the devil himself could conceive in his own most wicked mind."[20] Although supralapsarianism was Arminius's main foil, he realized that every form of Calvinism known to him (including what came to be called infralapsarianism, which says God only decreed to save and damn individuals in light of the Fall) fell on the same sword by making the fall of humanity necessary by divine decree, and then asserting that God unconditionally by decree saves only a portion of fallen humanity. The nub of Arminius's entire argument against Calvinism lies in this declaration:

> That creature necessarily sins, upon whom, left in his own nature, a law is imposed not performable by the powers of that nature: But [according to Calvinism] a law not performable by the powers of his nature was imposed upon man left in his own nature: therefore man left in his own nature nec-essarily sinned. And by consequent, God, who gave that law, and determined

---

[18]Arminius, "An Examination of Dr. Perkins's Pamphlet on Predestination," *Works,* 3:375.
[19]Arminius, "An Examination of the Theses of Dr. Franciscus Gomarus Respecting Predestina-tion," *Works,* 3:602.
[20]Ibid., p. 603.

to leave man in his own nature [by withdrawing the power not to sin], is the cause that man sinned.[21]

Arminius spoke harshly of the logical consequences of the conventional Calvinist view of divine determinism in the Fall, which resulted in sin and eternal damnation (because God decided to pass over many unconditionally to save others): "if this 'determination' denote the decree of God by which He resolved that the will should be depraved and that man should commit sin, then it follows from this that God is the author of sin."[22] Arminius pulled no punches: "From these premises [that all things follow necessarily by divine decrees, including the Fall] we deduce . . . that *God really sins. . . .* [t]hat *God is the only sinner . . . [t]hat sin is not sin.*"[23] But Arminius's argument against the Calvinist view is not that it violates free will! Rather, he said, "This doctrine is repugnant to the nature of God" and injurious to the glory of God.[24] Let it be clear that although Arminius was often, as in this particular context, talking about supralapsarianism, he occasionally went out of his way to note that "a second kind of predestination" (infralapsarianism) falls to the same objections by having God foreordain the Fall; thus he is the author of sin.[25] Throughout his writings against Calvinism and in favor of free will, Arminius appealed to the nature and character of God. He realized that Calvinists denied that God is the author of sin or in any way stained by the guilt of sin, but he insisted that it is nevertheless a fair inference from what they believe.[26]

Simon Episcopius. Arminius's Remonstrant followers echoed the Dutch Reformers' method of using God's character of goodness as the critical principle for rejecting divine determinism and monergism, and embracing evangelical synergism. Simon Episcopius dwelled at length on God's goodness as his primary and controlling attribute in his *Confession of Faith* (1622). He asserted that although God is free and not determined by any inner or outer necessity or cause, because of his nature God cannot will or cause evil or sin.[27] The "cannot" is not because God is unable, because, ac-

---

[21]Arminius, "Friendly Conference of James Arminius . . . with Mr. Franciscus Junius, About Predestination," *Works*, 3:214.

[22]Arminius, "Nine Questions," *Works*, 2:65.

[23]Arminius, "A Declaration of Sentiments," *Works*, 1:630.

[24]Ibid., pp. 623, 630.

[25]Ibid., p. 648.

[26]Arminius, "Theses of Dr. Franciscus Gomarus," *Works*, 3:654.

[27]Simon Episcopius, *Confession of Faith of Those Called Arminians* (London: Heart & Bible, 1684), p. 84.

cording to Episcopius, God is omnipotent, which means he can do anything not a contradiction or against his will. But God can do more than he will, and his will is guided by his nature, which is good. God's nature is perfect in goodness and justice; he never does wrong to anyone. "He is most good, both in himself, and toward his creatures."[28] Why is there sin and evil in God's creation if he is perfectly good and "the inexhaustible fountain of all things that are good"?[29] Because he values the liberty he gave his human creatures, and he will not abrogate it even though it means sin and evil enter creation. God permits, but does not will or cause, sin and evil "that he may not overthrow the order once settled by himself and destroy and void that liberty which he gave his creature."[30] But God never imposes sin or evil on anyone, which would violate God's character by making him the author of sin. God bestowed Adam and Eve with every gift necessary for obedience and blessedness, but they rebelled anyway, which is why they and all their posterity are condemned (unless they repent and have faith). For Episcopius, as for Arminius, Calvinism inexorably makes God the author of sin by rendering the Fall necessary through his decree and the withdrawal of sufficient grace not to sin. This opinion makes God unwise and unjust and "the true and proper author of sin."[31] Again, as with Arminius, Episcopius was not concerned with free will for its own sake but with God's nature and character.

Philip Limborch. Later, Philip Limborch, a Remonstrant defector from classical Arminianism, also appealed to God's goodness in refuting conventional Calvinism. Because God is inherently good, which means just, the fall of humanity into sin cannot have resulted from any secret counsel or determination of God. That would make God directly or indirectly the author of

---

[28]Ibid., p. 85.

[29]Ibid., p. 87.

[30]Ibid., p. 85. Note that even though it may sound like Arminius and Arminians make liberty an ultimate purpose of God in creation and thus a highest good, that is not really the case. When Arminius and Arminians say that God values his human creatures' free will and will not rob them of it, they do not mean because free will is a good in and of itself. Rather, God creates and preserves free will for the sake of a higher good, which is well expressed by Methodist theologian Thomas Oden as he explains why God permits sin: "God does not want sin, but permits sin in the interest of preserving free, compassionate, self-determined persons with whom to communicate incomparable divine love and holiness" (*John Wesley's Scriptural Christianity* [Grand Rapids: Zondervan, 1994], p. 172). In other words, the higher good that requires free will is a relationship of love, which, Arminians believe, cannot be determined by anyone other than the ones who love.

[31]Ibid., p. 104.

sin and evil.[32] In spite of the fact that he was not a very good representative of true Arminianism, especially in his doctrine of human moral ability after the Fall, Limborch spoke truly for all Arminians about the belief that God rendered the Fall certain by withdrawing from Adam and Eve (and by implication from humanity itself) sufficient grace not to sin:

> The unreasonableness (not to say worse) of this Argument appears at first view; for what can be supposed more unjust than for God by withholding his sufficient restraining grace to lay his creatures under a fatal necessity of sinning and then to punish them for what they could not avoid? If this be not making God the Author of sin and charging him with the highest injustice . . . I know not what is: and whether such a doctrine, so derogatory to the nature of God, be fit to be maintained, we leave the world to judge.[33]

Like all Arminians Limborch rejected the doctrine of unconditional election, and especially reprobation, not because it detracts from human free will but because it denigrates the divine character. He affirmed conditional election and predestination as bringing glory to God, but he appealed to the Scriptures (1 Tim 2:4; 2 Pet 3:9) to establish God's universal will for salvation and connected that with God's love as his basic attribute: "the doctrine of absolute reprobation is repugnant to the divine perfections of holiness, justice, sincerity, wisdom and love."[34] He also said:

> Now what can be more dishonorable, what more unworthy of God, than to make him the author of sin which is so highly inconsistent with his holiness, which he severely forbids and threatens to punish with no less than everlasting torments? Certainly this is so monstrous, that this single consideration might be enough to deter all who are concerned for the glory of God from embracing such a harsh and unbecoming doctrine.[35]

Conclusion. Notice the pattern in all of these arguments. None of these authors appealed to free will as the first principle of theological construction or critical principle for rejecting divine determinism and monergism. If the Calvinist critics were correct, we would find the Arminians saying something like "God's foreordination of all things, including the Fall, cannot be true because that would rob human beings of their free will." But this

---

[32]Philip Limborch, *A Complete System, or, Body of Divinity,* trans. William James (London: John Darby, 1713), pp. 68-69.
[33]Ibid., p. 88.
[34]Ibid., p. 371.
[35]Ibid., p. 372.

is not what we find in Arminian literature (as opposed perhaps to popular religious tracts or clichés uttered by people who think they are Arminians!). True Arminians have always based their belief in freedom of the will and denial of divine determinism, including compatibilist free will, on the first principle of God's goodness. Given so much evil in the world stemming from the Fall of humanity in the garden, free will rather than divine determination must be the cause or else God would be the author of it all, rendering his character morally ambiguous and his reputation questionable. This is the pattern of Arminian argument. Of course, Calvinists can still argue that Arminians are wrong about this, but they should not argue that Arminians are motivated by a "nearly idolatrous belief in free will" for its own sake (or even for the sake of fairness), because it is simply not in the literature, which reveals that Arminians are primarily concerned about God's goodness and not about free will or fairness.

John Wesley on God's Goodness

Eighteenth-century Arminian revivalist and Methodist founder John Wesley followed the same method as Arminius and the Remonstrants in rejecting Calvinism and affirming free will. He did not begin with a priori belief in free will and then proceed from there. He was not even absolutely committed to freedom of the will; he was willing to concede that sometimes God overwhelms the will and forces a person to do something God wants done.[36] His main concern was to protect God's goodness from the charge that God is the author of sin and evil. And Wesley could not see how Calvinism could escape that conclusion. For Wesley, any belief in unconditional election leads inevitably to double predestination, which includes unconditional reprobation of certain individuals to eternal condemnation and suffering. For Wesley, "the price of double predestinarian exegesis is far too high not only for moral accountability but for theodicy, evangelism, the attributes of God, the goodness of creation, and human freedom."[37] The crux of Wesley's argument, however, is that belief in double predestination, which follows necessarily from belief in unconditional election, subverts the moral attributes of God: "The merciful God appears as a capricious tyrant more de-

---

[36]According to leading Wesley scholar Thomas Oden, Wesley agreed with fellow Calvinist revivalist that some persons may be predestined by God for salvation, but he rejected any reprobation by divine decree as incompatible with God's goodness. See Thomas Oden, *John Wesley's Scriptural Christianity*, p. 253.

[37]Ibid., p. 257.

ceptive and cruel than the devil himself, and the human person an automaton."[38]

Wesley's sermon "Free Grace" represents the worst of Arminian polemics against Calvinism; even Wesley's own followers consider it an "intemperate sermon" that resulted in an unnecessary rift between Wesley and Calvinist Methodist George Whitefield during the Great Awakening and afterward.[39] Nevertheless, there Wesley's basic theological underpinnings become transparent; he did not appeal primarily to free will or fairness, but to God's nature and character as love. At the beginning Wesley established his foundation: "The grace or love of God, whence cometh our salvation, is free in all, and free for all."[40] He continued by sweeping away any accusation that his theology is based on appreciation for human merit or good works, including free decisions and actions: "Whatsoever good is in man, or is done by man, God is the author and doer of it."[41] (All true Arminians agree with Wesley about this, but we would never know this by reading Calvinist polemical literature on Arminianism or Wesley!) Then Wesley argued that Calvinist belief in "single predestination" logically entails double predestination, including unconditional reprobation and damnation of certain persons to hell without hope or regard to their genuinely free decisions or actions:

> You [Calvinists] still believe that in consequence of an unchangeable, irresistible decree of God the greater part of mankind abide in death, without any possibility of redemption: inasmuch as none *can* save them but God; and he *will not* save them. You believe *he hath absolutely decreed not to save them;* and what is this but decreeing to damn them? It is, in effect, neither more nor less; it comes to the same thing. For if you are dead, and altogether unable to make yourself alive; then if God hath absolutely decreed your everlasting death—you are absolutely consigned to damnation. So, then, though you use softer words than some, you mean the selfsame thing.[42]

Wesley went on to enumerate several reasons why this doctrine is false. Primarily, it conflicts with God's attribute of love revealed in Scripture: "Now what can possibly be a more flat contradiction than this, not only to

---

[38]Ibid., p. 259.
[39]Albert Outler, editor's note on John Wesley's "Free Grace," *The Works of John Wesley* 3:3 (Nashville: Abingdon, 1986), pp. 542-43.
[40]Wesley, "Free Grace," *Works* 3:3, p. 544.
[41]Ibid., p. 545.
[42]Ibid., p. 547.

the whole scope and tenor of scripture, but also to all those particular texts which expressly declare, 'God is love'?" "It destroys all [God's] attributes at once," and "it represents the most Holy God as worse than the devil, as both more false, more cruel, and more unjust." Finally, Wesley declared: "Whatever . . . Scripture proves, it can never prove this. Whatever its true meaning be, this cannot be its true meaning. . . . No Scripture can mean that God is not love, or that his mercy is not over all his works. That is, whatever it prove beside, no Scripture can prove predestination."[43]

Wesley was not denying the authority of Scripture or imposing an alien standard of truth or authority on Scripture; he was simply stating his own (and all Arminians') synoptic vision of the meaning of Scripture as a whole, which cannot be contradicted or overthrown by any particular troublesome passage. Scripture as a whole, and Jesus Christ in particular, identifies God as loving and just; if an individual passage (even a whole chapter) appears to contradict this, it must be interpreted in the light of the whole of revelation and not be allowed to dominate, control and ultimately overturn the true meaning of God's self-disclosure as good. The pattern of hermeneutical and theological authority seen in Arminius and the Remonstrants is repeated by Wesley: God's goodness (his love and justice) is the primary content of revelation, and divine determinism and monergism cannot be brought into harmony with it.

Wesley scholar Jerry Walls elucidates Wesley's method by uncovering his basic assumption of metaphysical realism; God has a nature that limits and controls the use of his power. Although God could practice double predestination, he will not because of his innate goodness. Walls contrasts this with Luther's and Calvin's nominalism, which leads to a voluntaristic notion in which God's power is more basic than his goodness. The result is a hidden God who foreordains evil, which Wesley could not stomach. For Wesley, there is no hidden God behind the God revealed in Jesus, and the God revealed in Jesus is, without qualification, good. To the charge that this ignores God's transcendence, in which God's goodness could be different than our notions of goodness, Wesley relied on what Walls calls "moral reliabilism" and eschewed "moral fideism." "It is simply unthinkable for Wesley that God has created us in such a way that our strongest moral feelings cannot be trusted. Such a thought, as he put it (in words also used elsewhere),

---

[43]Ibid., pp. 552, 555, 556.

'makes one's blood run cold.'"[44] Such a God, whose goodness bears no real analogy to the best of human goodness or to goodness as revealed and commanded in Scripture, is unreliable and unable to be trusted. Such a God can only be feared and is barely distinguishable from the devil. For Wesley, the only alternative to this cold-blooded view of God is belief in freedom of the will.

Nineteenth-Century Methodists on God's Goodness

Richard Watson. Wesley's nineteenth-century evangelical followers adhered to the same pattern of argument: from God's goodness to free will. Early Methodist Richard Watson, for instance, did not begin with free will but with God's goodness. When commenting on the Calvinist scheme of unconditional election (with its concomitant of unconditional reprobation), Watson said:

> The difficulties of reconciling such a scheme as this to the nature of God, not as it is fancied by man, but as it is revealed in his own word; and to many other declarations of Scripture as to the principles of the administration both of his law and of his grace; one would suppose insuperable by any mind, and indeed, are so revolting, that few of those who cling to the doctrine of election will be found bold enough to keep them steadily in sight.[45]

To those who argue that God's goodness is somehow mysteriously compatible with divine determinism and monergism, including unconditional consignment of some persons to hell, Watson declared:

> It is most egregiously to trifle with the common sense of mankind to call that a righteous procedure in God which would by all men be condemned as a monstrous act of tyranny and oppression in a human judge, namely, to punish capitally, as for a personal offense, those who never could will or act otherwise.[46]

This is a prime example of what Walls calls moral reliabilism, the only alternative to which is moral fideism, which simply asserts that God is good against every notion of goodness known to humanity or revealed in Scripture.

---

[44]Jerry Walls, "Divine Commands, Predestination, and Moral Intuition," in *The Grace of God, The Will of Man*, ed. Clark H. Pinnock (Grand Rapids: Zondervan, 1989), p. 273.
[45]Richard Watson, *Theological Institutes* (New York: Lane & Scott, 1851), 2:339.
[46]Ibid., p. 439.

William Burton Pope. Nineteenth-century Methodist theologian William
Burton Pope also argued against Calvinism and for free will on the basis of
God's goodness revealed in Jesus Christ. For him, as for all Arminians, "God
Himself, with every idea we form of His nature, is given to us by the revelation of Christ."[47] Whereas Christ reveals God as love, Calvin's doctrine of unconditional election and reprobation implies that "all is of the absolute, unquestionable, despotic sovereignty of God."[48] Finally, Pope declared, "Surely
it is dishonorable to the name of God to suppose that He would charge on
sinners a resistance which was to them a necessity, and complain of outrage
on His Spirit Whose influence were only partially put forth."[49] As with Wesley and Watson, Pope based belief in free will and conditional election on
God's goodness.

John Miley. When considering monergism versus synergism, John Miley,
another nineteenth-century Methodist theologian, also began with the priority of divine love. Rather than establishing first and foremost, as Calvinist
critics of Arminianism would have it, that human beings have free will, he
began with God's love and worked toward freedom of the will.

> No theistic truth is more deeply emphasized in the Scriptures than love. . . .
> Any notion of God without love is empty of the most vital content of the true
> idea. The very plenitude of other perfections, such as infinite knowledge and
> power and justice, would, in the absence of love, invest them with the most
> fearful terrors—enough, indeed, to whelm the world in despair.[50]

According to Miley, divine determinism renders any viable theodicy—
justification of the ways of God—impossible. Apart from belief in free will,
all evil must be placed to the divine account.[51] When approaching the doctrine of predestination Miley did not reject it on the basis that it is incompatible with free will. Rather, he rejected unconditional election and reprobation, which he said must go together, because they make God unjust,
unloving, arbitrary and insincere. The character of God is at stake: "A reprobation for unavoidable sin must be contrary to the divine justice," and
"The doctrine of reprobation is disproved by the universality of the atone-

---

[47]William Burton Pope, *A Compendium of Christian Theology* (New York: Phillips & Hunt, n.d.),
      2:345.
[48]Ibid., p. 352.
[49]Ibid., p. 346-47.
[50]John Miley, *Systematic Theology* (Peabody, Mass.: Hendrickson, 1989), 1:204-5.
[51]Ibid., p. 330.

ment; by the divine sincerity in the universal overture of salvation in Christ; by the universal love of God."[52] Finally, Miley pointed out that unconditional election and reprobation can only be based on arbitrary choice because there can be nothing in the character or nature of a person that causes God to elect him or her.[53] All of this, then, is contrary to the biblical portrait of God as merciful, just, compassionate and loving. Free will follows this discernment about the impossibility of divine determinism; it does not control such discernment.

Twentieth Century and Contemporary Arminians on God's Goodness
What about twentieth- and twenty-first-century Arminians? Do they keep to the pattern of Arminius, Episcopius, Limborch, Wesley, Watson, Pope, Miley and many other older Arminians? Do they base their Arminianism on a vision of God's character rather than a preconceived and a priori belief in free will? Space precludes a thorough treatment of all of them. Suffice it to say that any critic would be hard-pressed to find any true Arminian, past or present, who holds free will up as the first principle of his or her theology. God's love as the controlling motif of Arminian theology is reiterated many times by the authors of *The Grace of God, the Will of Man*. Editor Clark Pinnock speaks for all the authors when he states the basic question underlying the Arminian-Calvinist conflict: "Is God the absolute Monarch who always gets his way, or is God rather the loving Parent who is sensitive to our needs even when we disappoint him and frustrate some of his plans?"[54] Pinnock asks his readers, "Does God love the people next door or has God perhaps excluded them from salvation?"[55] But can't the two be combined? Might not God love and exclude the same persons? Arminians resoundingly answer no. There is no way to combine real love with exclusion when exclusion is unconditional and to everlasting suffering. One evangelical Calvinist suggests that God loves all people, including the reprobate, in some ways but only some people (the elect) in every way. This makes no sense to Arminians. In what way could God be loving toward those he has unconditionally decreed to consign to the flames of hell for eternity? To say that God loves them anyway (even if only in *some* way) is to make *love* an equivocal term, emptying it of meaning. Might

---

[52]Ibid., p. 265.
[53]Ibid., p. 266.
[54]Clark Pinnock, ed., *The Grace of God, the Will of Man* (Grand Rapids: Zondervan, 1989), p. ix.
[55]Ibid., p. x.

not God be a God of love even if he dictates and determines people's eternal destinies, including some to endless torment? Again, what would *love* mean in that case? And how would such a God be different from the devil, other than in terms of the total population of hell? To quote Wesley again, "Is not this such love as makes your blood run cold?"

Arminian theologian Fritz Guy rightly avers that for Arminianism "God's love is the inner content of all the doctrines of Christianity. It is what they are all *about*," and "In the reality of God, love is more fundamental than, and prior to, justice or power."[56] This is because God's character is definitively revealed in Jesus Christ; it is not because Arminians prefer a sentimental or nice God. Arminian theologian William G. MacDonald makes the fundamental issue clear:

> When doing theology, we always must ask the supreme question concerning God, *"What is his name?"* (Exodus 3:14). His true identity is ultimately the issue in every doctrine. What kind of God has manifested himself in history, culminating in the infallible revelation in Christ? What does a particular doctrine like election teach and imply about the nature of God? God's character is on the line in every doctrine and especially in the doctrine of election.[57]

MacDonald concludes, "Attempts to make individualistic election the absolute of a theological system finally succeed in doing so by backing away from the contingencies of grace for the certainties of decrees that people are helpless against. God's love for the whole world is then called into question."[58]

The point is that for these and other modern and contemporary Arminians, the controlling belief is not free will but God's good character, which is manifested in love and justice. Free will enters in only because without it God becomes the all-determining reality, who is necessarily the author of sin and evil, whether directly or indirectly. This makes God morally ambiguous and flies in the face of especially the New Testament revelation of God.[59]

---

[56]Fritz Guy, "The Universality of God's Love," in *The Grace of God, the Will of Man*, ed. Clark Pinnock (Grand Rapids: Zondervan, 1989), p. 35.

[57]William G. MacDonald, "The Biblical Doctrine of Election," in *The Grace of God, the Will of Man*, ed. Clark Pinnock (Grand Rapids: Zondervan, 1989), p. 207.

[58]Ibid., pp. 224-25.

[59]Some Calvinist exegetes have tried to say that in John 3:16 (and other passages) where God is said to be love or that he loves the *whole world*, what is meant is "all kinds of people" or "people from every tribe and nation of the world." Arminians see this as forced theological interpretation and not true exegesis.

MYTH 5

Arminian Theology
Denies the Sovereignty of God

Classical Arminianism interprets God's sovereignty and providence differently than Calvinism without in any way denying them; God is in charge of everything without controlling everything.

OCCASIONALLY I, LIKE MANY ARMINIANS, AM asked the accusatory question, You don't believe in God's sovereignty, do you? It is usually asked by a Calvinist who knows I am an Arminian; many Calvinists learn in their churches and educational institutions that Arminians do not believe in the sovereignty of God. Even some Arminians believe that Calvinists affirm and Arminians deny God's sovereignty and providence. This is simply not true. And yet some version of this misconception pops up frequently in Calvinist thought. A leading evangelical Calvinist theologian, writer and radio speaker told an audience that though Arminians claim to believe in divine sovereignty, when their claim is examined carefully very little of God's sovereignty remains. Calvinist pastor and theologian Edwin Palmer flatly says that "the Arminian denies the sovereignty of God."[1]

Arminians are more than slightly puzzled by these Calvinist claims about Arminian theology. Have they read Arminius on God's providence? Have they read any classical Arminian literature on this subject, or are they simply using second-hand reports about Arminian theology? My impression is that many Calvinist critics of Arminianism have never perused Arminius or

---

[1]Edwin H. Palmer, *The Five Points of Calvinism* (Grand Rapids: Baker, 1972), p. 85.

Arminian theology. They seem to derive their opinions about Arminianism from Jonathan Edwards (who wrote against New England Arminianism of the head, which was becoming unitarian and deistic); nineteenth-century Princeton theologians Archibald Alexander, Charles Hodge and B. B. Warfield; turn-of-the-century Baptist theologian Augustus Hopkins Strong; and twentieth-century Calvinist theologians such as Louis Berkhof and Loraine Boettner. While some of these authors had some sound knowledge of Arminian theology, they seem to have given it a decidedly uncharitable interpretation that is less than fully faithful to what Arminius and his followers meant. Whether this is true or not, it is apparent to Arminians that distorted information about Arminian theology plagues contemporary Calvinist students, pastors and lay people. A decidedly erroneous notion of Arminian belief about God's sovereignty plays a large part. Simply denying that Arminians believe in God's sovereignty, as Palmer does, is so blatantly false that it boggles Arminians' minds.

Of course, when Calvinists say that Arminians do not believe in God's sovereignty, they undoubtedly are working with an a priori notion of sovereignty such that no concept but their own can possibly pass muster. If we begin by defining *sovereignty* deterministically, the issue is already settled; in that case, Arminians do not believe in divine sovereignty. However, who is to say that *sovereignty* necessarily includes absolute control or meticulous governance to the exclusion of real contingency and free will? Does *sovereignty* entail these meanings in human life? Do sovereign rulers dictate every detail of their subjects' lives, or do they oversee and govern in a more general way? And yet even this analogy does not sufficiently illustrate Arminian belief in divine sovereignty and providence. Classical Arminianism goes far beyond belief in general providence to include affirmation of God's intimate and direct involvement in every event of nature and history. The only thing the Arminian view of God's sovereignty necessarily excludes is God's authorship of sin and evil. Faithful followers of Arminius have always believed that God governs the entire universe and all of history. Nothing at all can happen without God's permission, and many things are specifically and directly controlled and caused by God. Even sin and evil do not escape God's providential governance in classical Arminian theology. God permits and limits them without willing or causing them.

In classical Christian thought, God's sovereignty is expressed most generally in the doctrine of providence; predestination is also an expression of sovereignty, but follows the more general idea of providence. God's providence is usually considered both general and special (particular) and is divided into three categories: preserving or sustaining, concurring, and governing. God's sustaining sovereignty is his providential upholding of the created order; even natural laws such as gravity are regarded by Christians as expressions of general divine providence. If God should withdraw his sustaining power, nature itself would run down and stop; chaos would replace order in creation. Deists may say that this exhausts God's providence, but classical Christian orthodoxy, whether Eastern, Roman Catholic or Protestant, confesses further senses of God's providential sovereignty in relation to the world. Arminians, together with Calvinists and other Christians, affirm and embrace God's special providence, in which he not only sustains the natural order but also acts in special ways in relation to history, including salvation history. God's concurrence is his consent to and cooperation with creaturely decisions and actions. No creature could decide or act without God's concurring power. For someone to lift his or her hand requires God's concurrence; God loans, as it were, the power sufficient to lift a hand, and without God's cooperation even such a trivial act would be impossible.

Most attention and controversy in the doctrine of God's providence surrounds the third aspect: governance. How does God govern the world? While preservation and concurrence might be considered forms of government, for the most part theologians regard governance as going further into the particular details of creaturely and human affairs. Does God govern by meticulously determining the entire course of every life, including moral choices and actions? Or does God allow humans a realm of freedom of choice and then responds by drawing them into his perfect plan for history's consummation? Calvinists (and some other Christians) believe God's control over human history is always already *de facto*—fully accomplished in a detailed and deterministic sense; that is, nothing can ever thwart the will of God. Arminians (and some other Christians) believe God's control over human history is always already *de jure*—by right and power if not already completely exercised—but at present only partially de facto. God can and does exercise control, but not to the exclusion of human liberty and not in such a way as to make him the author of sin and evil. After all, Jesus taught his disciples to pray "Thy will be done, on earth as it is in heaven" (Mt 6:10 RSV). If God's sovereignty were already completely exercised de facto, why would anyone need to pray for God's will to be done on earth? In that case, it would always already be done on earth. The distinction between God's sovereignty de facto and de jure is required by the Lord's Prayer.

If the Calvinist wishes to say the Arminian distinction between sovereign control de facto and de jure is false, and that sovereignty *means* not only rule by right but also rule in detailed, deterministic reality to the exclusion of creatures' power to thwart God's will at any point, then the Arminian account of divine providence would fall short of true sovereignty. But Arminians reject the narrow definition of sovereignty—absolute and meticulous control—because it cannot avoid making God the author of sin and evil, in which case, Arminians believe, God would be morally ambiguous. The word *sovereignty* simply does not mean absolute control.

The Calvinist account of sovereignty is simply incongruous with sovereignty as we know it in the world. Even though Calvinists may express it in softer language, Arminians believe "absolute and meticulous control" is the classical Calvinist view. Calvin's own account of the doctrine of providence in *Institutes of the Christian Religion* provides concrete examples of events that may seem accidental but are not because, according to Calvin, nothing happens fortuitously or by chance. There are no accidents; everything that happens is foreordained by God for a purpose, and God renders everything certain efficaciously even if not by direct, immediate causation.[2] According to Calvin, if a man wanders away from his traveling companions and is set upon by thieves and robbed and murdered, Christians should consider that event, as everything else, planned and directed by God and not a happenstance.[3]

Edwin Palmer made no secret of his belief in such meticulous providence extending even to sin and evil: "All things, including sin, are brought to pass by God," and "the Bible is clear: God ordains sin."[4] In his book on providence British evangelical philosopher and theologian Paul Helm stops short of Palmer's claim that God ordains sin, but he avers that nothing at all falls outside the plan and control of God: "Not only is every atom and molecule, every thought and desire, kept in being by God, but every twist and turn of each of these is under the direct control of God."[5] Arminians find it interesting that many Calvinists, like Helm and even Calvin, fall into using language of "per-

---

[2]John Calvin, *Institutes of the Christian Religion*, 1.16.9, ed. John T. McNeill, trans. Ford Lewis Battles (Philadelphia: Westminster Press, 1960), pp. 208-10. In this context Calvin says "God by the bridle of his providence turns every event whatever way he wills" (p. 209).

[3]Ibid., pp. 208-10.

[4]Palmer, *Five Points of Calvinism*, pp. 101, 103.

[5]Paul Helm, *The Providence of God* (Downers Grove, Ill.: InterVarsity Press, 1994), p. 22.

mission" and "allowing" when discussing God's providential governance of sin and evil.[6] Because of their all-encompassing divine determinism, however, we can fairly assume that they mean what Palmer boldly called "efficacious permission." In other words, God does not merely look at and permit sin and evil but plans, guides and directs it, indirectly causing it to happen; God renders it certain because he wants it to happen for some greater good and ultimately for his own glory. Here the foil for the Arminian account of God's sovereignty and providence will be the Calvinist interpretation as expressed by Palmer:

> Foreordination [synonymous with sovereignty and providence] means God's sovereign plan, whereby He decides all that is to happen in the entire universe. Nothing in this world happens by chance. God is in back of everything. He decides and causes all things to happen that do happen. . . . He has foreordained everything. . . . [E]ven sin.[7]

It is this view of sovereignty and providence to which Arminius objected; he did not object to a doctrine of God's sovereignty and providence that avoids making God the author of sin and evil. To Arminians, the typical Calvinist view cannot avoid it by good and necessary consequence—if not by blatant admission!

Classical Arminians do believe in God's sovereignty and providence over human history. These are not doctrines foreign or alien to Arminianism; many Arminian authors, beginning with Arminius himself, emphasize them and explain them in great detail. Fair-minded Calvinists must recognize that Arminians really are concerned to explain and defend God's sovereignty (even if the Calvinists cannot agree with the Arminian account).

Arminius's View of God's Sovereignty and Providence
Arminius's own theology clearly teaches that God has the right and the power to dispose of his creation, including his creatures, in any way he sees fit. The Dutch theologian allowed no inherent limitation of God by creation but only by God's own character, which is love and justice. "God can indeed do what He wills with His own; but He cannot will to do with His own what He cannot rightfully do, for His will is circumscribed within the bounds of

---

[6]Ibid., p. 101. Helm, like most Calvinists, cannot bring himself to say that God caused the fall of humanity with its terrible consequences. He says only that God permitted it. This seems inconsistent with his earlier statement that every twist and turn of every thought and desire is controlled by God, and with his overall insistence on meticulous providence.

[7]Palmer, *Five Points of Calvinism*, p. 25.

justice."[8] In this Arminius was not arguing that God is limited by human justice; Arminius did not believe that God is beholden to human notions of justice. However, he did believe that God's justice cannot be so foreign to the very best understandings of justice, especially as communicated in God's Word, that it is emptied of meaning. Thus, although God has the right and the power to do whatever he wishes with any creature, God's character as supreme love and justice makes certain acts of God inconceivable. Among them would be foreordaining sin and evil. This is Arminius's only main concern; he agreed with the main outlines of the Augustinian doctrine of God's providence as expressed in Luther and Calvin, but he had to reject divine determinism in meticulous providence insofar as it leads inevitably to God being the author of sin.

Much to the surprise of many Arminians, to say nothing of Calvinists, Arminius affirmed a very strong doctrine of God's providential sovereignty. For him, God is the cause of everything but evil, which he only permits.[9] And anything that happens, including evil, must be permitted by God; it cannot happen if God does not allow it.[10] God has the ability to stop anything from happening, but to preserve human liberty he permits sin and evil without approving them.[11] Arminius said of God's providence: "It preserves, regulates, governs and directs all things, and that nothing in the world happens fortuitously or by chance."[12] He elucidated this to mark his own view off from Calvinism's:

> "Nothing is done without God's ordination" [or appointment]: If by the word "ordination" is signified "that God appoints things of any kind to be done," this mode of enunciation is erroneous, and it follows as a consequence from it, that *God is the author of sin.* But if it signify, that "whatever it be that is done, God ordains it to a good end," the terms in which it is conceived are in that case correct.[13]

[8]James Arminius, "Friendly Conference with Mr. Francis Junius," quoted in Alan P. F. Sell, *The Great Debate: Calvinism, Arminianism and Salvation* (Grand Rapids: Baker, 1982), p. 13.
[9]Arminius, "A Declaration of the Sentiments of Arminius," *Works,* 1:658.
[10]Arminius, "An Examination of Dr. Perkins's Pamphlet on Predestination," *Works,* 3:369.
[11]Arminius, "A Letter Addressed to Hippolytus A Collibus," *Works* 2:697-98. Again, it is important to point out that human liberty is not the main end or purpose of God in creating humans or giving them prevenient grace. Rather, liberty is necessary for the higher purpose of loving relationship; according to Arminian theology relationship that is not entered into freely by both (all) parties cannot be truly loving or personal.
[12]Arminius, "Declaration of Sentiments," *Works,* 1:657.
[13]Ibid., p. 705.

In other words, whatever happens, including sin (e.g., the Fall of Adam), is at least allowed by God, but if it is positively evil, and not only evil to a mistaken understanding, it is not authored or authorized by God. God permits it "designedly and willingly," but not efficaciously. Furthermore, God controls (ordains, appoints, limits, directs) it *in the sense that* he points it to a good end. "God knows how to educe the light of his own glory, and the advantage of his creatures, out of the darkness and mischief of sin."[14] Thus, for Arminius, God's governing providence is comprehensive and active without being all-controlling or omnicausal.

Arminius's account of God's providence could hardly be higher or stronger without being identical with Calvinism's divine determinism. For him, God is intimately involved in everything that happens without being the author of sin and evil, or without infringing on the moral liberty of human beings. To diplomat Hippolytus A Collibus, Arminius wrote:

> I most solicitously avoid two causes of offense,—that God be not proposed as the author of sin,—and that its liberty be not taken away from the human will: Those are two points which if anyone knows how to avoid, he will think upon no act which I will not in that case most gladly allow to be ascribed to the Providence of God, provided a just regard be had to the Divine pre-eminence.[15]

Arminius was puzzled about the accusation that he held corrupt opinions respecting the providence of God, because he went out of his way to affirm it. He even went so far as to say that every human act, including sin, is impossible without God's cooperation! This is simply part of divine concurrence, and Arminius was not willing to regard God as a spectator. His only two exceptions to God's providential control were stated in his letter to Hippolytus A Collibus—that God does not cause sin, and that human liberty (to commit sin freely) not be abridged. In the same letter he offered the opinion that the accusation arose from his denial that Adam's fall was made necessary by any decree of God. And yet he went so far as to argue that Adam sinned "infallibly" (inevitably?) even though not "necessarily." In other words, according to Arminius, Adam's fall came as no surprise or shock to God. God knew it was going to happen. But no necessity was imposed on Adam to sin. For Arminius the conventional Calvinist explanation that Adam fell because God withdrew his morally sustaining grace and

---

[14]Arminius, "The Public Disputations of James Arminius," *Works*, 2:172.
[15]Arminius, "Letter Addressed to Hippolytus A Collibus," *Works*, 2:697-98.

power from Adam amounts to the claim that Adam sinned by necessity. This Arminius could not abide because it stains the character of God.

That Arminius held a high view of God's sovereignty and did not fall into a deistic mode of thinking about providence is proven by his account of divine concurrence. According to this, God does not permit sin as a spectator; God is never in the spectator mode. Rather, God not only allows sin and evil designedly and willingly, although not approvingly or efficaciously, but he cooperates with the creature in sinning without being stained by the guilt of sin. God both permits and effects a sinful act, such as the rebellion of Adam, because no creature can act apart from God's help. In several of his writings Arminius carefully explained divine concurrence, which is without doubt the most subtle aspect of his doctrine of sovereignty and providence. For him God is the first cause of whatever happens; even a sinful act cannot occur without God as its first cause, because creatures have no ability to act without their Creator, who is their supreme cause for existence. Thus, even sin requires

> the Divine Concurrence, which is necessary to produce every act; because nothing whatever can have any entity except from the First and Chief Being, who immediately produces that entity. The Concurrence of God is not his immediate influx into a second or inferior *cause,* but it is an action of God immediately *[influens]* flowing into *the effect* of the creature, so that the same effect in one and the same entire action may be produced simultaneously *[simul]* by God and the creature.[16]

Arminius argued that when God has permitted an act, God never denies concurrence to a rational and free creature for that would be contradictory. In other words, once God decides to permit an act, even a sinful one, he cannot consistently withhold the power to commit it. However, in the case of sinful or evil acts, whereas the same event is produced by both God and the human being, the guilt of the sin is not transferred to God, because God is the effecter of the act but only the permitter of the sin itself.[17] This is why Scripture sometimes attributes evil deeds to God; because God concurs with them. God cooperates with the sinners who commit them. But that does not mean God is the efficacious cause of them or wills them, except according to his "consequent will." God allows them and cooperates with them unwill-

---

[16]Arminius, "Public Disputations," *Works,* 2:183.
[17]Arminius, "Examination of Dr. Perkins's Pamphlet," *Works,* 3:415.

ingly in order to preserve the sinners' liberty, without which sinners would not be responsible and repentant persons would not enter into a truly personal and loving relationship with God.

A distinction between two modes of God's will is absolutely crucial to Arminius and his followers: the antecedent and the consequent wills of God. The first has priority; the second exists because God reluctantly allows human defection in order to preserve and protect the integrity of the creature. In his antecedent will "God judged that it was the province of His most omnipotent goodness rather to produce good from evils, than not to allow evils to be."[18] This will of God precedes sin itself; it precedes the Fall and is the reason the Fall could happen. In his consequent will God cooperates with the sinner in sin after and as a consequence of the sinner's free decision to sin (with God's permission). Sin then is not within God's will in the same way; it is only within the will of God antecedently insofar as God determines to permit sin within his creation. Sin is only within God's will consequently insofar as it is necessary to preserve liberty and bring about some greater good. Arminius also used this distinction to explain why not all are saved. "God seriously wills that all men be saved; yet, compelled by the pertinacious and incorrigible wickedness of some, He wills them to make shipwreck of the faith, that is, to be condemned."[19] Thus, even though God does not approve of sin, sin does not thwart the will of God. God antecedently wills to permit sin and consequently wills to allow unrepentant sinners to be condemned.

Arminius apparently assumed a perfect or ideal will of God as part of God's antecedent will, in which no one would ever sin, but he believed in a "relaxed will" of God in relation to human creatures, which includes a divine self-limitation for the sake of their integrity as free beings. Sin's entrance into the world, permitted and supported by God without approval, requires a prior self-limitation of God. But this self-limitation does not mean that God becomes uninvolved or a mere spectator, wringing his hands pathetically over the waywardness of his creatures. God knows what he is doing. Out of love he is respecting the freedom of his creatures for the sake of genuineness of relationship. Out of justice he is not coercing or predetermining their actions. As a result of this divine self-limitation and the consequent fall of creation, God has to act differently than he would have acted

---

[18]Ibid., p. 408.
[19]Ibid., pp. 430-31.

if humanity did not fall away. All of this is only possible because of God's sovereign relaxation of his perfect will, which is part of his antecedent will—the part that does not get its way because sin intervenes.[20]

The charge that Arminius denied the sovereignty of God or in any way diminished it is impossible to sustain. He held a very high view of God's providence. It would be impossible to hold a higher or stronger view without falling into divine determinism. According to Arminius, everything is governed by God's eternal, though not equal, decrees, and nothing at all can happen without God's permission and cooperation. God's dominion is comprehensive even though some things, such as sin and damnation, take place within it that God only permits and does not approve. God can and does limit sin and evil, and he makes them fit into his overall plan for history.

God's Sovereignty and Providence in Post-Arminius Arminianism

Simon Episcopius. Arminian theologians after Arminius followed his lead with regard to the doctrines of divine sovereignty and providence. Their main concern was always to protect the character of God from any hint of authorship of sin or evil. But alongside that they promoted strong appreciation for God's all-encompassing dominion over creation, which extends far beyond mere preservation (sustaining) to governance. Arminius's heir Episcopius echoed his mentor's horror at any doctrine of providence that made God appear to be the author of sin. Of high Calvinism he wrote that it makes God unwise and unjust, and "the true and proper author of sin" because it necessarily implies of the reprobate that God "did fatally destine

---

[20]See William Gene Witt, *Creation, Redemption and Grace in the Theology of Jacob Arminius* (Ph.D. diss., University of Notre Dame, 1993), pp. 494-506, on God's self-limitation and "relaxed will." Witt's treatment of Arminius's doctrine of providence is superior to Richard Muller's *God, Creation, and Providence in the Thought of Jacob Arminius* (Grand Rapids: Baker, 1991). The latter tends to distort the true picture of Arminius's thought. For example, Muller suggests that Arminius moved away from belief in divine omnipotence toward divine self-limitation under the influence of the beginnings of modern cosmology (*God, Creation, and Providence,* p. 240). But I see no such move or influence in Arminius! Arminius's option for divine self-limitation in God's "relaxed will" poses no limitation of God's omnipotence. God simply chose not to use all the power he has or could use. For Arminius, God always remains omnipotent in the most radical sense possible within a metaphysically realistic frame of reference (i.e., God's power conditioned by his character). Also, Arminius's apparent belief in divine self-limitation arose from his obsession with the character of God as love and justice, which is derived from divine revelation in Jesus Christ and Scripture, and not from early modern cultural influences.

him to this eternal evil."[21] On the other hand, Episcopius, like Arminius, affirmed that God governs and directs all human actions and all events in creation.[22] Episcopius excepted only one class of actions from God's direct and immediate ordination and causation: "As touching disobedience or sins, although he hate it with the greatest hatred, yet doth he wittingly and willingly permit or suffer it to be, yet not with such a permission [that] disobedience cannot but follow . . . by this means God would be altogether the author of sin."[23] He meant that God willingly and purposefully permits sin but does not cause it, even by withdrawing sufficient grace and power to avoid sinning. Episcopius's high view of God's sovereignty is well expressed in the declaration "There is therefore nothing that comes to pass any where in the whole world rashly or by chance; that is, God either not knowing of it or not regarding it or only idly looking on."[24]

Episcopius agreed with Arminius that God concurs with the will of the free and rational creature without laying any necessity on it of doing well or ill.[25] God bestows the gift of free will on people and controls it by putting boundaries around what it can do.[26] In other words, for Episcopius and all real Arminians, free will is never autonomous or absolute. (That Arminians believe it to be is another frequently encountered myth!) God hedges free will; only God's freedom is absolute.[27] Human free will is always only situated free will; it exists and is exercised within a limiting context, and God's limitation of it is one factor in that context. Apparently Arminius and Episcopius believed that God hinders acts of free will that could not be directed toward the good. But God never directs the will toward evil or decrees evil actions: "He never decrees evil actions that they should be; nor does he approve them, nor love them; neither does he ever properly bid or command them: much less so as to cause or procure them, or to stir up or force anyone to them."[28]

Philip Limborch. The later Remonstrant Philip Limborch may have departed from Arminius and the early Remonstrants on total depravity and the absolute necessity of restorative grace for any exercise of a good will to-

---

[21]Simon Episcopius, *Confession of Faith of Those Called Arminians* (London: Heart & Bible, 1684), p. 104.
[22]Ibid.
[23]Ibid., p. 109.
[24]Ibid., p. 115.
[25]Ibid., pp. 114-15.
[26]Ibid., p. 110.
[27]Arminius, "Public Disputations," *Works,* 2:190.
[28]Episcopius, *Confession of Faith,* p. 110.

ward God, but he agreed completely with them about divine sovereignty
and providence. Limborch affirmed God's preservation of nature, concurrence with every event and governance of all things:

> The government of providence is that powerful act of God whereby he admin-
> isters and disposes of all things with the highest wisdom so as shall best tend
> to the advancement of his glory and the eternal welfare of mankind. This gov-
> ernment extends itself to all things so that there is nothing in the whole uni-
> verse but what is under the guidance of providence.[29]

Limborch argued that God limits both himself and human beings so that
his own will is exercised in relation to human free will, and the latter is unable to do anything except what is permitted by God and can be directed to
the good. God's concurrence is necessary for all creaturely decisions and actions. God is not the author of any evil actions but always the author of good
actions in that he bestows the ability to do them on humans. In general,
God's sovereignty means that no person can act apart from God's willing
permission and assistance: "Doubtless a man cannot so much as conceive in
his mind, much less can he execute his own actions, unless by the knowledge, permission, and assistance of God," but "we urge . . . that God does
not excite and predetermine men to every action, even those that are evil,
which we are sure the [Scriptures] will [never] allow of."[30]

Like Arminius, Episcopius and Limborch held to a high and strong doctrine of God's sovereignty and providence. They only exempted from God's
decrees and direct action (causation) sinful acts. Although they did not discuss calamities, we can safely assume they would consider them part of God's
providential governance. Later Arminians would begin to question this and
widen the scope of God's consequential will to include many natural disasters
along with sinful and immoral actions of people. Even sinful acts (and calamities), however, do not escape God's governance, although they are in a separate category than good acts. Sinful and evil acts are never planned or decreed by God; God only decrees to allow them. God never instigates them or
renders them certain (e.g., by withdrawing the grace necessary to avoid
them). There is neither a secret impulse of God toward evil nor a hidden God
who manipulates people to sin. Yet evil decisions and actions are circum-

---

[29]Philip Limborch, *A Complete System, or, Body of Divinity*, trans. William Jones (London: John
Darby, 1713), p. 149.
[30]Ibid., pp. 160, 162.

scribed by God so that they fit into his purposes, and he directs them toward the good end he had in mind for creation. And they cannot happen without God's permission and cooperation. The reason God permits and cooperates with them is to preserve human liberty (and thus integrity of personal reality) and bring good out of them. This strong belief in divine sovereignty completely overturns the impression that Arminians believe only in general providence (preservation, sustaining of creation) and not in special providence, or that they do not believe in divine sovereignty.

John Wesley. John Wesley did not write very much about the doctrine of providence, but he clearly believed in God's sovereignty but rejected any idea of a fixed determinism divine or otherwise. He defended free will against the Calvinism of his day and carefully balanced it with divine sovereignty. For him, "God's sovereignty is manifested through free will, not undermined by it."[31] Wesley was neither a philosopher, although he knew philosophy, nor a systematic theologian; his focus was on preaching and commenting on Scripture rather than on resolving every doctrinal dilemma. The doctrine of providence took a back seat to his arguments against unconditional predestination. However, his sermons "On Divine Providence" and "On God's Sovereignty" included ringing endorsements of classical Christian teachings about God's preservation, concurrence and governance of every part of creation. He denied a mere general providence, which was gaining popularity among deists to the exclusion of particular, detailed providence. He called that view "self-contradictory nonsense"[32] and challenged his listeners and readers to

> Either, therefore, allow a particular providence, or do not pretend to believe
> any providence at all. If you do not believe that the Governor of the world gov-
> erns all things in it, small and great; that fire and hail, snow and vapour, wind
> and storm, fulfill his word; that he rules kingdoms and cities, fleets and
> armies, and all the individuals whereof they are composed (and yet *without*
> *forcing the wills of men or necessitating any of their actions*); do not affect to believe
> that he governs anything.[33]

---

[31]John Wesley, quoted in Thomas C. Oden, *John Wesley's Scriptural Christianity* (Grand Rapids: Zondervan, 1994), p. 267.

[32]John Wesley, "On Divine Providence," quoted in Oden, *John Wesley's Scriptural Christianity,* p. 116.

[33]John Wesley, "An Estimate of the Manners of the Present Times," quoted in Oden, *John Wesley's Scriptural Christianity,* p. 116.

But Wesley added that free will is no diminution of God's sovereignty, power or providential governance; it falls within them as God allows it and delimits it for his own good purposes. According to Wesley, however, sin must not be attributed to God's foreordination or even secret impulsion even though God only permits evil that clears the way for a greater good.[34]

God's Sovereignty and Providence in Nineteenth-Century Arminianism

The leading Arminian theologians of the nineteenth century repeated Arminius's theology of God's sovereignty and providence while adding their own spins to them. Nevertheless, even among these Methodist theologians who are supposed by many to have formed a bridge between early Arminianism and twentieth-century liberal theology, God's sovereign governance of nature and history remains intact and even in some ways deepened. One cannot read Richard Watson, William Burton Pope, Thomas Summers or John Miley without acknowledging their faithful commitment to God's sovereign preservation, concurrence and governance of the universe, including human affairs. At the same time, they all found the conventional Calvinist accounts seriously defective in making God the author of sin and evil by elevating sovereignty to comprehensive control and diminishing human free will to the vanishing point.

Richard Watson. According to Watson, "That the sovereignty of God is a Scriptural doctrine no one can deny; but it does not follow that the notions which men please to form of it should be received as Scriptural."[35] Most especially he rejected as unscriptural any doctrine of God's sovereignty that results in making God the author of sin, because this is incompatible with God's goodness.[36] He acknowledged that most Calvinists do not attribute sin to God's causality, but he also argued that their explanation of why Adam fell in the garden necessarily includes or leads to divine causality, even if only indirectly. His own position was that there is no answer to why God allowed the Fall except that God could have prevented it but decided it was better to allow it.[37] Clearly, for Watson the Fall was not foreordained by God or included in God's antecedent perfect will, but resulted from hu-

---

[34]Ibid., p. 115.
[35]Richard Watson, *Theological Institutes* (New York: Lane & Scott, 1851), p. 2:442.
[36]Ibid., p. 429.
[37]Ibid., p. 435.

man self-determination and self-assertion against God, which was allowed by God in his consequent will.

Watson contributed two relatively new ideas to the stream of Arminian theology, although not all Arminians picked them up from him. First, he argued against what he called the "philosophical theory" of free will, which is now generally known as compatibilist free will. This is the idea of free will advocated and defended by Jonathan Edwards, but its roots can be found at least as far back as Augustine. The idea is that the will is controlled by motives, and motives are provided by something external to the self, such as God. Most Calvinists, when pushed to explain why persons act in certain ways or choose certain things, appeal to the strongest motive as explanation and then add that motives are not self-determined but given to persons by someone or something. In this theory people are "free" when they act in accordance with their desires, when they do what they want to do, even if they could not do otherwise. This "free will" is compatible with determinism. Watson rejected it as incompatible with responsibility: "For if the will is thus absolutely dependent upon motives, and the motives arise out of uncontrollable circumstances, for men to praise or to blame each other is a manifest absurdity and yet all languages abound in such terms."[38] According to Watson, the will is not mechanically controlled by motives instilled by something or someone; rather the mind and the will are capable of judging motives and deciding between them. Moral liberty, he argued, consists in thinking, reasoning, choosing and acting based on mental judgment.[39] Clearly, for Watson, free will means being able to discern and choose between conflicting motives; it includes being able to do other than one wants to do and other than one does. That is the essence of libertarian (incompatibilist) free will. Watson's first contribution was in providing a critique of the Calvinist doctrine of free will (the "philosophical doctrine") and recommending its alternative.

Watson's second contribution to Arminian theology was his denial of God's timelessness, or the "eternal now" theory of God's eternity. He also denied divine immutability. Not all Arminians have agreed with Watson about these matters, but he opened the door to later developments within Arminianism, such as open theism. More importantly, however, he wrestled creatively and constructively with the issue of God's relationship with time in view of the reality of free will and creatures' interactions with God. Until Watson,

---

[38]Ibid., pp. 440-41.
[39]Ibid., p. 442.

most Arminian theologians, including Arminius, held to the Augustinian interpretation of God's eternity; that is, there is no duration of God's being in or through time, or there is no real succession of past, present and future in God. Even for Arminius, God's awareness of creation is such that all times are simultaneously before God's eyes. Watson could see no sense in this in light of human free will and its ability to affect God's knowledge (i.e., God foreknows free decisions and actions without causing them). Watson's main concern was to protect free will in order to protect God's character (love) and human responsibility. For him, the doctrines of immutability and eternity as an eternal now were speculative and not biblical.[40] On the basis of biblical narratives illustrating how free and rational creatures affect God, Watson rejected the idea that God cannot change in any way. According to him, God's knowledge of the possible is timeless and not derived from events in the world, while God's knowledge of the actual is temporal and derived from events in the world.[41] Nevertheless, God is sovereign in that he is fully capable of responding appropriately to whatever human beings (or other creatures) do and fitting it in with his overall purpose and plan; God is also sovereign in that whatever happens is foreknown and permitted by God.

William Burton Pope. William Burton Pope also protested against the Calvinist doctrine of God's sovereignty as meticulous providence. That theology, he argued, leads inevitably to the conclusion that "All is of the absolute, unquestionable, despotic sovereignty of God."[42] He asserted that the Arminian/Remonstrant teaching about God's sovereignty not only preserves God's character and human responsibility but is also the faith of the ancient church before Augustine.[43] This is also precisely the argument made about a century later by Methodist theologian Thomas C. Oden in *The Transforming Power of Grace.* Oden agrees entirely with Pope, saying, "The Remonstrance represented a substantial reapropriation of pre-Augustinian eastern patristic consensus."[44] In spite of his rather acerbic description and rejection of the Calvinist doctrine of sovereignty, Pope did not hesitate to affirm and proclaim God's detailed, minute supervision of all events in nature and history:

---

[40]Watson, *Theological Institutes,* 2:400-401.

[41]Ibid., pp. 402-4.

[42]William Burton Pope, *A Compendium of Christian Theology* (New York: Phillips & Hunt, n.d.), 2:352.

[43]Ibid., p. 357.

[44]Thomas C. Oden, *The Transforming Power of Grace* (Nashville: Abingdon, 1994), p. 152.

As He is present everywhere in His infinite power, all providential relation must be minute and special: to think otherwise of the Divine control of the laws of nature and the actions of men is inconsistent with the first principles of the doctrine. This is the glory of the Scriptural teaching, that it knows nothing of a Divine general care which does not descend to the minutest particulars.[45]

However, in good Arminian fashion Pope noted that God's providential governance of history necessarily includes the free will of humans. His argument is that the very concept of providence or rulership loses much of its meaning if the objects of governance are subjected to "the unbending government of a soul that must act out its destiny."[46] Rather, true government seeks to guide and persuade and teach, not control. "Hence, the most impressive view that may be taken of this doctrine regards it as the slow but sure guidance of all creatures whose state is not yet eternally fixed to the consummation of their destiny as foreappointed of God."[47]

Thomas Summers and John Miley. Thomas O. Summers and John Miley joined Watson and Pope in rejecting divine sovereignty as absolute control while affirming a high doctrine of providence. According to Miley (in full agreement with Summers, who cannot be quoted here due to limitations of space), "A theory of providence which must either render moral action impossible or make God the determining agent in all evil can have no place in a true theology."[48] God's providence is not coercion but enlightenment and persuasion in the sphere of moral freedom. Nevertheless, it is not limited because "God rules in all the realms of nature, and in their minutiae as in their magnitudes."[49] For Miley, and most if not all later Arminians, God's primary way of ruling over human affairs is through persuasion, but God's persuasive power is greater than any creature's. God's influence lies directly on every subject so that nothing can happen without being pulled or pushed by God toward the good. However, free and rational creatures have the power to resist the influence of God. This power was given to them by God himself. Miley's theology assumes a divine self-limitation for the sake of human liberty. Against the main alternative theory of divine sovereignty, he wrote:

If the agency of providence must be absolute, even in the moral and religious

---

[45]Pope, *Compendium of Christian Theology*, 1:444.
[46]Ibid., p. 452.
[47]Ibid., pp. 452-53.
[48]John Miley, *Systematic Theology* (1983; reprint, Peabody, Mass.: Hendrickson, 1989), 1:329.
[49]Ibid., p. 309.

sphere, there can be no approach toward a theodicy. All evil, physical and moral, must be directly placed to the divine account. Man can have no personal or responsible agency in either. For good and evil he is but the passive subject of an absolute providence. In the light of reason, and conscience, and Scripture there is no such a providence over man.[50]

The exposition of Arminian theology in this chapter so far should be sufficient to disprove critics' claims that Arminianism lacks any doctrine of divine sovereignty or rejects God's special providence in favor of a general providence of preservation and conservation only. From Arminius on, Arminians of the heart, as opposed to those Arminians who veered into deism or later liberal theology, heartily embraced and promoted the concurrence and governance of God, even in the details of history. But they sought to develop a concept of God's sovereignty that would avoid making God the author of sin and evil, something they believed Calvinism could not do. This necessarily involved the idea of God's voluntary self-limitation in relation to creation for the sake of human liberty. They believed that this does not detract from God's sovereign oversight of human decisions and actions; thus God is able to make everything work together for the good in his plan and purpose. Above all, these Arminians affirmed that nothing can happen apart from God's permission. God is sufficiently powerful to stop anything from happening, but he does not always exercise that power, because to do so would be to rob his free and rational creatures, created in his image, of their distinct reality and liberty. Pope especially made it clear that this liberty is a function of human probation; it will not exist in the same way into eternity.

Twentieth-Century Arminianism on God's Sovereignty and Providence

Thomas Oden. But what about twentieth-century Arminians? Do they also believe and teach a high doctrine of God's sovereignty? Although he does not call himself an Arminian, Thomas Oden's Methodist theology follows the Arminian pattern. In *The Transforming Power of Grace* he explains how human freedom does not limit divine sovereignty. The freedom to say no to God is granted by God himself, but it is unable to thwart God's ultimate plans and purposes.

Though temporarily freedom is able to resist divine grace, God's purpose in

---

[50]Ibid., p. 330.

history will in the long run be carried out, even if in the short run thwarted by human defiance. It is not a limitation of the divine sovereignty that God grants this temporary and finite freedom to humanity, but an expression of the greatness of God's compassion and parenting care and joy in companionship. This does not limit God's capacity, but stands as a freely given self-constraint of God's actual scope of activity within and for the wretched history of sin.[51]

Henry Thiessen. Evangelical theologian Henry C. Thiessen stepped confidently and correctly in the path of earlier Arminian thought about providence even though he was seemingly unaware that he was an Arminian! And though he (or his editor) incorrectly labeled the semi-Pelagian theory of original sin "Arminianism," his soteriology was thoroughly Arminian. Of providence he wrote that it is

> that continuous activity of God whereby He makes all the events of the physical, mental, and moral phenomena work out His purposes; and that this purpose is nothing short of the original design of God in creation. To be sure, evil has entered the universe, but it is not allowed to thwart God's original, benevolent, wise and holy purpose.[52]

Ray Dunning. Nazarene theologian H. Ray Dunning strongly objects to the deterministic sovereignty of Calvinism:

> A deterministic worldview, whether philosophical or theological, avoids the question [of evil] but abandons any meaningful personal dimension in God's relation to the world. If men are pawns that . . . the Sovereign Chessmaster moves in a unilateral, even capricious, way, the personal character of the divine-human relation is effectively eliminated.[53]

Yet, according to Dunning, God exercises detailed "watchcare" over creation, not using deterministic control but powerful persuasion and occasional miracles to turn the tide of history toward his desired ends. The only thing God does not do is coerce people.[54]

Jack Cottrell. Twentieth-century Church of Christ theologian Jack Cottrell has examined and rejected the Calvinist idea of divine sovereignty and adopted an Arminian perspective.[55] He argues that all attempts to moderate and modify strict determinism within Calvinist systems are unsuccessful. The

---

[51]Oden, *Transforming Power of Grace*, pp. 144-45.
[52]Henry C. Thiessen, *Lectures in Systematic Theology* (Grand Rapids: Eerdmans, 1949), p. 177.
[53]H. Ray Dunning, *Grace, Faith, and Holiness* (Kansas City, Mo.: Beacon Hill, 1988), pp. 257-58.
[54]Ibid., p. 258.

twin problems are divine omnicausality (even if using secondary causes) and unconditionality of purpose and ordination.[56] His conclusion is that "this idea of unconditionality completely rules out any meaningful notion of human freedom" with the result that it is inconsistent with God's goodness and human responsibility.[57] Cottrell presents an alternative concept of sovereignty that is wholly consistent with classical Arminianism even though, unlike most Arminians, he uses the term *control* to describe God's governance. In this view, God limits himself in relation to creation in order to allow room for creaturely liberty; some of God's decrees are conditional and some are unconditional. Regardless of what people do with their liberty, God will bring about his kingdom, but who will be included in the kingdom is determined not by God but by humans making use of the gift of free will. God exercises absolute and total control over every part of creation without determining everything. He does this through his foreknowledge and intervention in creaturely affairs whenever it is necessary to accomplish his purposes.[58]

> Even though he bestowed relative independence on his creatures, as Creator he reserved the right to intervene if necessary. Thus he is able not only to *permit* human actions to occur, but also to *prevent* them from occurring if he so chooses. . . . In addition, God's foreknowledge also enables him to plan his own responses to and uses of human choices even before they are made. Thus he remains in complete control and is able to carry out his purposes, especially regarding redemption.[59]

Some Arminians are troubled by Cottrell's admission that God on occa-

---

[55]Although Church of Christ theologians do not usually use the Arminian label for their theology, I asked Cottrell whether he is an Arminian and received an affirmative response. And in "The Nature of the Divine Sovereignty" (see footnote 56) he calls his view "Arminian."

[56]Jack Cottrell, "The Nature of the Divine Sovereignty," in *The Grace of God, The Will of Man*, ed. Clark H. Pinnock (Grand Rapids: Zondervan, 1989), pp. 106-7.

[57]Ibid., p. 103.

[58]Ibid., p. 111. Some Arminians, especially open theists such as John Sanders, are troubled by Cottrell's assumption that absolute divine foreknowledge provides God with a providential advantage. How can God intervene *because* of something he foresees when he foresees everything, including his own future intervention? On this problem and challenge see John Sanders, *The God Who Risks* (Downers Grove, Ill.: InterVarsity Press, 1998), pp. 200-206. An alternative view (to Cottrell's) is provided by evangelical philosopher Dallas Willard, who denies that God is "a great unblinking cosmic stare, who must know everything whether he wants to or not" (*The Divine Conspiracy* [San Francisco: HarperSanFrancisco, 1998], pp. 244-45). According to Willard (and open theists) God can choose not to know everything of the future so that he can intervene in response to prayer. According to Willard and open theists this does nothing to detract from God's sovereignty because God is omnipotent and omniresourceful.

[59]Ibid., p. 112.

sion may have to violate free will in order to accomplish his purposes in history, but he does not mean that God determines their moral or spiritual choices. Apparently, Cottrell is suggesting that God controls history by foreseeing when it may veer from his plan and intervening to steer it back onto course. And in doing so he may even override human volition in matters that have nothing to do with individuals' spiritual condition or eternal destiny. An example would be God's hardening of Pharaoh's heart in the Exodus narrative. Pharaoh was not a good man whom God made evil. Rather, Pharaoh was an evil man whose heart momentarily began to falter, but God harden his resolve so that Israel could escape.

Conclusion

One thing should be absolutely clear from all these examples of Arminian accounts of divine sovereignty and providence—the common accusation that Arminianism lacks a strong or high view of God's sovereignty is false. Every classical Arminian shares with every classical Calvinist the belief that God is in charge of and governs the entire creation, and will powerfully and perhaps unilaterally bring about the consummation of his plan. Arminians demur from Calvinism's divine determinism because it cannot avoid making God the author of sin and evil. When the Calvinist responds that Calvinism avoids that, the Arminian asks about the origin of the very first impulse to evil in creation.

If God is the all-determining reality and creatures have no incompatibilist (libertarian) freedom, then where did that first evil motive or intent come from? If the Calvinist says from God, which is logically consistent with divine determinism, then God is most certainly the author of sin and evil. If the Calvinist says from autonomous creatures, then this opens up a hole in divine determinism so large that it consumes it. Can anything at all arise without God's determining ordination and power? To Arminians, a question mark remains over Calvinism's intelligibility. It does not seem intelligible to assert absolute divine determinism on the one hand and affirm that any part of creation falls outside that on the other hand.

It may be assumed that Paul Helm speaks for all consistent Calvinists when he writes that every thought and desire is under the direct control of God.[60] What does "control of God" mean? Arminians are eager to affirm

---

[60]Helm, *Providence of God*, p. 22.

God's control only if it means that God permits, cooperates with and brings good out of human freedom for his own ultimate plans and purposes. Surely it means something more in Helm and in Calvinism generally. The inner logic of Calvinism—exhaustive divine determinism—drives toward saying that because nothing happens that God has not foreordained and rendered certain, God is the ultimate cause of every wicked thought and desire because he seeks glory for himself even through damning the wicked. To Arminians this must be the case even though Calvinists do not admit it. This is the main reason Arminians are Arminians rather than Calvinists—to preserve the goodness of God's character and human sole responsibility for sin and evil.[61]

---

[61]By pointing out this apparent inconsistency in Calvinism I am not suggesting that every Calvinist embraces what Arminians see as the logically good and necessary consequence of their affirmation of divine determinism. Most Calvinists certainly do not regard God as the cause of every wicked thought and desire. My point is simply to say that this would seem to be logically required by divine determinism (such as Paul Helm's account of providence). Here many Calvinists appeal to mystery and turn away from embracing the logically good and necessary consequence of their doctrine of providence. I admitted earlier that Arminianism also has its problems. However, one of the reasons Arminians are Arminians and not Calvinists is because they realize that were they to embrace the Calvinist account of divine providence they would have to also accept that God is the author of the very first impulse toward evil because that seems to them logically implied by divine determinism. They do not see any similarly insuperable difficulties (i.e., logical inconsistencies) in their own theology. They recognize that their own theology has to appeal to mystery at some points, as do all theologies, but they do not think Arminianism has to avoid affirming the logically good and necessary consequences of any of its essential tenets. Calvinists may disagree, of course.

MYTH 6

Arminianism Is a
Human-Centered Theology

*An optimistic anthropology is alien to true Arminianism,
which is thoroughly God-centered. Arminian theology confesses human depravity, including bondage of the will.*

ONE OF THE MOST PREVALENT AND damaging misconceptions about Arminianism is that it is human-centered because it believes in the innate ability
of humans to exercise good will toward God and to contribute to salvation
even after the fall of Adam. Another way of expressing the myth is that
Arminianism does not believe that the consequences of the fall of humanity
are truly devastating; thus it believes that in the moral and spiritual realm
human free will survived the Fall, and at worst people are damaged goods,
but not totally depraved. While this high view of humanity and its moral
freedom and power (and sometimes even goodness) is a hallmark of much
contemporary Western society, including much of Christianity, it is not the
classical Arminian view. Classical Arminianism takes the Fall and its consequences very seriously.

Some Calvinist accusations against Arminian theology demonstrate a
nearly complete lack of knowledge or understanding of classical Arminian
literature. Calvinist theologian Edwin H. Palmer is guilty of just such egregious distortion of Arminianism when he wrote that Arminians "believe that
at times the natural, nonregenerate man has enough goodness in him so
that if the Holy Spirit assists him he will want to choose Jesus. Man chooses
God, and then God chooses man." He also claimed that "the real nub of the
matter [between Calvinism and Arminianism] is that the Arminian [says]
that the unsaved is able in his own strength, with an assist of the Holy Spirit,

to ask Jesus to save him."[1] Of course, Palmer's statements about Arminian-ism here seem to contain an inconsistency. If Arminians believe that people need an assist of the Holy Spirit in order to believe in Christ, how can that be in their own strength? In fact, classical Arminianism does say that people can choose God, but only with the help of the Holy Spirit. This is called pre-venient grace. And according to Arminius and his true followers, whenever people choose God, that is proof they are not "natural, unregenerate" peo-ple but persons already under the supernatural influence of the Holy Spirit. Then, to add insult to injury, Palmer accused Arminians of robbing God of his glory and giving it to humans: "Does man keep just a little bit of glory for himself—the ability to believe? Or does all the glory go to God? The teaching of total depravity is that God gets all the glory, and man none."[2]

Palmer was certainly not alone in making this accusation against Armin-ianism. In *Whatever Happened to the Gospel of Grace?* noted Calvinist pastor and theologian James Montgomery Boice, who was one of my seminary profes-sors, discussed "people who cannot give God glory." The first group is unbe-lievers. The second is Arminians! Boice's description of Arminian belief about sin and salvation is insulting because of its ridiculing tone. He more than implied that Arminians do not believe in salvation by grace alone and that they believe in natural human ability to initiate and contribute to salva-tion. "They want to glorify God. Indeed, they can and do say 'to God be glory,' but they cannot say 'to God *alone* be glory,' because they insist on mixing human will power or ability with the human response to gospel grace."[3] Boice continued by saying that in heaven an Arminian will have to boast "I chose to believe. I, by my own power, received Jesus Christ as my Sav-ior." Then he concluded, "A person who thinks along these lines does not understand the utterly pervasive and thoroughly enslaving nature of human sin."[4] There it is—the calumny that Arminians do not take sin seriously and that they believe in the natural human ability to cooperate with grace; thus they contribute something to their own salvation. This is simply false. And Boice should have known it.

Other critics of Arminianism have fallen into the same error as Palmer and Boice. In fact, the error is so widespread that many Arminians have

[1]Edwin H. Palmer, *The Five Points of Calvinism* (Grand Rapids: Baker, 1972), pp. 27, 19.
[2]Ibid.
[3]James Montgomery Boice, *Whatever Happened to the Gospel of Grace?* (Wheaton, Ill.: Crossway, 2001), p. 167.
[4]Ibid.

come to believe it and rejected the Arminian label while remaining true Arminians. Once again we encounter the charge that Arminianism is tantamount to semi-Pelagianism, which is the belief that humans can and must initiate salvation by exercising a good will toward God before God responds with saving grace. Semi-Pelagianism, which was condemned by the Second Council of Orange in A.D. 529, denies total depravity and bondage of the will to sin. Michael Horton, executive director of the largely Calvinist organization the Alliance of Confessing Evangelicals, wrote in 1992 that "Arminius revived Semi-Pelagianism."[5] In theological parlance this is shorthand for the criticisms made by Palmer and Boice. Horton explicitly stated that Arminianism is a human-centered theology and that it has negatively affected the American evangelical movement.[6] "One can readily see how a shift from a God-centered message of human sinfulness and divine grace to a human-centered message of human potential and relative divine impotence could create a more secularized outlook."[7] Immediately before this statement, Horton mentioned Arminianism so that the context makes clear what "message" he has in mind. Classical Arminianism is not a "message of human potential and relative divine impotence." Nor do Arminians believe, as Horton suggested, that "we save ourselves with God's help."[8]

W. Robert Godfrey, president of Westminster Theological Seminary California, chimes in with Palmer, Boice, Horton and other Calvinists by implying that Arminianism is closely related to Pelagianism. In a 1992 article in *Modern Reformation* he said the conflict between Calvinism and Arminianism is "related to the conflict between Augustine—the champion of grace—and Pelagius—who insisted that man's will was so free that it was possible for him to be saved solely through his own natural abilities."[9] For Godfrey, the influence of Arminianism is pernicious because it undermines total reliance on God and elevates human ability. It even affects evangelical worship: "Does one seek to entertain and move the emotions and will of men whose salvation is ultimately in their own hands? Or does one present the claims of God

---

[5]Michael Horton, "Evangelical Arminians," *Modern Reformation* 1 (1992): 18. Since 1992 Horton has modified his attitude toward Arminius and Arminians without entirely retracting what he previously wrote. In personal communications with me, he has affirmed his belief that Arminians can be evangelicals but that Arminianism is faulty theology not consistent with the basic impulses of the Reformation.

[6]Ibid., pp. 15-19.

[7]Ibid, p. 16.

[8]Ibid., p. 17.

[9]W. Robert Godfrey, "Who Was Arminius?" *Modern Reformation* 1 (1992): 7.

as clearly as possible while recognizing that ultimately fruit comes only from the Holy Spirit?"[10] Of course, true Arminians would answer the latter positively, right alongside Calvinists! Arminians do not believe that salvation is ultimately in their own hands. It is all of grace.

Even some very well-informed Calvinists who have read Arminian theology with at least some degree of a hermeneutic of charity usually fall short of stating the Arminian view of human ability. Richard A. Muller, a leading Calvinist expert on Arminius, got it wrong when evaluating Arminius's belief in natural human ability to know God. He contrasts Arminius's theology with Reformed theology and says that "Arminius's thought evinces, therefore, a greater trust in nature and in the natural powers of man to discern God in nature than the theology of his Reformed contemporaries."[11] The implication (made clear in context) is that Arminius did not take the effects of the Fall seriously enough; he allegedly believed that some goodness and ability to know God survived it. This can only arise from a jaundiced reading of Arminius through the lens of Roman Catholic theology. During his own lifetime Arminius was falsely accused of being a secret Jesuit! (The Jesuits were believed to be mortal enemies of the Dutch Protestants.) Muller's claim that Arminius was a "modified Thomist" (a follower of the theology of medieval Catholic theologian Thomas Aquinas) seems designed to distance him from the Reformed tradition.[12] Arminians who know Arminius's theology will not deny that he was influenced in some ways by the medieval scholastic tradition and by Thomas Aquinas, but that is not to say he was a "modified Thomist," which clearly puts him closer to the Catholic than the Protestant tradition.

Even the usually irenic authors of *Why I Am Not An Arminian*, Robert Peterson and Michael Williams, charge Arminianism with holding an optimistic anthropology. They acknowledge that Arminius and the early Remonstrants (and later Arminians) believe in the absolute necessity of grace for even the first exercise of a good will toward God. They also admit that Arminianism is not Pelagian or semi-Pelagian. These two Calvinists correctly note that Arminius and the Arminians

> held that the human will has been so corrupted by sin that a person cannot seek grace without the enablement of grace. They therefore affirmed the ne-

---

[10]Ibid., p. 24.
[11]Richard A. Muller, *God, Creation, and Providence in the Thought of Jacob Arminius* (Grand Rapids: Baker, 1991), p. 234.
[12]Ibid., p. 271.

cessity and priority of grace in redemption. Grace must go before a person's response to the gospel. This suggests that Arminianism is closer to Semi-Augustinianism than it is to Semi-Pelagianism or Pelagianism.[13]

For this clear acquittal of heresy Arminians are grateful. However, later in the book these usually precise and charitable Calvinist authors take back some of what they gave. They refer to "Arminius's optimistic view of human free will and his synergistic view of redemption," the Remonstrant (Arminian) belief that "[prevenient] grace is merely persuasive," and the "almost idolatrous [Arminian] doctrine of the autonomous human being."[14] The problem with these statements is not only that they contradict real Arminian theology but they also contradict their own admissions about Arminian theology's belief in prevenient grace—right in the context where they are made! For example, how can prevenient grace be merely persuasive, as if the will were already able to accept God but needed persuasion, when "under prevenient grace, the will is restored so that sin does not impede the will's response to the gospel"?[15] The authors' description of the Arminian doctrine of prevenient grace is better than their conclusions about Arminianism's anthropology, which are not justified by it. If what they say about prevenient grace is true (and much of it is), then how could Arminianism hold to a doctrine of the autonomous human being? It does not. In redemption and in creation, human beings are wholly dependent on God's sustaining and renewing power for anything good, including an exercise of good will toward God and acceptance of God's offer of free salvation.

The only conclusion possible is that many Calvinist critics of Arminianism have wittingly or unwittingly borne false witness against Arminius and Arminians; they have distorted beyond recognition Arminian theology about humanity. Anyone who reads real, historical Arminian literature on this subject will be amazed at the discrepancies between what is widely said about Arminian doctrine and what Arminians have actually written about humanity.

Arminius's Pessimistic Anthropology
Contrary to much scholarly and popular opinion, Arminius did not believe

---

[13]Robert A. Peterson and Michael D. Williams, *Why I Am Not an Arminian* (Downers Grove, Ill.: InterVarsity Press, 2004), p. 39.
[14]Ibid., pp. 115, 116, 117.
[15]Ibid., p. 116.

in natural human moral ability after the fall of Adam; he believed in total depravity, including bondage of the will to sin. Arminius scholar William Witt correctly says, "Whatever may be true of successors to Arminius's theology, he himself held to a doctrine of the bondage of the will which is every bit as trenchant as anything in Luther or Calvin."[16] Witt demonstrates conclusively from Arminius's own writings that although he was influenced by Thomas Aquinas in some areas of his thought, he did not follow Aquinas or the Catholic tradition in holding lightly to the doctrine of inherited depravity. Arminius believed strongly in original sin as inherited corruption that affects every aspect of human nature and personality, and renders human persons incapable of anything good apart from supernatural grace. Witt rightly notes that Arminius's theology was not Pelagian or semi-Pelagian in any sense because Arminius rested every good in human life, including ability to respond to the gospel with faith, on prevenient grace that restores free will. The free will of human beings in Arminius's theology and in classical Arminianism is more properly denoted *freed* will. Grace frees the will from bondage to sin and evil, and gives it ability to cooperate with saving grace by not resisting it. (Which is not the same as contributing something to its work!) Witt contradicts Boice about Arminians' ability to boast in heaven; for Arminius the saved person cannot boast because *even faith is a gift of God.*[17]

Arminius distanced himself as far as possible from Pelagianism and semi-Pelagianism, referring to "the whole troop of Pelagians and Semi-Pelagians in the Church itself," which he calls "ignorant" of spiritual matters.[18] Arminius refuted the charge of Pelagianism leveled against him (or against his doctrine) by English Calvinist William Perkins, saying that the power to believe and obtain salvation is not a part of the human person's natural equipment but "Divinely conferred upon the nature of man."[19] Arminius could not have made clearer his belief that human beings are utterly helpless and totally dependent on grace for their salvation. Chapter nine will elucidate his doctrine of salvation by grace alone. In this chapter I will focus on Arminius's doctrine of the human condition consequent to the fall of Adam.

That Arminius rejected the charges of Pelagianism and semi-Pelagianism

---

[16]William Gene Witt, *Creation, Redemption and Grace in the Theology of Jacob Arminius* (Ph.D. diss., University of Notre Dame, 1993), p. 479.

[17]Ibid., p. 662.

[18]Arminius, "Examination of Dr. Perkins's Pamphlet on Predestination," *Works*, 3:273.

[19]Ibid., p. 482.

is patent; it can be read in various places throughout his writings. Can his denials be sustained? If he believed that fallen people are incapable of exercising a good will toward God or even not resisting the grace of God for salvation, then the accusation that he held an optimistic anthropology is false. Some critics appear to be charmed by an unexamined assumption that any synergistic soteriology is automatically humanistic and is based on an optimistic view of humans and their spiritual abilities. That Arminius believed humans must cooperate with God's grace for salvation is beyond dispute. But critics need to consider what he and Arminians in general mean by cooperation, and on what they base the human ability to cooperate with God. These concepts are susceptible of various meanings. For Arminius the human ability to cooperate with God's grace is itself a gift of God; it is not a natural human ability, which was lost when Adam sinned, and all of his posterity inherit that inability.

In his "Declaration of Sentiments" delivered to the Dutch state officials one year before his death Arminius declared of human beings:

> In his lapsed and sinful state, man is not capable, of and by himself, either to think, to will, or to do that which is really good; but it is necessary for him to be regenerated and renewed in his intellect, affections or will, and in all his powers, by God in Christ through the Holy Spirit, that he may be qualified rightly to understand, esteem, consider, will, and perform whatever is truly good. When he is made a partaker of this regeneration or renovation, I consider that, since he is delivered from sin, he is capable of thinking, willing, and doing that which is good, but yet not without the continued aids of Divine grace.[20]

This confession is so clear that it should close the case against him with acquittal. How could someone with an optimistic or humanistic anthropology say this? How could a Pelagian or semi-Pelagian say it? Clearly Arminius was none of these. He was optimistic about grace, not about human nature! Because of his belief in the fallen human condition of spiritual helplessness and bondage of the will Arminius attributed everything in salvation to grace:

> I ascribe to grace THE COMMENCEMENT, THE CONTINUANCE AND THE CONSUMMATION OF ALL GOOD,—and to such an extent do I carry its influence, that a man, though already regenerate, can neither conceive,

---

[20]Arminius, "A Declaration of the Sentiments of Arminius," *Works*, 1:659-60.

will nor do any good at all, nor resist any evil temptation, *without this preventing and exciting, this following and co-operating grace*—From this statement it will clearly appear, that I am by no means injurious or unjust to grace, by attributing, as it is reported of me, too much to man's free-will: For the whole controversy reduces itself to the solution of this question, "Is the grace of God a certain irresistible force?" That is, the controversy does not relate to those actions or operations which may be ascribed to grace, (for I acknowledge and inculcate as many of these actions or operations as any man ever did,) but it relates solely to the mode of operation,—*whether it be irresistible or not.* With respect to which, I believe, according to the scriptures, that many persons resist the Holy Spirit and reject the grace that is offered.[21]

Clearly then Arminius did believe people are totally dependent on grace for any and every good they have or do. Grace is the beginning and continuation of spiritual life, including the ability to exercise a good will toward God. And for Arminius this prevenient grace (which his translators call "preventing grace") is supernatural and not merely the common grace universally spread abroad within creation to hold back the power of sin and evil. In his "Letter to Hippolytus A Collibus" Arminius further explained his view of bondage of the will and grace in order to make clear that the grace that frees the will and gives humans the ability to cooperate with saving grace is special, not general:

Free will is unable to begin or to perfect any true and spiritual good, without Grace. That I may not be said, like Pelagius, to practice delusion with regard to the word "Grace," I mean by it that which is the Grace of Christ and which belongs to regeneration. . . . I confess that the mind of *[animalis]* a natural and carnal man is obscure and dark, that his affections are corrupt and inordinate, that his will is stubborn and disobedient, and that the man himself is dead in sins.[22]

How anyone could read these passages from Arminius and then label his theology Pelagian or even semi-Pelagian is beyond comprehension. The only way this can be done is to redefine Pelagianism and semi-Pelagianism in such a way as to include Arminius; but this would arbitrarily broaden the borders of those two heresies. Whether there is integrity in that is doubtful. Arminius finally put to rest any doubt about his Protestant orthodoxy in this area of doctrine when he affirmed that belief in Christ is never a possibility apart from

---

[21]Ibid., p. 664.
[22]Arminius, "A Letter Addressed to Hippolytus A Collibus," *Works*, 2:700-701.

special grace: "No man believes in Christ except him who has been previously disposed and prepared by preventing or preceding grace."[23]

Arminius made clear that the fallen human condition, which can rightly be called total depravity, stems from Adam's defection from God's will. He denied that God is in any way the cause of that first sin, and he believed high Calvinism cannot avoid imputing such to God because of God's claimed foreordination and withdrawing of necessary grace. Rather, the efficient cause of humanity's fall is humanity itself as stimulated by the devil.[24] God merely permitted it and is in no way guilty because "He neither denied nor withdrew any thing that was necessary for avoiding this sin and fulfilling the law; but He had endowed Him [Adam] sufficiently with all things requisite for that purpose, and preserved him after he was thus endued."[25] Arminius agreed with Augustine and Calvinism that one result of Adam's fall is the fallenness of his posterity; as the Puritans said, "in Adam's fall we sinned all":

> The whole of this sin . . . is not peculiar to our first parents, but is common to the entire race and to all their posterity, who, at the time when this sin was committed, were in their loins, and who have since descended from them by the natural mode of propagation, according to the primitive benediction: For in Adam "all have sinned." (Rom. v, 12.) Wherefore, whatever punishment was brought down upon our first parents, has likewise pervaded and yet pursues all their posterity: So that all men "are by nature the children of wrath," (Ephes. ii, 3,) obnoxious to condemnation, and to temporal as well as to eternal death; they are also devoid of that original righteousness and holiness. (Rom. v, 12, 18, 19.) With these evils they would remain oppressed for ever, unless they were liberated by Christ Jesus; to whom be glory for ever.[26]

Glory to whom? To God, not to humans. This crystal clear confession of Arminius puts down all opinions that he was a Pelagian or semi-Pelagian, or

---

[23]Arminius, "Certain Articles to Be Diligently Examined and Weighed," *Works*, 2:724.

[24]Arminius, "Public Disputations," *Works*, 2:152.

[25]Ibid., pp. 152-53.

[26]Ibid., pp. 156-57. Arminius denied that children are born condemned because Adam's sin is not imputed to them for Christ's sake. In other words, he did not believe in natural innocence even of children. Rather, he believed that Christ's death on the cross set aside the guilt of original sin so that Adam's federal headship of the race is broken. However, he did not believe the same about the corruption of original sin. For Arminius, all inherit a corrupt humanity that makes actual sins of presumption and guilt inevitable. Notice, however, that he does not say that humans are not guilty of Adam's sin! They are except insofar as Christ intervenes. It is a dialectical concept of original sin as both inherited guilt and guilt removed by Christ.

that he held an optimistic view of humanity. If humans have any free will in spiritual matters, it is a freed will because of Jesus Christ and not because of any surviving relic of goodness in them.

Remonstrants' and Wesley's Views of the Human Condition

Simon Episcopius. The first generation of Remonstrants, led by Simon Episcopius, followed Arminius's theology closely; this is nowhere clearer than in Episcopius's doctrine of original sin and inherited depravity. Like his mentor, Episcopius adamantly denied any necessity in the fall of humanity; Adam was not forced to rebel, nor was his rebellion rendered certain by any divine decree. There was no hidden determination or necessitation by God or the devil.[27] "Nor did he [Adam] fall into sin through any withdrawing or denying . . . of any divine virtue or action necessary for the avoiding of sin."[28] According to Episcopius, if it were the case that Adam fell because God foreordained it and rendered it certain by withdrawing grace and power necessary to avoid it, God would be the author of sin, and sin would not really be sin.[29] The Fall was instigated by Satan but caused solely by Adam, who involved all of his posterity in death and misery with him.[30] Episcopius revealed his own belief in total depravity in the process of recommending the necessity of grace for anything good:

> Without it we can neither shake off the miserable yoke of sin nor do anything truly good in religion at all, nor lastly ever escape eternal death or any true punishment of sin. Much less are we at any time able without it and of ourselves, or by any other creatures, to obtain eternal salvation.[31]

Episcopius denied any natural human ability to initiate salvation or contribute anything causative to it; he regarded the human condition as absolute and utter helplessness in spiritual matters apart from special grace:

> Man . . . hath not saving faith of or from himself; nor is he born again or converted by the power of his own free will: seeing in the state of sin he cannot so much as think, much less will or do any good which is indeed savingly good . . . of or from himself: but it is necessary that he be regenerated and wholly

---

[27]Simon Episcopius, *Confession of Faith of Those Called Arminians* (London: Heart & Bible, 1684), p. 118.
[28]Ibid.
[29]Ibid.
[30]Ibid., pp. 120-21.
[31]Ibid., p. 127.

renewed of God in Christ by the Word of the gospel and by the virtue of the Holy Spirit in conjunction therewith: to wit, in understanding, affections, will, and all his powers and faculties, that he may be able rightly to understand, meditate on, will and perform these things that are savingly good.[32]

Clearly then Episcopius was not guilty of the charge often leveled against Remonstrants of departing from the Protestant doctrines of total depravity and *sola gratia*—grace alone. In their natural, fallen state, apart from God's special, prevenient grace, humans have no free will to do anything spiritually good. Their wills are bound to sin.

Philip Limborch. Now we come reluctantly to the special case of later Remonstrant leader and spokesman Philip Limborch, who defected from Arminius's theology, especially in this area of the human condition. The accusation that Arminianism has an optimistic anthropology is probably based on someone's reading of Limborch, who was repudiated (at this point) by all later classical Arminians, such as the nineteenth-century Methodist theologians and by twentieth-century Nazarene theologian Wiley.

According to Limborch, who no doubt was influenced by the late-seventeenth-century Enlightenment and perhaps by Socinianism, the fall of humanity did not result in bondage of the will or total depravity, but only in a "universal misery," which inclines people toward sinful acts. He called this condition an "inherited misfortune" but failed to explicate its exact nature.[33] It seems that for him, humans after Adam are born without guilt or such corruption as would make actual, presumptuous sinning inevitable. However, a network of sin within the human race seduces people to commit actual sins for which they become condemned.[34] He explicitly denied inherited depravity or habitual sin (sin residing within the nature). Limborch seems a bit inconsistent at times because in some places he did admit to the reality of inherited original sin in human life:

> But here it may be asked whether there be not any Original Sin with which all men are tainted at their birth? In answer to this we say that the phrase *original sin* is no where to be met with in Scripture and it is likewise very improper since it cannot properly be said that sin which is voluntary is innate to us. But if by *original sin* they mean the misfortune which happened to mankind upon

---

[32]Ibid., p. 204.

[33]Philip Limborch, *A Complete System, or, Body of Divinity,* trans. William Jones (London: John Darby, 1713), p. 192.

[34]Ibid., pp. 209-10.

Adam's transgression we very readily grant it, though it cannot in proper sense be said to be sin. We likewise own that infants are born in a less degree of purity than Adam was created and have a certain inclination to sin which they derived not from Adam but from their next immediate parents.[35]

This is a somewhat confusing statement about the human condition. However, in the larger context of Limborch's work, it seems to imply that after Adam's fall, humans are all influenced to sin by their parents even if they do not inherit a corrupt and sinful nature. Yet he did admit that infants are born in a "less degree of purity" than Adam.

The upshot is that Limborch held a more optimistic view of humanity's condition than either Arminius or Episcopius. That can be seen clearly in his account of salvation, which is semi-Pelagian. According to him, "seeds of religion" remain in all people in spite of humanity's collective misery and misfortune because of Adam, and everyone may exercise those seeds of religion to worship God truly.[36] For him, "All men are not by nature unteachable and wicked; for indocility is not owing to our nature, nor is it born with us, but 'tis acquired by a vicious education and a bad custom."[37] What could constitute a clearer denial of the doctrines of total depravity and absolute necessity of special grace for even the first exercise of a good will toward God? Limborch also confused common grace and prevenient grace so that the latter does not need to be supernatural even though it does "excite" people's free will toward the good. All in all, Limborch deviated from Arminius so far that he does not deserve to be called a true Arminian. John Mark Hicks is right to distinguish clearly between Arminius on the one hand and Limborch on the other: "Arminius ought to be regarded as a theologian of the Reformation, but Limborch, and his Remonstrant brethren, ought to be seen as the advocates of a theology which undermines the distinctives of the Reformation."[38] It is important to mark a clear line between true, classical Arminianism and Remonstrantism that follows Limborch and later Arminians of the head, most of who became deists, unitarians and free thinkers.

John Wesley. John Wesley recovered true Arminianism and struggled to res-

---

[35]Ibid., p. 192.

[36]Ibid., p. 199.

[37]Ibid., p. 409.

[38]John Mark Hicks, *The Theology of Grace in the Thought of Jacobus Arminius and Philip van Limborch* (Ph.D. diss., Westminster Theological Seminary, 1985), p. 3.

cue it from the bad reputation given by Limborch. His doctrine of original sin returned to Arminius and Episcopius, and did not follow the more optimistic view of Limborch. Wesley was an optimist of grace, not an optimist of free will or human potential. Thomas Oden correctly distances Wesley from Pelagianism and semi-Pelagianism.[39] Wesley denied that any natural goodness in humanity survived the Fall. He may have at one time preferred the term *deprivation* to *depravity*, but that does not mean he believed in innate human goodness or moral ability. He did not. It seems that Wesley may have misunderstood the Reformed doctrine of total depravity as teaching that humans are as bad as they can possibly be. As an optimist of grace Wesley could never affirm that any creature made in the image and likeness of God could become positively evil. Thus we find his occasional preference for *deprivation* to describe humanity's corruption and loss of righteousness.[40]

Wesley confessed that all humans (except Christ) are "dead in trespasses and sins" until God calls their dead souls to life.[41] According to him, all the "souls of men" are dead in sin by *nature* even if the universal prevenient grace of God is working in them. In his sermon "On Original Sin" he presented a testimony to the fallen condition of humanity that would make any Augustinian proud! He decried a modern tendency to emphasize the "fair side of human nature" and argued that humanity in his time was no different than it was before the flood of Noah's day—wholly evil with nothing good left except what is wrought by God's grace. "In his natural state every man born into the world is a rank idolater."[42] He even went so far as to say, perhaps homiletically, that fallen humans bear the image of the devil and tread in Satan's steps.[43] How could anyone be clearer about the human con-

---

[39]Thomas C. Oden, *John Wesley's Scriptural Christianity* (Grand Rapids: Zondervan, 1994), pp. 251, 269.

[40]On Wesley's view of original sin as deprivation see Charles W. Carter, "Harmartiology: Evil, the Marrer of God's Creative Purpose and Work," in *A Contemporary Wesleyan Theology*, ed. Charles W. Carter (Grand Rapids: Francis Asbury Press, 1983), 1:268-69. Carter rightly notes that for Wesley original sin results in both deprivation (of something of the image of God and of righteousness) and depravity (corruption, inclination to sin).

[41]John Wesley, "On Working out Our Own Salvation," in *The Works of John Wesley*, ed. Albert C. Outler (Nashville: Abingdon, 1986), 3:206-7.

[42]John Wesley, "On Original Sin," *John Wesley*, ed. Stephen Rost, abridg. ed. (Nashville: Thomas Nelson, 1989), pp. 23-24, 29.

[43]Surely Wesley did not mean this literally, because it would conflict with humanity in the image of God; Wesley never denied and even upheld the shattered image of God surviving as a relic in human nature after the Fall. It is no doubt an example of sermonic hyperbole, but it reveals something about Wesley's view of humanity and undermines the claim made by critics that he did not believe in total depravity!

dition in sin as totally depraved than one who said and wrote:

> Here is the *shibboleth:* Is man by nature filled with all manner of evil? Is he void
> of all good? Is he wholly fallen? Is his soul totally corrupted? Or, to come back
> to the text, is "every imagination of the thoughts of his heart evil continually?"
> Allow this, and you are so far Christian. Deny it, and you are but a heathen still.[44]

Wesley's estimation of fallen human nature shows also in his insistence
on supernatural grace as the ground of anything good. He never tired of re-
iterating it; it runs throughout virtually every sermon and treatise. Far from
allowing any glory to humans, Wesley reserved all glory for God so that even
all good works are unholy and sinful. "Neither is salvation of the works we
do when we believe: for *it is then God that worketh in us,* and, therefore, that
he giveth us a reward for what he himself worketh, only commendeth the
riches of his mercy, but leaveth us nothing whereof to glory."[45]

 Conclusion. With the sole exception of Limborch and some of his followers, then, Arminius and his seventeenth- and eighteenth-century followers
embraced the doctrines of original sin and total depravity. They affirmed
the bondage of the will to sin in a manner reminiscent of Luther and Calvin.
Unfortunately, most critics of Arminianism are not acquainted with this history; they seem to know only the legacy of Limborch and the later Remonstrants, whose theology is rejected by classical Arminians, and this has become Arminianism for them. However, this is not a fair treatment of
Arminianism. It is analogous to describing Calvinism as synonymous with
supralapsarianism or hyper-Calvinism or even with Schleiermacher, the father of liberal theology, who claimed to be a Calvinist! Just like Calvinism,
Arminianism has suffered its defections and revisions by people who retained the label. Calvinists and other critics of Arminianism should be careful to distinguish between true Arminianism, which is optimistic about
grace but not about human nature, and Remonstrantism following Limborch (and manifested in Finney), which modified true Arminian theology
into something more akin to semi-Pelagianism.

Nineteenth-Century Arminians on the Human Condition

Some critics of Arminianism are aware that Arminius and Wesley held firmly

---

[44]Ibid., p. 34.
[45]John Wesley, "Salvation by Faith," *John Wesley,* ed. Stephen Rost, abridg. ed. (Nashville: Thomas
Nelson, 1989), pp. 91, 98.

to original sin and total depravity, but they think that after Wesley, Arminianism fell into the heresy of semi-Pelagianism or worse. That is false. The leading Arminian thinkers of the nineteenth century held firmly to these doctrines and strictly avoided semi-Pelagianism. Richard Watson, William Burton Pope, Thomas Summers and John Miley all affirmed inherited depravity and bondage of the will apart from special, supernatural grace. Some of them were harshly critical of Limborch and Remonstrantism, and distanced true Arminianism from them. Due to space limitations, treatments of these four true Arminians and their doctrines of sin will necessarily be brief. The conclusion, however, is the same as with Arminius and Wesley: the nineteenth-century Arminians of the heart were not optimistic about human potential; they were optimistic about grace.

Richard Watson. Watson stated the matter unequivocally: "The true Arminian, as fully as the Calvinist, admits the doctrine of the total depravity of human nature in consequence of the fall of our first parents."[46] He pointed to the gulf fixed between Arminius's own doctrine of original sin and semi-Pelagianism, and embraced the former:

> That the corruption of our nature, and not merely its greater liability to be corrupted [as with Limborch], is the doctrine of Scripture, will presently be shown. This [semi-Pelagian sentiment] was not the opinion of Arminius, nor of his immediate followers. Nor is it the opinion of that large body of Christians, often called Arminians, who follow the theological opinions of Mr. Wesley.[47]

Watson drew the same connection between Adam and his posterity as Arminius—a federal headship of Adam resulting in the fall of the entire race into corruption and spiritual death. He explicitly acknowledged *both* deprivation *and* depravation.[48] Limborch came in for serious and harsh criticism from this early Methodist systematician; Watson accused Limborch of defecting from Arminius and true Arminianism by reducing the inheritance of original sin to sinful tendencies or propensities. By contrast Watson regarded all of Adam's descendents (except Christ) as born sinners guilty and condemned apart from Christ's atoning death, and helpless to do anything at all toward the good without the special prevening grace of God. Even repentance is a gift of God; sinful men and women are

---

[46]Richard Watson, *Theological Institutes* (New York: Lane & Scott, 1851), 2:48.
[47]Ibid., p. 45. Unfortunately, like too many Methodists, Watson did not seem to know that there are non-Methodist Arminians!
[48]Ibid., pp. 53-55.

not capable of repentance apart from God's grace![49] This is hardly an optimistic anthropology.

William Burton Pope. Like Watson, later Methodist theologian William Burton Pope affirmed a high doctrine of original sin and condemned Limborch and the later Remonstrants' departures from it. He defined original sin as "the hereditary sin and hereditary sinfulness of mankind derived from Adam its natural head and representative."[50] It brings condemnation and corruption such that all humans (except Christ) are by inheritance inclined only to evil. "Original sin is utter powerlessness to good: it is in itself a hard and absolute captivity."[51] Pope drove a stake in semi-Pelagianism's heart (and in the heart of the criticism that Arminianism is semi-Pelagian!):

> No ability remains in man to return to God; and this avowal concedes and vindicates the pith of original sin as internal. The natural man . . . is without the power even to co-operate with Divine influence. The co-operation with grace is of grace. Thus it keeps itself for ever safe from Pelagianism and semi-Pelagianism.[52]

Thomas Summers. Thomas Summers and John Miley, two later nineteenth-century Methodist theologians, echoed Watson and Pope. Summers portrayed true Arminianism as a via media between the extremes of Augustinianism and Pelagianism. The former imputes the guilt of Adam's sin to every human baby (except Jesus Christ) and the latter denies inherited corruption. Summers burst out against those who identify Arminius as a Pelagian: "What ignorance or impudence have those men who charge Arminius with Pelagianism, or any leaning thereto!"[53] He clearly delineated the differences between Arminianism and the semi-Pelagianism of Limborch and other later Remonstrants, and said that "all true Arminians . . . firmly believe in the doctrine of original sin."[54] Summers affirmed total depravity in the strongest terms possible and condemned a "new divinity" (beginnings of liberal theology) that reduces human moral inability. For him, "Apart from grace the will is bad, because the man's nature is so bad that of himself he

---

[49]Ibid., p. 99.

[50]William Burton Pope, *A Compendium of Christian Theology* (New York: Phillips & Hunt, n.d.), 2:47.

[51]Ibid., p. 60.

[52]Ibid., p. 80.

[53]Thomas O. Summers, *Systematic Theology* (Nashville: Publishing House of the Methodist Episcopal Church, South, 1888), 1:34.

[54]Ibid.

cannot choose that which is right."[55]

John Miley. Agreeing entirely with his nineteenth-century Methodist forebears and colleagues, John Miley said, "As the offspring of Adam, we all inherit the depravity of nature into which he fell through transgression."[56] However, Miley underscored more forcefully than previous Arminians that original sin does not include condemnation. His motto was "Native depravity without native demerit."[57] Apparently, for him, the guilt of original sin does not need to be set aside by Christ's atonement (as in Watson, Pope and Summers) because no such guilt exists. Individual persons cannot be guilty of others' sins, but they can inherit a corrupt and fallen nature. However, Miley did believe that all humans except Christ are guilty of their own actual sins, which are inevitable because of their inherited depravity of nature. He affirmed that free will is lost by the Fall, especially in the spiritual and moral realms; the power of choice to do the good is a "gracious endowment" and not a native ability.[58] Only with the help of the Holy Spirit can Adam's descendents recover free will; the work of moral regeneration is entirely that of the Holy Spirit and not a human achievement.[59] Humanity's natural condition apart from the Holy Spirit is "a state of alienage from the true spiritual life, and utterly without fitness for a state of holy blessedness. Nor have we any power of self-redemption."[60]

Conclusion. No doubt one reason critics abuse Arminianism by accusing it of having an optimistic anthropology is because these nineteenth-century Methodist theologians, building on especially Wesley's theology, affirmed a universal healing of total depravity by the grace of God through the atoning work of Christ on the cross. According to Watson, "As all are injured by the offence of Adam, so all are benefited by the obedience of Christ."[61] For him and the later Arminians of the nineteenth century, Christ's death not only resolved the guilt issue of original sin, so Adam's sin is not imputed to every child born, but it also mitigated the corruption of inherited depravity. From the cross flowed into humanity a power of spiritual renewal "removing so much of their spiritual death as to excite in them various degrees of reli-

---

[55]Ibid., pp. 64-65.
[56]John Miley, *Systematic Theology* (Peabody, Mass.: Hendrickson, 1989), 1:509.
[57]Ibid., 1:521.
[58]Ibid., 2:305.
[59]Ibid.
[60]Ibid., 2:529.
[61]Watson, *Theological Institutes,* 2:57.

gious feelings, and enabling them to seek the face of God, to turn at his rebuke, and, by improving that grace, to repent and believe the gospel."[62]
Pope agreed. Christ's life and death, he averred, provided a free gift to all
humanity. "The gift was the restoration of the Holy Spirit; not indeed as the
indwelling Spirit of regeneration, but as the Spirit of enlightenment, striving, and conviction."[63] This common (not universal) Arminian doctrine of
universal prevenient grace means that because of Jesus Christ and the Holy
Spirit no human being is actually in a state of absolute darkness and depravity. Because of original sin, helplessness to do good is the natural state of humanity, but because of the work of Christ and the operation of the Holy
Spirit universally no human being actually exists in that natural state. Wesley
connected this with an elevated conscience present in everyone as a work of
God through Christ and by the Holy Spirit. That does not mean everyone
has an equal opportunity for salvation. It only means that people everywhere have some ability to hear and respond to the gospel freely.

In their book *Why I Am Not an Arminian* Robert Peterson and Michael
Williams go after this Arminian doctrine and treat it as tantamount to a denial of original sin and total depravity. They charge that in spite of apparent agreement between Arminianism and Calvinism on the subject of original sin, the difference is still vast and great. That is because, so they argue
(basing much of their argument on the words of one contemporary Wesleyan scholar), in Arminian theology nobody is actually depraved! Depravity and bondage of the will is only hypothetical and not actual. This seems
a bit disingenuous, however, because they know very well that Arminians
do affirm total depravity as the natural state of human beings. What would
they think of a person who said of a man who is legally blind but with special glasses can see a little bit that he is only "hypothetically blind"? Or what
would they think of a person who said of a woman who is deaf but with special hearing aids can hear a little that she is only "hypothetically deaf"?
What would they think of a Roman Catholic who accused all Protestants of
believing in a mere hypothetical unrighteousness of regenerate and justified believers because of the Reformation doctrine of imputed righteousness? The doctrine of *simul justus et peccator* lies at the heart of the Protestant Reformation. It says that Christians are always at best simultaneously
sinners and righteous because their righteousness is Christ's imputed to

[62]Ibid., p. 58.
[63]Pope, *Compendium of Christian Theology*, 2:57.

their account. To Catholic eyes this appears a subterfuge, but to Protestant eyes it is the very heart of the gospel! Surely these two Reformed authors would reject any claim that they believe in a purely hypothetical unrighteousness of believers. In classical Protestant theology neither sinfulness nor righteousness is a fiction.

So it is for Arminians. The moral ability to respond to the gospel freely—by the graciously freed will—is a free gift of God through Christ to all people in some measure. It does not mean that anyone can now seek and find God using natural ability alone! It is a supernatural endowment that can be and usually is rejected or neglected. According to Arminian theology, because of Christ and by the power of the Holy Spirit all people are being influenced toward the good; the deadly wound of Adam's sin is being healed. And yet their fallen nature is still with them. This dual reality is analogous to the *simul justus et peccator,* or the war between flesh and Spirit within every Christian. The inability to will the good is not merely hypothetical; it is the state of nature in which every person (except Jesus Christ) lives. But no person is left by God entirely in that state of nature without some measure of grace to rise above it if he or she cooperates with grace by not resisting it. Arminians agree with Peterson and Williams that "without the Holy Spirit there would be *no faith and no new birth*—in short, *no Christians.*"[64] The only question is whether Christians are preselected by God out of the mass of others (who have no hope and no chance to respond to the gospel because God has chosen to pass over them and not give them the gift of irresistible grace) or whether they have responded freely to the gospel because they made use of the gift of prevenient grace extended to all. If Peterson and Williams are right, God's heart is totally closed to all but the elect, and the rest of humanity is never even given the ability to hear and respond to the gospel. What kind of God is it who glorifies himself that way?

Twentieth-Century Arminians and Human Depravity
Nothing has significantly changed in twentieth-century Arminianism. Like their spiritual and theological ancestors, modern and contemporary classical Arminians affirm inherited sinfulness and moral helplessness to exercise a good will toward God apart from prevenient grace. Nazarene theologian H. Orton Wiley said, "Not only are all men born under the penalty of death,

---

[64]Peterson and Williams, *Why I Am Not An Arminian,* p. 172.

as a consequence of sin, but they are born with a depraved nature also, which in contradistinction to the legal aspect of penalty, is generally termed inbred sin or inherited depravity."[65] He described this inheritance as alienated affections, darkened intellect and perverted will. "Depravity is total in that it affects the entire being of man."[66] For Wiley, as for all real Arminians, humans are totally unable to do anything good in spiritual matters apart from a special communication of grace. He preferred to call this condition "impotence to the good" rather than "bondage of the will," but the effect seems to be the same.[67] Wiley agreed with Wesley and the nineteenth-century Arminians that total depravity is mitigated by universal prevenient grace stemming from the cross of Christ through the Holy Spirit, which gives a "gracious ability" to fallen persons to hear and respond to the gospel. It frees the will from bondage and allows the person who hears the gospel to respond positively. Is this merely a hypothetical inability? No. It is both an actual inability and an actual ability alongside each other. One is natural and the other is supernatural. It is just like the Christian who struggles between the flesh (fallen nature) and the indwelling Spirit. No one would say the regenerate Christian has a merely hypothetical fallen human nature in spite of the fact that the Spirit within mitigates the power of the flesh and gives the Christian an ability to overcome it.

Wiley speaks for virtually all twentieth-century classical Arminians; many others could be named and quoted, but their statements would not substantially differ from those already offered here. The only conclusion that can be drawn from all the material offered in this chapter is that given by Charles Cameron in his article "Arminius—Hero or Heretic?" It applies equally to all real Arminians: "It should not . . . be supposed that Arminius has a man-centered emphasis which directs our attention away from the grace of God."[68] True Arminianism gives God all the glory and humans none; salvation is all of God even if people must freely choose not to resist it. But even that ability to not resist saving grace is of God; it is not a part of humanity's natural equipment.

At this point, of course, we know that some Calvinists will object that Arminianism is still nevertheless human-centered insofar as the person be-

---

[65]H. Orton Wiley, *Christian Theology* (Kansas City, Mo.: Beacon Hill, 1941), 2:98.
[66]Ibid., p. 129.
[67]Ibid., p. 138.
[68]Charles M. Cameron, "Arminius—Hero or Heretic?" *Evangelical Quarterly* 64, no. 3 (1992): 223.

ing saved makes a free choice and thus contributes the decisive element to his or her own salvation. Arminians reject that. The decisive element of salvation is grace; the only "contribution" of the human person is nonresistance. Saying that mere acceptance of a gift is the decisive element is bizarre. Imagine a woman on the verge of bankruptcy boasting that her endorsement and deposit of a gift check that saved her from financial ruin was the decisive element in her financial rescue. Anyone who heard her and knew the true circumstances of her situation would consider her either an ingrate or a lunatic. The decisive element was the gift of the check. If a Calvinist says that those who are saved according to the Arminian understanding can boast that they did something the nonsaved did not do, an Arminian can turn the tables and suggest that in the Calvinist scheme those who are saved because of unconditional election and irresistible grace can also boast because God chose them and not others. The Calvinist will object that this is foreign to Calvinism; the Arminian will respond that so is boasting foreign to Arminianism. All glory to God.

MYTH 7

Arminianism Is Not
a Theology of Grace

The material principle of classical Arminian thought is prevenient grace. All of salvation is wholly and entirely of God's grace.

THAT CLASSICAL ARMINIANISM IS NOT A theology of grace is a frequently expressed myth; we can find it in most books by Calvinists that touch on Arminianism. Calvinism is said to include "the doctrines of grace" as if other traditions of Christianity know little of grace. A widely held misconception is that Arminian theology focuses on free will to the exclusion of grace; its soteriology is believed to revolve around the human's choice of God rather than God's saving mercy and power. Once again the specter of semi-Pelagianism rears its ugly head. The common accusation is that Arminianism is a form of semi-Pelagianism that places the initiative in salvation on the human side and requires what amounts to meritorious good work toward righteousness for salvation. At worst the charge is that Arminians believe they save themselves rather than being saved by God. All these claims about Arminianism are false; classical Arminian theology has always given to God alone all the glory for salvation and reserved none for humans. It has always denied righteousness by performance or good works and warmly embraced salvation by grace alone through faith alone.

Calvinist theologian Edwin Palmer expressed the myth about Arminianism most bluntly. Speaking of Arminian theology he offered this analogy:

The theory that gives man a little credit for his salvation by granting him the ability to believe, pictures man as drowning. His head is bobbing up and down in the water as he flails his arms, trying to keep above water. If someone doesn't save him, he will die. He may have his lungs partially filled with water, even lose consciousness for a moment or two, but he still has enough presence of mind and ability to wave and yell to the lifeguard to save him. If he calls to the guard, the guard will rescue him.[1]

The problem with Palmer's analogy is that classical Arminianism does not depict human beings as able to initiate or aid in their own salvation; humans are dead in trespasses and sins until the prevenient grace of God awakens and enables them to exercise a good will toward God in repentance and faith. Even repentance and faith are gifts of God in traditional Arminian theology, although they are gifts that must be accepted by a bare decision not to resist them. Palmer's analogy is a complete distortion of the true Arminian picture of the human situation and the grace of God. A better illustration using water would be a man who has fallen into a pit and is unconscious. God calls to the man and offers help. The man awakens to consciousness. God pours water into the pit and encourages the injured person to float on the water out of the pit. All the man has to do is allow the water to lift him out by not struggling against it or holding on to the bottom. That is a picture (however homely and feeble) of prevenient grace. How could a person thus rescued boast of aiding in the rescue operation? All he did was relax and allow the water (grace) to save.

The key distinctive doctrine of Arminianism is *prevenient grace*. It may not be a biblical term, but it is a biblical concept assumed everywhere in Scripture. It is the powerful but resistible drawing of God that Jesus spoke about in John 6. Contrary to what some Calvinist commentators argue, the Greek word *elkō* (e.g., John 6:44) does not have to mean "drag" or "compel" (as claimed, for example, by Calvinist theologian R. C. Sproul in *Chosen by God*).[2] According to various Greek lexicons it can mean draw or attract.[3] Arminians believe that if a person is saved, it is because God initiated the relationship and enabled the person to respond freely with

---

[1]Edwin H. Palmer, *The Five Points of Calvinism* (Grand Rapids: Baker, 1972), p. 18.

[2]R. C. Sproul, *Chosen by God* (Wheaton, Ill.: Tyndale House, 1994), p. 69.

[3]Here I am indebted to the careful unpublished exegetical study "The 'Drawings' of God" by Steve Witzki. Witzki points to *A Greek-English Lexicon of the New Testament and Other Early Christian Literature*, 3rd. ed., *The Analytical Lexicon to the Greek New Testament, Greek-English Lexicon to the New Testament, Analytical Lexicon of the Greek New Testament, Greek and English Lexicon to the New Testament* and *The New Analytical Greek Lexicon*.

repentance and faith. This prevenient grace includes at least four aspects or elements: calling, convicting, illuminating, and enabling.[4] No person can repent, believe and be saved without the Holy Spirit's supernatural support from beginning to end. All the person does is cooperate by not resisting. This doctrine of prevenient grace is the focus of this chapter, which will demonstrate the falsity of Palmer's and other Calvinists' claims about Arminianism and grace.

Palmer is not the only scholar who failed correctly to understand or communicate Arminian doctrine about this grace. Even if someone disagrees with the Arminian position, he or she should always express it as an Arminian would express it, which includes an emphasis on prevenient grace. Calvinists Michael Horton and Robert Godfrey fail at this point.[5] In his articles "Who Saves Who?" and "Evangelical Arminians?" Horton equates Arminius's theology with semi-Pelagianism and argues that in Arminian theology God does not do all the saving; the individual person does at least some of it. He sums up his whole argument against Arminianism with the declaration that "if one does not believe in the doctrine of unconditional election, it is impossible to have a high doctrine of grace."[6] This is meant as a jab at Arminianism. But it misses the target because classical Arminianism does have a high doctrine of grace in spite of rejecting unconditional election. Horton ignores or neglects Arminianism's reliance on prevenient grace. Surely many of his readers did not know of this key Arminian doctrine unless they had read classical Arminian literature. Robert Godfrey is even harsher in his rejection of Arminianism on the ground that it allegedly denies salvation by grace: "Arminius ultimately failed to have a true theology of grace. . . . Jesus is no longer the actual Savior of His people," and "Arminius's teaching turns faith from an instrument that rests on the work of Christ to a work of man, and tends to change faith from that which receives the righteousness of Christ to that which is righteousness itself."[7] These and other attacks on Arminius's theology and on classical Arminianism are serious distortions.

Grace heals the deadly wound of sin and enables humans, who are otherwise in bondage of the will to sin, to respond freely to the message of the

---

[4]Stanley J. Grenz, *Theology for the Community of God* (Grand Rapids: Eerdmans, 2000), pp. 412-514.

[5]I confidently hope they have changed their rhetoric since 1992 when *Modern Reformation* published the distortion-filled special issue on Arminius and Arminianism!

[6]Michael S. Horton, "Who Saves Who?" *Modern Reformation* 1 (1992): 1.

[7]W. Robert Godfrey, "Who Was Arminius?" *Modern Reformation* 1 (1992): 6-7.

gospel.[8] Grace brings God's undeserved and unmerited favor to humans who exercise faith with repentance and trust in Christ alone for salvation. In order to demonstrate Arminian theology's truly high doctrine of grace, some reminders of the doctrine of sin (including depravity) and anticipations of the doctrine of justification (which is by faith) will be necessary. Knowledgeable Calvinists (and other non-Arminians) may already be anticipating questions and answers such as, Isn't the bare human decision to accept and not resist God's grace and mercy unto salvation a meritorious work? Arminians respond with a resounding no. In sum, and by way of preview, classical Arminianism argues that anyone who shows the first inkling or inclination of a good will toward God is already being influenced by grace. Grace is the first cause of genuine free will as liberation from bondage to sin, and grace is the source of anything good. In its prevenient (going before) form, it is the "quickening ray" Charles Wesley wrote about in his famous Arminian hymn "And Can It Be?" It awakens the prisoner lying helpless in the dungeon of nature's night and breaks off his chains so the he can rise up and follow Christ. There is no hint in traditional Arminian theology of salvation by works righteousness; all good is attributed solely to God's grace.

Arminius on the Grace of God in Salvation

Anyone who reads Arminius's theology with a fair and open mind cannot miss his passionate commitment to the grace of God. Nowhere did he attribute any causal efficacy for salvation to human goodness or even will power. William Witt rightly says that "Arminius's theology is throughout a theology of *sola gratia*. It has nothing in common with Semi-Pelagianism or Lutheran synergism."[9] Also, according to Witt, "Arminius has a very high theology of grace. He insists emphatically that grace is gratuitous because it is obtained through God's redemption in Christ, not through human effort."[10] Arminius went out of his way to elevate grace as the sole efficient cause of salvation and even of the first exercise of a good will toward God, including the desire to receive the good news and respond positively to it. Internal grace as inward calling rather than outward, common or general

---

[8]This chapter will necessarily contain some overlap with chap. 6 on human depravity and with chap. 9 on justification by faith. Grace, of course, connects the two.

[9]William Gene Witt, *Creation, Redemption and Grace in the Theology of Jacob Arminius* (Ph.D. diss., University of Notre Dame, 1993), p. 193.

[10]Ibid., pp. 259-60.

grace was his focus. According to Arminius no person can even desire God apart from a special interior, renovating operation of grace.

In his "Declaration of Sentiments" Arminius stated the matter as clearly as anyone could, leaving no doubt about his commitment to grace alone:

> I ascribe to grace THE COMMENCEMENT, THE CONTINUANCE AND THE CONSUMMATION OF ALL GOOD,—and to such an extent do I carry its influence, that a man, though already regenerate, can neither conceive, will nor do any good at all, nor resist any evil temptation, *without this preventing and exciting, this following and co-operating grace.*—From this statement it will clearly appear, that I am by no means injurious or unjust to grace, by attributing, as it is reported of me, too much to man's free-will: For the whole controversy reduces itself to the solution to this question, "Is the grace of God a certain irresistible force?" That is, the controversy does not relate to those actions or operations which may be ascribed to grace, (for I acknowledge and inculcate as many of these actions or operations as any man ever did,) but it relates solely to the mode of operation,—*whether it be irresistible or not.* With respect to which, I believe, according to the scriptures, that many persons resist the Holy Spirit and reject the grace that is offered.[11]

For Arminius, then, the issue was not whether salvation is all of grace but whether grace is resistible. Of course, Calvinists then and today argue that if grace is resistible, salvation is not all of grace. Arminians simply do not see any sense in that claim. A gift that can be rejected is still a gift if freely received. A gift freely received is no less a gift than one received under compulsion.

As if Arminius's statement about grace was insufficient, he offered something just as strong if not stronger: "That teacher obtains my highest approbation [approval, applause] who ascribes as much as possible to Divine Grace; provided he so pleads the cause of Grace, as not to inflict an injury on the Justice of God, and not to take away *the free will to that which is evil.*"[12] In other words, Arminius was protecting God from the authorship of sin and evil by affirming the free will of fallen people to sin without any secret impulse or compulsion by God. Lest anyone doubt his high doctrine of grace Arminius drove it home by saying of the supernatural operation of the Holy Spirit on the human soul that "as the very first commencement of every good thing, so likewise the progress, continuance and confirmation,

[11]Arminius, "A Declaration of the Sentiments of Arminius," *Works,* 1:664.
[12]Arminius, "A Letter by the Rev. James Arminius, D.D.," *Works,* 2:700-701.

nay, even the perseverance in good, are not from ourselves, but from God through the Holy Spirit."[13] For Arminius, then, grace in the form of the liberating and empowering work of the Holy Spirit precedes every positive movement of the freed will in relation to salvation. It also accompanies and makes possible the regenerate person's perseverance in grace.

What can we make of Calvinist critics' claims about Arminius's semi-Pelagianism and denial of *sola gratia* in light of these clear confessions? Either they do not know Arminius first hand, or they read him but misunderstood him, or they understood him but decided to misrepresent him anyway. Perhaps a fourth alternative comes closer to the truth: Arminius's critics understand him but consider him inconsistent. For all his affirmations of the necessity of grace from beginning to end in the process of salvation, he still affirmed that the person under the influence of grace can resist it and, in order to be saved, must freely accept it of his or her own volition by not resisting it. For them, this is to take back with one hand what Arminius gave with the other. Fine. We will have to disagree about that. However, fairness requires that they at least mention Arminius's strong affirmations of grace: it is the ground and cause of everything spiritually good that a person can do, including the first movement of the heart toward God. Too many Calvinist critics do not mention this and undermine their credibility, which raises questions about their integrity.

Arminius was a strong believer in prevenient grace as regenerative. That is, for him, prevenient grace is not only persuasive; it also renews the person in the image of God and liberates the will so that the person can for the first time exercise a good will toward God in repentance and faith. It even communicates the gifts of repentance and faith to the person, who must only accept and not resist them. First, the carnal person is incapable of faith: "For as that act of faith is not in the power of a natural, carnal, sensual *[animalis]*, and sinful man; and as no one can perform this act except through the grace of God; but as all the grace of God is administered according to the will of God," so "evangelical faith is an assent of the mind, produced by the Holy Spirit, through the Gospel, in sinners, who through the law know and acknowledge their sins, and are penitent on account of them."[14] Repentance and faith, then, are produced in the sinner by God's Spirit and are not works of "autonomous man." But the person must receive and not resist

---

[13]Arminius, "Public Disputations," *Works*, 2:195.
[14]Arminius, "Private Disputations," *Works*, 2:394, 400.

them in order to be saved. Nevertheless, Arminius ascribed all of the effi-
ciency in salvation to God and his grace: "as the very first commencement
of every good thing, so likewise the progress, continuance and confirmation, nay, even the perseverance in good, are not from ourselves, but from
God through the Holy Spirit."[15]

Arminius's biographer Carl Bangs was right that Arminius's objective was
"a theology of grace which does not leave man a 'stock or a stone.'" This is
because for him "grace is not a force; it is a Person."[16] Arminius was concerned not only that God not be made the author of sin but also that the
God-human relationship not be merely mechanical but genuinely personal.
For him the high Calvinist doctrine reduced the person being saved to an
automaton and the God-person relationship to the level of the relationship
between a person and an instrument. Therefore, he had to leave room for
resistance, but never did he so much as hint that the person being saved became a cause of salvation. He adamantly denied it. The whole tenor of
Arminius's soteriology is that "the capacity to believe does belong to nature,
but actual believing belongs to grace, and no one actually does believe without prevenient and accompanying grace."[17] It seems that for Arminius even
regeneration precedes conversion; that is, God begins the renewal of the
soul that is often called being "born again" before the human person exercises repentance and faith. Calvinism insists that regeneration precedes
conversion; otherwise repentance and faith would be autonomous works of
the human. This would mean the person is not really depraved but is capable of compelling the grace of God, which would no longer be sheer gift.
For Arminius, however, there is an intermediate stage between being unregenerate and regenerate.

The intermediate stage is when the human being is not so much free to
respond to the gospel (as the semi-Pelagians claimed) but is *freed* to respond
to the good news of redemption in Christ. Arminius thus believes not so
much in free will but in a freed will, one which, though initially bound by
sin, has been brought by the prevenient grace of the Spirit of Christ to a
point where it can respond freely to the divine call.[18]

This intermediate stage is neither unregenerate nor regenerate, but per-

---

[15]Arminius, "Public Disputations," *Works,* 2:195.
[16]Carl Bangs, *Arminius* (Grand Rapids: Zondervan, 1985), pp. 195, 343.
[17]Witt, *Creation, Redemption and Grace,* pp. 629-30.
[18]Ibid., pp. 636-37.

haps post-unregenerate and pre-regenerate. The soul of the sinner is being regenerated but the sinner is able to resist and spurn the prevenient grace of God by denying the gospel. All that is required for full salvation is a relaxation of the resistant will under the influence of God's grace so that the person lets go of sin and self-righteousness and allows Christ's death to become the only foundation for spiritual life.

Was Arminius's soteriology then synergistic? Yes, but not in the way that is often understood. Calvinists tend to regard synergism as equal cooperation between God and a human in salvation; thus the human is contributing something crucial and efficacious to salvation. But this is not Arminius's synergism. Rather, his is an evangelical synergism that reserves all the power, ability and efficacy in salvation to grace, but allows humans the God-granted ability to resist or not resist it. The only "contribution" humans make is nonresistance to grace. This is the same as accepting a gift. Arminius could not fathom why a gift that must be freely received is no longer a gift, as Calvinists contend. To explain the "concurrence and agreement of divine grace with free will" he offered an analogy:

> To explain the matter I will employ a *simile*, which yet, I confess is very *dissimilar;* but its dissimilitude is greatly in favour of my sentiments. A rich man bestows, on a poor and famishing beggar, alms by which he may be able to maintain himself and his family. Does it cease to be a pure gift, because the beggar extends his hand to receive it? Can it be said with propriety, that "the alms depended partly on *the liberality* of the Donor, and partly on *the liberty* of the Receiver," though the latter would not have possessed the alms unless he had received it by stretching out his hand? Can it be correctly said, *because the beggar is always prepared to receive,* that "he can have the alms, or not have it, just as he pleases?" If these assertions cannot be truly made about a beggar who receives alms, how much less can they be made about the gift of faith, for the receiving of which far more acts of Divine Grace are required![19]

At this point, of course, some Calvinist critics still maintain that Arminius makes the free acceptance of the gift of salvation, including faith, the decisive factor in salvation; so the human act of acceptance, and not God's grace, becomes the ground of righteousness. No Arminian, including Arminius, will agree with the formula that the person's mere acceptance of redemption from Christ is "the decisive factor" in salvation. For Arminius,

---

[19]Arminius, "The Apology or Defence of James Arminius, D.D.," *Works,* 2:52.

as for all classical Arminians, the decisive factor is the grace of God—from beginning to end. Using Arminius's analogy of the rich man and the beggar, would it be normal speech to say that the beggar's acceptance of the rich man's money was the decisive factor in his family's survival? Who would say that? All attention in such a case would focus on the benefactor and not on the poor receiver of benefaction. We might extend the analogy a bit and suggest that the rich man bestowed the gift in the form of a check, which needs only to be endorsed and deposited in the poor man's bank account. What if someone claimed that the act of endorsing the check and depositing it was the decisive factor in the poor man's family's survival? Surely even the Calvinist must see that no reasonable person would say that. So it is with Arminian evangelical synergism; the bare act of deciding to rely totally on God's grace for salvation and to accept the gift of eternal life is not the decisive factor in salvation. That status belongs to God's grace alone.

Post-Arminius Remonstrant and Wesleyan Accounts of Grace

Simon Episcopius. Arminius's theological heir, Simon Episcopius, confessed just as strongly as his mentor the absolute dependence of humans on grace for anything good and grace's sufficiency for everything needed for salvation:

> Man therefore hath not saving faith of or from himself; nor is he born again or converted by the power of his own free will: seeing in the state of sin he cannot so much as think, much less will or do any good which is indeed savingly good . . . of or from himself: but it is necessary that he be regenerated and wholly renewed of God in Christ by the Word of the gospel and by the virtue of the Holy Spirit in conjunction therewith; to wit, in understanding, affections, will, and all his powers and faculties, that he may be able rightly to understand, meditate on, will and perform these things that are savingly good.[20]

According to Episcopius, prevenient grace is regenerative; it can, however, be resisted. Salvation comes from not resisting it. The grace of calling becomes efficacious and saving grace when the human hearing the Word of God does not resist it.[21] For Episcopius, prevenient grace normally enters a person's life when the Word of God is heard, giving him or her everything necessary and sufficient for faith and obedience. In fact, prevenient grace

---

[20]Simon Episcopius, *Confession of Faith of Those Called Arminians* (London: Heart & Bible, 1684), p. 204.
[21]Ibid., p. 202.

is "wrought" by the Word of God.[22] This means that for Episcopius, in distinction from Wesley, who came later, prevenient grace is not necessarily universal. God is not an equal-opportunity Savior. Arminius left this question open; he did not answer it definitively but only hinted in his writings that those who never hear the Word of God proclaimed may by God's grace and mercy nevertheless come to a saving knowledge of God. He did not explain how and tended to restrict the reach of prevenient grace to the scope of the evangelized.

Philip Limborch. Episcopius left no doubt about his commitment to grace. How anyone can read this confession and think Arminianism does not have a high view of grace is a mystery: "Faith, conversion, and all good works, and all pious saving actions, which anyone can think of, are wholly to be ascribed to the grace of God in Christ as their principal and primary cause."[23] The only solution to the mystery of this myth about Arminianism may be the influence of Philip Limborch eclipsing Episcopius. Even people who never heard of Limborch generalized his theology onto all Arminians without distinguishing between his later Remonstrantism and true Arminianism. In all fairness to Limborch, however, he was committed to prevenient grace as the ground of all moral ability or goodness in humans, including the first exercise of a good will toward God. According to Limborch, in concert with Arminius and Episcopius, "the grace of God revealed to us by the gospel is the beginning, progress, and completion of all saving good without the cooperation of which we could not so much as think of, much less perform, anything conducing to salvation."[24] Limborch's problems began when he tried to explain the relationship between grace and faith; faith begins to float away from its Arminian grounding in grace as its sole cause, and Limborch moves toward grounding it in free will.

Limborch wanted to say that even faith is caused by God. "The primary and efficient cause of faith is God from whom, as from the father of lights, every good and perfect gift cometh."[25] Unfortunately, he did not leave matters there. He felt the need to elevate the human being's role in synergism and did so in such a way that the person becomes an equal partner with God in producing faith. In fact, he seemed to reverse himself and make the hu-

---

[22]Ibid., pp. 201, 207.

[23]Ibid., p. 205.

[24]Philip Limborch, *A Complete System, or, Body of Divinity,* trans. William Jones (London: John Darby, 1713), p. 412.

[25]Ibid., p. 504.

man will the ground of faith: "We therefore say that *faith* is at the very first
an act even of the will, not indeed acting by its own natural faculty alone but
excited and rendered capable of believing by the divine grace preventing
and assisting it."[26] It appears that Limborch believed the will of the fallen
human needs only assistance and not renewal; he seems to have believed
that the primary role of prevenient grace is to strengthen the natural ability
of the person and communicate knowledge and understanding about God
and the gospel. Limborch scholar John Mark Hicks sums up Limborch's
doctrine of prevenient grace:

> Grace does not restore freedom to the will, but strengthens the free will which
> remains. . . . Grace, therefore, is only necessary to assist man's fallen capabili-
> ties so that he is able to regain the integrity of Adam. Fallen man is not sub-
> stantially different from created man. The only differences are ones of
> degree, not kind. Man is weakened in his capabilities (the will has a propensity
> to evil, the intellect has lost its "natural guidance" system), but they are still
> intact and potent. Consequently, grace simply works with those capabilities
> which remain.[27]

In other words, whereas classical Arminianism before and after Limborch speaks of a personal work of the Holy Spirit beginning to regenerate
the human soul, including the will, through the Word, Limborch spoke
only of a boost or assist of the soul by prevenient grace. The assistance of
grace is primarily information; the unregenerate person needs enlightenment but not regeneration in order to exercise a good will toward God.
Hicks correctly compares and contrasts Arminius and Limborch:

> Both believe that original sin is fundamentally a deprivation, but their defini-
> tion *[sic]* of deprivation is radically different. For Arminius man is deprived of
> the actual ability to will the good, but for Limborch man is only deprived of
> the knowledge which informs the intellect, but the will is fully capable within
> itself, if it is informed by the intellect, to will and perform anything truly
> good.[28]

Later Arminians, such as Richard Watson, noted the same error in Limborch's thinking about grace and rejected his semi-Pelagian slant in favor
of prevenient grace as regenerative. Unfortunately, nineteenth-century re-

---

[26]Ibid., p. 506.
[27]John Mark Hicks, *The Theology of Grace in the Thought of Jacobus Arminius and Philip van Limborch*
(Ph.D. diss., Westminster Theological Seminary, 1985), p. 177.
[28]Ibid., p. 286.

vivalist and theologian Charles Finney followed Limborch's model (as mediated to him by Nathaniel Taylor) and that has come to be misunderstood as the classical Arminian position. This is simply incorrect insofar as Arminius sets the gold standard for true Arminianism.

John Wesley. John Wesley returned to the classical Arminianism of Arminius and Episcopius by stressing the supernatural, regenerating power of prevenient grace; for him it clearly transcends enlightenment or elevation of the intellect. It is the absolutely necessary personal power of the Holy Spirit working on the soul of the person, giving him or her the ability and opportunity to not resist saving grace. Thomas Oden rightly notes that for Wesley

> grace works ahead of us to draw us toward faith, to begin its work in us. Even the first fragile intuition of conviction of sin, the first intimation of our need of God, is the work of preparing, prevening grace, which draws us gradually toward wishing to please God. Grace is working quietly at the point of our desiring, bringing us in time to despair over our own unrighteousness, challenging our perverse dispositions, so that our distorted wills cease gradually to resist the gift of God.[29]

For Wesley, this work of prevenient grace is comparable to God's initial creation ex nihilo (out of nothing). Just as God created us ex nihilo, so "God recreates our freedom to love from its fallen condition of unresponsive spiritual deadness."[30]

Wesley anticipated the Calvinist accusation that by affirming even grace-enabled free will he was opening the door to Pelagianism or semi-Pelagianism. He rejected that criticism as invalid, attributing all goodness in human beings to God's supernatural grace: "Whatsoever good is in man, or is done by man, God is the author and doer of it."[31] His entire sermon "On Working Out Our Own Salvation" is a response to the charge of Pelagianism made against his Arminianism by Calvinist critics. Albert Outler, editor of Wesley's collected works, said, "If there were ever a question as to Wesley's alleged Pelagianism, this sermon alone should suffice to dispose of it decisively."[32] Commenting on the paradox-of-grace passage Phil-

---

[29] Thomas C. Oden, *John Wesley's Scriptural Christianity* (Grand Rapids: Zondervan, 1994), p. 246.
[30] Ibid., p. 249.
[31] John Wesley, "Free Grace," in *The Works of John Wesley,* ed. Albert C. Outler (Nashville: Abingdon, 1986), 3:545.
[32] Albert C. Outler, in the introduction to John Wesley, "On Working Out Our Own Salvation," in *The Works of John Wesley,* ed. Albert C. Outler (Nashville: Abingdon, 1986), 3:199.

ippians 2:12-13, Wesley declared:

> This position of the words, connecting the phrase of "his good pleasure" with
> the word "worketh," removes all imagination of merit from man, and gives
> God the whole glory of his own work. Otherwise we might have had some
> room for boasting, as if it were our own desert, some goodness in us, or some
> good thing done by us, which first moved God to work. But this expression
> cuts off all such vain conceits, and clearly shows his motive to work lay wholly
> in himself—in his own mere grace, in his unmerited mercy.[33]

Wesley went on in the sermon to leave no doubt about the primary role
of grace in salvation, without denying a certain synergistic cooperation between humans and the saving God. For him, as for all true Arminians, "God
works; therefore you *can* work. . . . God works; therefore you *must* work."[34]
Lest anyone misunderstand, however, Wesley did not mean by "you *must*
work" that salvation depends on good works. That would be an egregious
distortion of his soteriology. The sermon makes crystal clear that every good
in a human comes from God as a free gift. This includes the first good desire, the first motion of the will toward the good as well as both inward and
outward holiness. These are all breathed into people by God and worked by
God in them.[35] In fact, Wesley could not have put the matter stronger than
when he said that all persons are "dead in trespasses and sins" until God
calls their dead souls to life.[36] Clearly, for him prevenient grace is regenerative even though actual salvation necessarily involves the person's free and
willing cooperation with it by not resisting its saving work. Even that nonresistance is a work of God. All the human has to do is receive it.

Nineteenth-Century Arminians on Grace

Did the mainstream nineteenth-century Arminian theologians follow
Arminius's and Wesley's high doctrine of grace? They did. The calumny
that Arminianism neglects the grace of God in salvation ignores the nine-
teenth-century evangelical Methodist theologians and focuses on Charles
Finney, who no doubt defected from true Arminianism (if he ever was an
Arminian!).

Richard Watson. Richard Watson, perhaps the first Methodist systematic

---

[33]John Wesley, "Working Out Our Own Salvation," p. 202.
[34]Ibid., p. 206.
[35]Ibid., p. 203.
[36]Ibid., pp. 206-7.

theologian, criticizes Limborch and the later Remonstrants for deviating from Arminius's high view of grace. According to Watson, Limborch and the later Remonstrants "very materially departed from the tenets of their master."[37] Throughout his discussion of the Remonstrant defection, Watson quoted John Calvin freely and approvingly on the subject of human depravity and the necessity of grace for every good. Against Limborch and with Calvin, Watson averred that the consequence of the Fall is not merely an infusion of evil (misfortune, misery) but a *loss* of spiritual life.[38] The only remedy for this is Christ's atoning sacrifice and prevenient grace, which is the renewing and life-giving presence of the Holy Spirit. Even repentance, Watson claimed, is a gift of God and not a human work. But not even the gift of repentance saves a sinner; only Christ's death on the cross saves.[39] Prevenient grace, the Methodist theologian said, works by "removing so much of [the humans'] spiritual death as to excite in them various degrees of religious feeling, and enabling them to seek the face of God, to turn at his rebuke, and, by improving that grace, to repent and believe the gospel."[40] Watson noted that prevenient grace is irresistible in its first coming; it is given by God through the Spirit independently of human seeking or desiring. However, once it comes it can then be resisted and must be "improved upon," which does not mean added to but cooperated with by nonresistance.[41] Watson left no doubt about his commitment to grace as the initiative and enablement of salvation:

> Equally sacred is the doctrine to be held, that no person can repent or truly believe except under the influence of the Spirit of God; and that we have no ground of boasting in ourselves, but that all the glory of our salvation, commenced and consummated, is to be given to God alone, as the result of the freeness and riches of his grace.[42]

William Burton Pope. William Burton Pope wrote just as forcefully as Watson about prevenient grace. Unlike some other Arminians, he seems to tie prevenient grace especially to the proclamation of the Word of God. He believed that Christ's atoning death on the cross spread throughout humanity

---

[37]Richard Watson, *Theological Institutes* (New York: Lane & Scott, 1851), 2:77.
[38]Ibid., p. 81.
[39]Ibid., p. 102.
[40]Ibid., p. 58.
[41]Ibid., pp. 447-49.
[42]Ibid., p. 447.

a new spiritual impulse, but "by the special appointment and will of God the Word has grace connected with it, sufficient for every purpose for which it is sent."[43] This grace is

> the sole, efficient cause of all spiritual good in man: of the beginning, contin-
> uance, and consummation of religion in the human soul. The manifestation
> of Divine influence which precedes the full regenerate life receives no special
> name in Scripture; but it is so described as to warrant the designation usually
> given it of Prevenient Grace.[44]

Prevenient grace includes God's striving, drawing and demonstrating truth, and piercing the human heart with conviction. It breaks the bondage of the will to sin and frees the human will to decide against sin and submit to God. It is completely a work of the Holy Spirit through the Word.[45] Pope made clear the superiority of grace over human ability or cooperation: "The Grace of God and the human will are co-operant, but not on equal terms. Grace has the pre-eminence."[46]

Pope admitted that a mystery lies at the heart of this cooperation between the human will and the grace of God (the Holy Spirit). Here the
Methodist theologian expressed the paradox of grace as it is believed by
every true Arminian:

> In the secret recesses of man's nature the grace is given disposing and en-
> abling him to yield. Though the will must at last act from its own resources and
> deliberate impulse, it is influenced through the feeling and the understand-
> ing in such a manner as to give it strength. It is utterly hopeless to penetrate
> this mystery: it is the secret between God's Spirit and man's agency. There is a
> Divine operation which works the desire and acts in such a manner as not to
> interfere with the natural freedom of the will. The man determines himself,
> through Divine grace, to salvation: never so free as when swayed by grace.[47]

Without doubt, classical Calvinists will jump on the last part of this statement: "man determines himself . . . to salvation." That would be wrong, however, because Pope (and other classical Arminians) did not mean that the
human being is the efficient cause of salvation but the instrumental cause,

---

[43]William Burton Pope, *A Compendium of Christian Theology* (New York: Phillips & Hunt, n.d.), 2:345.
[44]Ibid., p. 359.
[45]Ibid, pp. 363-64.
[46]Ibid., p. 364.
[47]Ibid., p. 367.

without whose free assent (nonresistance) prevenient grace would never turn into saving grace. The real determination to salvation is God, who calls, convicts and enables, and subsequently responds with the free gifts of regeneration and justification to a positive human response.

Thomas Summers. Thomas Summers agreed completely with Watson and Pope about Limborch and the later Remonstrants. Summers bemoaned the fact that people were calling Limborch's system Arminianism, ignoring the differences between true Arminianism and Remonstrantism.[48] Also in harmony with Watson and Pope, Summers attributed all the power in salvation and every good to God's prevenient grace, which "precedes our action, and gives us the capacity to will and to do right, enlightening the intellect, and exciting the sensibility."[49] According to Summers, the only role of the human person in salvation is nonresistance to the grace of God.[50] This must be free; God will not select people against their will or without their free consent. So, prevenient grace overcomes the natural and automatic resistance of fallen people to the gospel, and makes them able to decide freely between resistance and nonresistance. For Summers, freedom of the will in spiritual matters is God's free and necessary gift to the soul, for without it responsibility would be destroyed. This freedom of the will must be "power of contrariety," ability to do otherwise. Summers clearly linked incompatibilist freedom with responsibility: "Freedom and responsibility would be destroyed or set aside, if we were necessitated to act according to motives over which we have no control, as truly as if some stronger power were to lay hands upon us, and mechanically force us to do any act contrary to our will."[51] He then connected this with the will to repent and believe (i.e., not resist the gifts of God's grace) in evangelical synergism:

> God alone regenerates the soul; but he will not regenerate anyone whom he does not justify—and God alone justifieth; but he will not justify any one who does not renounce his sins by repentance, and embrace the Savior by faith. We need hardly say that though no one can repent or believe without the aid of God's grace, yet God can neither repent nor believe for any man.[52]

---

[48]Thomas O. Summers, *Systematic Theology* (Nashville: Publishing House of the Methodist Episcopal Church, South, 1888), 2:34.
[49]Ibid., p. 68.
[50]Ibid., p. 83.
[51]Ibid., p. 68.
[52]Ibid., p. 120.

Therein lies the offense of Arminian evangelical synergism to Calvinism, but Arminians question the alternative. Summers was arguing that if divine determinism is true, the person is made into a stone, in spite of Calvinist objections to the contrary.

John Miley. Late-nineteenth-century Methodist theologian John Miley agreed completely with Summers. Free will as the personal power of choice over motives and between alternatives (ability to do otherwise) is a "gracious endowment," not a natural human ability in spiritual matters.[53] He even argued that prevenient grace reconciles monergism and synergism by attributing all the work of regeneration, from beginning to end, to the work of the divine Spirit while acknowledging that human agency must cooperate by choosing the good.[54] For Miley the liberty granted the soul by the Spirit is never arbitrary volition or indifference; that is, even under the regenerating power of prevenient grace, people do not receive the ability to do everything. Contrary to what some critics allege, Arminian free will is not absolute freedom of indifference; it is situated freedom under the influence of the call to the good *and* the pull of the fallen nature. Miley expressed true Arminian belief in free will best: "It is the freedom of personal agency, with power for required choices. It is sufficient for the sphere of our responsible life."[55] This is not the free will of the Enlightenment or of Immanuel Kant, who spoke of the "transcendental self" of the human person as if free will were a Godlike quality within humanity. Arminian free will is a creation of God and is limited in its range of possibilities, and it is still under the influence of fallen human nature as well as God's Spirit.

Grace in Modern and Contemporary Arminian Theology

H. Orton Wiley. Twentieth-century Nazarene theologian H. Orton Wiley followed in the footsteps of his nineteenth-century Arminian forebears. He defined prevenient grace as

> that grace which "goes before" or prepares the soul for entrance into the initial state of salvation. It is the preparatory grace of the Holy Spirit exercised toward man helpless in sin. As it respects the guilty, it may be considered mercy; as it respects the impotent, it is enabling power. It may be defined,

---

[53]John Miley, *Systematic Theology* (Peabody, Mass.: Hendrickson, 1989), 2:305.
[54]Ibid.
[55]Ibid., pp. 306-7.

therefore, as that manifestation of the divine influence which precedes the full regenerate life.[56]

He repeated, almost word for word, the doctrines of grace and free will found in Watson, Pope, Summers and Miley. Grace has the preeminence, and prevenient grace is irresistible in its initial arrival so that "man may [later] resist it but he cannot escape it."[57] Prevenient grace stimulates and persuades toward cooperation, but it will not overwhelm or violate the free will it has granted. On evangelical synergism, he quoted earlier Arminian theologian Adam Clarke approvingly: "God gives the power [to believe], man uses the power thus given, and brings glory to God: Without the power no man can believe; with it, any man can."[58] I wish Wiley had expressed inherited depravity and the regenerating work of prevenient grace more fully and forcefully. A hint of Limborch's semi-Pelagianism infects Wiley's account in places. He argued, for example, that the will's power of volition was not destroyed by the Fall, but the "bent to sinning" determines the sinner's conduct by influencing the will.[59] We hear echoes of Limborch in Wiley's statement that "grace is needed, not to restore to the will its power of volition, nor thought and feeling to the intellect and sensibility, for these were never lost; but to awaken the soul to the truth upon which religion rests, and to move upon the affections by enlisting the heart upon the side of truth."[60]

On the other hand, he averred that free agency as well as repentance and faith flow from prevenient grace even though they also involve a free response by the human agent.[61] He moved away from Limborch and back into classical Arminianism by affirming that faith itself is both a work of God and a free response of the human.[62]

Ray Dunning. Later Nazarene theologian Ray Dunning teaches the absolute necessity of prevenient grace for anything spiritually good in human life. It is, he admits, "not a biblical term but a theological category developed to capture a central biblical motif."[63] Because of original sin a human is totally unable to initiate the divine-human relationship, so this

---

[56]H. Orton Wiley, *Christian Theology* (Kansas City, Mo.: Beacon Hill, 1941), 2:346.
[57]Ibid., p. 355.
[58]Adam Clarke, quoted in ibid., pp. 369-70.
[59]Ibid., p. 357.
[60]Ibid.
[61]Ibid., p. 360.
[62]Ibid., p. 369.
[63]H. Ray Dunning, *Grace, Faith, and Holiness* (Kansas City, Mo.: Beacon Hill, 1988), p. 338.

work is done by prevenient grace, which is grounded in God's nature as love. Prevenient grace is, Dunning says, "a direct inference from the New Testament understanding of God."[64] It restores true free will as freedom for God that was lost in the Fall. "It creates both awareness and capacity, but neither is saving unless responded to or exercised by one's grace-endowed freedom."[65] Prevenient grace, then, includes the moments or aspects of awakening, conviction and calling. The preaching of Christ is the primary vehicle through which the Holy Spirit most effectively and normatively works prevenient grace in the soul of the human being.[66] Faith is the proper response to prevenient grace, but faith is itself a work of the Spirit and not of humans. Dunning appeals to Wiley in saying that the Holy Spirit is the "efficient cause" of faith; the "instrumental cause" is the revelation of truth (the gospel message) concerning the need and possibility of salvation.

Other Arminians theologians. We can easily find the same sentiments about grace in the writings of numerous twentieth-century Arminian theologians. Larry Shelton, for example, says that "salvation is all of grace. Although the human will must respond to the offer of grace at every level of spiritual development, the will does not initiate or merit grace or salvation."[67] Free Will Baptist theologian Leroy Forlines embraces bondage of the will to sin under the conditions of the Fall: "If anyone [takes] *freedom of the will* to mean that an unconverted person could practice righteousness *and not sin,* he misunderstands the meaning of freedom of the will for fallen human beings."[68] According to Forlines, even faith is a gift of God because it would be impossible without divine aid. "The Holy Spirit must work before there can be a successful communication of the gospel to the sinner and before there will be conviction and response from the sinner."[69] In other words, prevenient grace goes before conversion and makes it possible. There is no idea of repentance and faith being works of an autonomous creature. They are works of God in the sense that they are impossible apart from God's enablement.

[64]Ibid., p. 339.
[65]Ibid.
[66]Ibid., p. 435.
[67]R. Larry Shelton, "Initial Salvation: The Redemptive Grace of God in Christ," in *A Contemporary Wesleyan Theology,* ed. Charles W. Carter (Grand Rapids: Francis Asbury Press, 1983), 1:485.
[68]F. Leroy Forlines, *The Quest for Truth* (Nashville: Randall House, 2001), p. 158.
[69]Ibid., p. 160.

British Methodist New Testament scholar I. Howard Marshall likewise refers freedom to choose God to prevenient grace:

> *In every case it is God who takes the initiative in salvation* and calls men to him, and works in their hearts by his Spirit. Salvation is never the result of human merit, nor can anybody be saved without first being called by God. Men cannot in any sense save themselves. It must be declared quite emphatically that *the non-Calvinist affirms this as heartily as the Calvinist* and repudiates entirely the Pelagianism which is often (but wrongly) thought to be inherent in his position. When a person becomes a Christian, he cannot do anything else but own that it is all of grace—and even see that he has been affected by the prayers of other people. . . . The effect of the call of God is to place man in a position where he can say "Yes" or "No" (which he could not do before God called him; till then he was in a continuous attitude of "No").[70]

Although he does not call himself an Arminian, Arminianism has no better twentieth-century exponent than evangelical Methodist theologian Thomas Oden, whose book *The Transforming Power of Grace* is an exemplary expression of classical Arminian theology. Oden attributes all goodness in unregenerate and regenerate people to the grace of God. Whereas evil is always our own doing, good is always God's doing in us:

> To the extent that we fall from grace, it is our own act of diminishing the sufficient grace given. To the extent that we turn to receive grace, it is God's own act enabling our act. We cannot turn to God except as God arouses and helps us to a good will. Yet when we turn away from God, we do so without the help of God, by our own absurd willfulness.[71]

Prevenient grace, Oden declares, is supernatural; it is not merely an intensification of common grace. It provides every enablement for the good, including the first stirring of a good will toward God: "God prepares the will and coworks with the prepared will. Insofar as grace precedes and prepares free will it is called prevenient. Insofar as grace accompanies and enables human willing to work with divine willing, it is called cooperating grace."[72] "Only when sinners are assisted by prevenient grace can they begin to yield their hearts to cooperation with subsequent forms of grace." "The need for

---

[70]I. Howard Marshall, "Predestination in the New Testament," in *Grace Unlimited,* ed. Clark H. Pinnock (Minneapolis: Bethany Fellowship, 1975), p. 140.

[71]Thomas C. Oden, *The Transforming Grace of God* (Nashville: Abingdon, 1993), p. 49.

[72]Ibid., p. 47. Many Arminians do not make this distinction and include cooperating and assisting grace under prevenient grace.

grace to prevene is great, for it was precisely when 'you were dead in your transgressions and sins' (Eph. 2:1) that 'by grace you have been saved' (Eph. 2:8)."[73]

Conclusion. We have to wonder what critics of Arminianism are thinking when they condemn or criticize it as lacking a doctrine of grace or diminishing grace without mentioning the all-important Arminian concept of prevenient grace. They may disagree with the belief, but they should not fail at least to mention it as the linchpin of the Arminian soteriology! Howard A. Slaatte is right that true Arminian theology is far removed from naive religiosity (by which he means moralistic idealism). "True Arminian theology always shows a profound respect for the primacy of the faith-related grace of God and the doctrine of the sinfulness of man, while at the same time pleading for man's consistent responsibility in the saving relationship."[74]

---

[73]Ibid.

[74]Howard A. Slaatte, *The Arminian Arm of Theology* (Washington, D.C.: University Press of America, 1979), p. 24.

MYTH 8

Arminians Do Not Believe
in Predestination

*Predestination is a biblical concept that classical Armin-
ians accept, though they interpret it differently than Calvinists. Predestination is God's sovereign decree to elect believers in Jesus Christ, and it includes God's foreknowledge
of those believers' faith.*

FEW OF ARMINIANISM'S THEOLOGICAL CRITICS would claim that Arminians do
not believe in predestination in any sense; they know that classical Arminianism includes belief in God's decrees respecting salvation and God's foreknowledge of believers in Jesus Christ. They also know that Arminians interpret predestination in light of Romans 8:29, which connects predestination
with God's foreknowledge of believers. They know that Arminius set forth
an alternative to Calvinism's interpretation of God's decrees and predestination. Only the most cynical scholar could claim that Arminius and Arminians deny predestination, and the claim would be refuted immediately—
even by other non-Arminian scholars. Nevertheless, some Calvinists dispute
the Arminian interpretation of predestination as unbiblical and illogical;
Arminians often return the favor.

In spite of widespread scholarly acknowledgment that Arminians do believe in predestination, popular Christian opinion has become firmly convinced that the difference between Calvinists and Arminians is that the
former believe in predestination and the latter believe in free will. That has
been elevated to the status of a truism in American pop theology and folk
religion. But it is false. The fact is that many Calvinists believe in free will
that is compatible with determinism. They distinguish it from libertarian

freedom, which is incompatible with determinism and is the Arminian view of free will. It is also a fact that all true Arminians believe in predestination, but not in Calvinist foreordination. That is, they believe that God foreknows every person's ultimate and final decision regarding Jesus Christ, and on that basis God predestines people to salvation or damnation. But Arminians do not believe God predetermines or preselects people for either heaven or hell apart from their free acts of accepting or resisting the grace of God. Furthermore, Arminians interpret the biblical concept of unconditional election (predestination to salvation) as corporate. Thus, predestination has an individual meaning (foreknowledge of individual choices) and a collective meaning (election of a people). The former is conditional; the latter is unconditional. God's predestination of individuals is conditioned by their faith; God's election of a people for his glory is unconditional. The latter will comprise all those who believe.

This chapter will demonstrate widespread agreement among Arminian theologians that predestination, including election, is a biblical concept. We will also examine whether the concept of middle knowledge (Molinism) is compatible with or useful to true Arminianism and whether open theism is consistent Arminianism.

A brief discussion of terminology is in order. In general, theologians use *predestination* to designate God's foreordination (Calvinism) or foreknowledge (Arminianism) of both the saved and the damned. It is a more general term than *election,* which is usually used to signify God's predestination of certain persons or groups to salvation. *Reprobation* is a term rarely found in Arminian literature because of its connotation of foreordination to damnation. And yet, within an Arminian frame of reference, it could be used for God's foreknowledge of persons who will resist prevenient grace to the bitter end. But Arminians want to make clear that persons reprobate themselves; God does not really damn anyone, especially unconditionally.

All Christians, so far as I know, believe in predestination to service. That is, God calls some people, almost irresistibly if not absolutely irresistibly, to a special function within God's program of redemption. Saul, who became the apostle Paul, is a good example. But the debate over the nature of predestination revolves around whether God unconditionally elects individuals to salvation and damnation. Arminians believe this is incompatible with God's character.

Arminius and Predestination

Arminius defined *predestination* (as election) thus: "The decree of the good pleasure of God in Christ, by which he resolved within himself from all eternity, to justify, adopt and endow with everlasting life, . . . believers on whom he had decreed to bestow faith."[1] Clearly, Arminius did believe in predestination. His definition even contains a hint of foreordination, but further examination of Arminius's writings reveals that the predestination of individuals is conditional while corporate predestination is unconditional. The "believers" that God decrees from all eternity to justify, adopt and endow with everlasting life is simply that group of people who accepts God's offer of the gift of faith; that is, those who do not resist prevenient grace. Their individual identities are not definite, except insofar as God foreknows them. The main point here, however, is that Arminius did not cast aside predestination. He defined it differently than most Calvinists of his day but in harmony with many medieval theologians. He even went so far as to say, "Predestination, when thus explained, is the foundation of Christianity, and of salvation and its certainty."[2] Again, Arminius defined predestination in his "Letter Addressed to Hippolytus A Collibus": "It is an eternal and gracious decree of God in Christ, by which He determines to justify and adopt believers, and to endow them with life eternal, but to condemn unbelievers, and impenitent persons." In the same context he distinguished his view from that of his Calvinist colleagues: "But such a decree as I have there described is not that by which God resolves to save some particular persons, and, that He may do this, resolves to endow them with faith, but to condemn others and not to endow them with faith."[3]

What Arminius objected to in the Calvinist account of predestination is the exclusion of particular persons from any possibility of salvation and the unconditional bestowal of faith on particular persons. He even argued that it made God a hypocrite "because it imputes hypocrisy to God, as if, in His exhortation to faith addressed to such [i.e., the reprobate], He requires them to believe in Christ, whom, however, He has not set forth as a Savior to them."[4] In other words, if some particular individuals have already been

---

[1]Jacob Arminius, quoted by Gerrit Jan Hoenderdaal, "The Life and Struggle of Arminius in the Dutch Republic," in *Man's Faith and Freedom*, ed. Gerald O. McCulloh (Nashville: Abingdon, 1962), pp. 18-19.

[2]Arminius, "The Declaration of Sentiments of James Arminius," *Works*, 1:654.

[3]Arminius, "A Letter Addressed to Hippolytus A Collibus," *Works*, 2:698-99.

[4]Arminius, "Examination of Dr. Perkins's Pamphlet on Predestination," *Works*, 3:313.

foreordained unconditionally by God for damnation, then the universal call for them to believe in Christ cannot be sincere. In spite of what some Calvinists claim, in other words, the universal call to repent and believe the gospel for salvation cannot be a "well meant offer" either by God or by those who believe in that decree of predestination and practice evangelism. Furthermore, Arminius argued that high Calvinism's decree of predestination and especially reprobation is not scriptural but speculative:

> If you thus understand it [i.e., predestination],—that God from eternity . . . determined to display His glory by mercy and by punitive justice, and, in order to carry that purpose into effect, decreed to create man good, but mutable, ordained also that he should fall, that in this way there might be room for that decree;—I say that this opinion cannot, in my judgment at least, be established by any word of God.[5]

The Dutch Reformer concluded that *any* claim that God "decreed that man should fall" is unprovable from Scripture and inevitably makes God the author of sin.[6]

To those Calvinists who say they do not believe God foreordained the Fall (in disagreement with Calvin!), Arminius objects that they still undermine the character of God revealed in Jesus Christ and in the New Testament: "I should wish it to be explained to me how God can really from his heart will him to believe in Christ, whom He wills to be alien from Christ, and to whom He has decreed to deny the necessary helps to faith: for this is not to will the conversion of any one."[7] He based this argument and implied accusation on the clear New Testament expressions of God's will that no one "perish" but that "all" come to repentance and that all should be saved (1 Tim 2:4; 2 Pet 3:9). To those Calvinists who say they believe God did foreordain the Fall but only to permit the Fall and not to cause it Arminius says, "Actually, you explain that permission or non-prohibition in such a way as to coincide with that energetical decree of God [to bring about the Fall]."[8] Arminius was clearly dissatisfied and impatient with any notion that God wanted the Fall to happen or caused it or rendered it certain. He was equally impatient and dissatisfied with any notion that once the Fall happened, God willingly passed over a portion of humanity that he could have

---

[5]Ibid., p. 276.
[6]Ibid., p. 281.
[7]Ibid., p. 320.
[8]Ibid., p. 360.

saved—since he always saves only unconditionally. For Arminius, the Calvinist doctrine of predestination is shipwrecked on the rock of God's goodness at every turn.

So what is Arminius's alternative to the Calvinist understanding of predestination? The first and most important point is that he conceived predestination as *primarily the predestination of Jesus Christ to be the Savior of sinners.* Arminius considers the Calvinist doctrine insufficiently Christocentric. Jesus Christ seems to arrive as an afterthought to God's primary decree to save some and damn others. In place of that, Arminius described the supremacy of Jesus Christ in his view of predestination:

> Since God can love to salvation no one who is a sinner, unless he be reconciled to Himself in Christ, hence it follows that predestination cannot have place except in Christ. And since Christ was ordained and given for sinners, it is certain that predestination and its opposite, reprobation, could not have had place before the sin of man,—I mean, foreseen by God,—and before the appointment of Christ as Mediator, and moreover before His discharging, in the foreknowledge of God, the office of Mediator, which appertains to reconciliation.[9]

This crucial statement requires some unpacking. Arminius did not object to the Calvinist accounts of the sovereign decrees of God because they expressed God's sovereignty or were scholastic. He believed that the Calvinist schemes of God's decrees either treated humans as abstract entities, who were not yet created much less fallen when God decreed to save some and damn others (as in supralapsarianism), or treated Jesus Christ as secondary to the predestination of some fallen humans to salvation and others to damnation (as in infralapsarianism). In fact, supralapsarianism, Arminius was convinced, fell to the second objection also. He insisted on working out a scheme of the decrees of God that treats the objects of God's decrees—humans—as already fallen and as desired by God for salvation through Christ. In place of the various Calvinists schemes Arminius proposed the following one, which he saw as "most conformable to the word of God":[10]

> The FIRST absolute decree of God concerning the salvation of sinful man, is that by which he decreed to appoint his Son Jesus Christ for a Mediator, Redeemer, Saviour, Priest, and King, who might destroy sin by his own death, might by his obedience obtain the salvation which had been lost, and might

---

[9]Ibid., pp. 278-79.
[10]Arminius, "Declaration of Sentiments," *Works,* 1:653.

communicate it by his own virtue.

The SECOND precise and absolute decree of God, is that in which he decreed to receive into favour *those who repent and believe,* and, in Christ, for HIS SAKE and through HIM, to effect the salvation of such penitents and believers as persevered to the end; but to leave in sin and under wrath *all impenitent persons and unbelievers,* and to damn them as aliens from Christ.

The THIRD Divine decree is that by which God decreed to administer *in a sufficient and efficacious manner* the MEANS which were necessary for repentance and faith; and to have such administration instituted (1) according to the *Divine Wisdom,* by which God knows what is proper and becoming both to his mercy and his severity, and (2) according to *Divine Justice,* by which He is prepared to adopt whatever his wisdom may prescribe and to put it in execution.

To these succeeds the FOURTH decree, by which God decreed to save and damn certain particular persons. This decree has its foundation in the foreknowledge of God, by which he knew from all eternity those individuals who *would,* through his preventing [prevenient] grace, *believe,* and, through his subsequent grace *would persevere,*—according to the before-described administration of those means which are suitable and proper for conversion and faith; and, by which foreknowledge, he likewise knew those who *would not believe and persevere.*[11]

Arminius's scheme of the divine decrees differs from both Calvinist schemes (supralapsarian and infralapsarian) in crucial ways. First, it relates only decrees of redemption; it does not begin with creation. Arminius firmly believed it is wrong to tie creation and redemption together in such a way as to imply that creation is merely a stage for the Fall and redemption. Second, it begins with Jesus Christ as the predestined One. As did twentieth-century Reformed theologian Karl Barth, Arminius regarded Jesus Christ as the primary focus of predestination. Third, it does justice to God's love by leaving the number and identities of those humans elected in Christ open and indefinite. There is no predetermination that only some will be saved. Finally, it bases the election and reprobation of specific individuals on God's foreknowledge of their treatment of his offer of saving grace.

Some Calvinists are certain to object that according to Arminius humans elect God rather than vice versa. William Witt rightly corrects any such criticism by saying that "in Arminius's understanding of predestination, God

---

[11]Ibid., pp. 653-54.

elects believers, not vice versa."[12] While faith is the condition for being elected, God alone is the cause of election. In response to the fall of humanity, which was not in any sense willed or rendered certain by God, God chose Christ as the Redeemer for that group of people who repent and believe, and chose all who repent and believe in Christ as the elect. Corporate, indefinite election is one part of predestination. God chose that group of people who reject Christ as the condemned. Corporate, indefinite reprobation is the other part of predestination. Finally, with respect to particular individuals, God elected those he foreknew would enter Christ by faith to be his people and damned those he foreknew would reject Christ as not his people. Witt astutely observes the main difference with Calvinism: "Election and predestination are not the unconditional and mysterious choosing of certain individuals known only to God, but is rather the election and predestination of those who have faith in Christ their redeemer. Election is in Christ, but no one is in Christ without faith."[13]

And for Arminius faith is a gift. But it is resistible.[14] Nevertheless, he clearly wanted to attribute even conversion to God and not to autonomous people. His statement on the matter is somewhat paradoxical, but a perfect expression of evangelical synergism:

> Faith is so of the mere will of God that that will does not make use of omnipotent and irresistible motion to generate faith in men, but of gentle persuasion adapted to move the will of men by reason of its very liberty; and therefore that the total cause why this man believes, and that does not, is the will of God and the free choice of man.[15]

Predestination According to the Remonstrants and Wesley

Simon Episcopius. Simon Episcopius followed closely in the steps of his mentor Arminius, no less in this doctrine than others. He was appalled at the Calvinist doctrine of predestination as spelled out at the Synod of Dort, no less than at supralapsarianism, which Dort did not endorse. Episcopius did not hold himself back when addressing the Calvinist doctrine of predestination: "There is nothing so much an Enemy to religion as that fictitious fate

---

[12]William G. Witt, *Creation, Redemption and Grace in the Theology of Jacob Arminius* (Ph.D. diss., University of Notre Dame, 1993), p. 717.
[13]Ibid., p. 706.
[14]Ibid., p. 722.
[15]Arminius, "Examination of Dr. Perkins's Pamphlet," *Works,* 3:454.

of predestination, and unavoidable necessity of obeying and offending."[16] For him, as for Arminius, predestination breaks down into two categories— election (of some to salvation) and reprobation (of some to damnation). God decreed both but limited himself, so he does not unilaterally decide which particular individuals will fall into which category. And yet God foresees these choices without determining them. Episcopius also treated faith as a gift of God, but faith cannot be wrought in people without their cooperation. Resistance to the grace of the gospel and to faith will nullify God's work in that particular individual's life, and he or she will not be elect but reprobate.

Philip Limborch. For all his failings with regard to pure evangelical theology, Philip Limborch delivers a clear Arminian account of predestination. He appeals to Scriptures that affirm God's universal love and will for salvation to discredit Calvinist schemes of predestination. Especially "the doctrine of absolute reprobation is repugnant to the divine perfections of holiness, justice, sincerity, wisdom, and love."[17] On the other hand, and perhaps surprisingly, he agrees with Calvinists that "the end [purpose] of predestination both to election and reprobation was the demonstration of God's glory."[18] According to Limborch, following Arminius, Jesus Christ is the center of predestination; he is the predestined one, and others are either elect in him or reprobates, because they are by their own decisions and actions outside of him. God looks on people as either believers or unbelievers in Jesus Christ; thus Jesus is the foundation of election.[19] (Anyone familiar with Barth's doctrine of predestination cannot fail to see the similarities, although Barth would no doubt turn over in his grave if he were called an Arminian!) Limborch defined predestination as:

> That decree whereby before all worlds he decreed that they who believed in his son Jesus Christ should be elected, adopted as sons, justified, and upon their perseverance in faith should be glorified, and on the contrary, that the unbelievers and obstinate should be reprobated, blinded, hardened, and if they continued impenitent should be damned forever.[20]

---

[16]Simon Episcopius, *Confession of Faith of Those Called Arminians* (London: Heart & Bible, 1684), p. 52.

[17]Philip Limborch, *A Complete System, or, Body of Divinity,* trans. William Jones (London: John Darby, 1713), p. 371.

[18]Ibid., p. 344.

[19]Ibid, pp. 343-44.

[20]Ibid., p. 343.

Astute readers will note the strong similarities between Limborch's and Arminius's doctrines of predestination. Both are Christ-centered, corporate and conditional. Limborch also agreed completely with Arminius about God's foreknowledge as the ground and basis of his foreordination of individuals. One difference between the Remonstrants Episcopius and Limborch, on the one hand, and Arminius, on the other, has to do with perseverance. The Remonstrants denied the unconditional security of believers, or what is theologically termed *inamissible grace* (grace from which one can not fall). Both include *voluntary* perseverance with the assistance of grace among the conditions for election. Many, perhaps most, Arminians followed the Remonstrants in this. However, Arminius himself never settled the matter. His strongest statement about it was that "I should not readily dare to say that true and saving faith may finally and totally fall away."[21] Methodists and all their offshoots followed the Remonstrants and Wesley, who believed total apostasy is a possibility, while many Baptists followed Arminius or even held onto the Calvinist's perseverance.

John Wesley. John Wesley had nothing but harsh things to say about Calvinist belief in double predestination; he considered the unconditional decree of individual reprobation (even stated as God's "passing over" certain persons for salvation) anathema because of its injury to the love and justice of God. In his sermon "Free Grace" he lashed out against Calvinism with a list of reasons why its account of predestination is impossible in the light of Scripture, tradition and reason. However, perhaps somewhat inconsistently, he agreed with his Calvinist friend George Whitefield that *some* persons may be predestined by God for salvation. But he adamantly rejected any reprobation by divine decrees.[22] He even went so far as to refer to the unconditional decree of individuals to reprobation as "the cloven foot of reprobation!"[23] In general, Wesley viewed predestination as God's foreknowledge of faith and unbelief. For him, "God sees from all eternity who will and will not accept his atoning work. God does not coerce the acceptance of his offer. The Atonement is available for all, but not received by all."[24] And yet, Wesley went to great lengths to reject any suggestion that human beings earn or merit any part of their salvation; they must accept grace by not resisting it,

---

[21]Arminius, "Examination of Dr. Perkins's Pamphlet," *Works*, 3:454.

[22]See Thomas Oden, *John Wesley's Scriptural Christianity* (Grand Rapids: Zondervan, 1994), p. 253.

[23]Ibid., pp. 264-65.

[24]Ibid., p. 261.

but whatever good is in them is solely from the grace of God. Of salvation
he declared:

> It is free in all to whom it is given. It does not depend on any power or merit
> in man; no, not in any degree, neither in whole, nor in part. It does not in any
> wise depend either on the good works or righteousness of the receiver; not on
> anything he has done, or anything he is. It does not depend on his endeavors.
> It does not depend on his good tempers, or good desires, or good purposes
> and intentions; for all these flow from the free grace of God.[25]

Calvinists may think such a strong statement against human merit is inconsistent with equally strong statements about free will, which abound in
Wesley's writings. But they must at least admit that Wesley was not conscious
of attributing any part of salvation to human merit or goodness. For him,
election to salvation is not based on foreseen righteousness but solely on
foreseen free acceptance of the grace of God. And even that is only possible
because of the work of prevenient grace in humans.

In his sermon "On Predestination" Wesley echoed Arminius and the Remonstrants by defining predestination in terms of foreknowledge: "Who
are predestined? None but those whom God foreknew as believers."[26] Wesley insisted that God's foreknowledge is not determinative or causative. God
simply knows because things are. In modern terms Wesley's view is "simple
foreknowledge." It is as if God has a crystal ball, but his preview of human
decisions does not in any way render them inevitable. Rather, the decisions
cause God to know them. For Wesley there is no contradiction or tension
between God's foreknowledge of free acts and libertarian free will: "Men
are as free in believing or not believing as if he [God] did not know it at
all."[27] On the other hand, God does know who will believe, and his decree
of predestination is to save all in the Son who he knows will believe; he also
calls inwardly and outwardly (by the Spirit and the word) those he foreknows will believe.[28] There is no escaping the paradoxical nature of these
Wesleyan confessions. No doubt Wesley would approve of that. He was a

[25]John Wesley, "Free Grace," in *The Works of John Wesley*, ed. Albert C. Outler (Nashville: Abingdon, 1986), 3:545.

[26]John Wesley, "On Predestination," in *John Wesley*, ed. Stephen Rost, abridg. ed. (Nashville:
Thomas Nelson, 1989), p. 74. This is an example of how these terms are slippery. Here Wesley
uses *predestination* when he perhaps should have used *election*, but all theologians sometimes
use *predestination* in its wide sense and sometimes in its narrow sense.

[27]Ibid., p. 71.

[28]Ibid., p. 72.

proponent of neither rationalism nor irrationalism and recognized the suprarational character of much of divine revelation.

Nineteenth-Century Arminians on Predestination

The leading nineteenth-century Arminian thinkers Richard Watson, William Burton Pope, Thomas Summers and John Miley all held views on predestination very similar to Wesley's. They were, after all, Wesleyan Arminians.[29]

Richard Watson. Watson typifies nineteenth-century Arminian approach to predestination by affirming it unequivocally. He rejected unconditional individual election as strictly incompatible with the character of God as revealed in Scripture.[30] He warmly embraced unconditional election of classes or groups or people, however, and identified the church as the subject of God's electing grace in Christ.[31] Individual election is conditional and based on God's foreknowledge.[32] Watson, however, differed from Arminius and even Wesley at one possibly crucial point. He denied God's eternity as timelessness or as simultaneity with all times. He also rejected God's impassibility and absolute unchangeableness.[33] For him these ideas were speculative and not biblical; the God who responds to prayer and interacts with creatures cannot be outside of time, or timeless. Watson saw the conflict between simple foreknowledge and timelessness: How can a God without time come to know what is within time? If God's knowledge is derived from events happening in the world and is not based on foreordination as predetermination to cause things to happen, then it cannot be timeless knowing. A God who grieves over sin and evil cannot be impassible, and a God who is capable of suffering cannot be strictly immutable.

William Burton Pope. Pope also rejected unconditional individual election as in conflict with the divine goodness and dishonoring to God. "Surely it is dishonorable to the name of God to suppose that He would charge on sinners a resistance which was to them a necessity, and complain of outrage on His Spirit whose influences were only partially put forth."[34] The elect are

---

[29]Not all Arminians are Wesleyans. The ingredient that makes some Wesleyans, besides regarding Wesley as special, is belief in Christian perfection through entire sanctification.

[30]Richard Watson, *Theological Institutes* (New York: Lane & Scott, 1851), 2:340.

[31]Ibid., p. 337.

[32]Ibid., p. 357.

[33]Ibid., 1:353-400.

[34]William Burton Pope, *A Compendium of Christian Theology* (New York: Phillips & Hunt, n.d.), 2:346-47.

those who accept the divine call through the Word of God, to which grace is specially bound. The elect are the people of God, the church.[35] As applied to individuals, election is conditional and refers to God's foreknowledge of their response to the gospel. This, Pope argued, is the "faith of the ancient church before Augustine."[36]

John Miley. Miley agreed with Watson and Pope about the general contours of Arminian belief about predestination. In harmony with them (and with Arminius and Wesley) he condemned double predestination as contrary to the revealed character of God and insisted that "single predestination" is an impossibility: "The election of a part means the reprobation of the rest; otherwise God must have been blankly indifferent to their destiny."[37] Furthermore, "reprobation is contrary to the divine justice."[38] Miley's discussion of predestination is largely a refutation of Calvinism, but intertwined with it are his own affirmations, implicit as they may be. We cannot read him or Summers without realizing that they take Wesley's, Watson's and Pope's views of the matter for granted, and wish to spend their time and energy undermining the high Calvinism of the late nineteenth century, especially as expressed in the Princeton theologians Archibald Alexander and Charles Hodge. Both Summers and Miley expressed agreement with Arminius, Wesley and the early Remonstrants that predestination is conditional as applied to individuals, and is synonymous with God's foreknowledge of individual's faith or unbelief, and that the church is the unconditional object of God's electing grace. Election, again, is corporate and conditional.

Predestination in Twentieth-Century Arminianism

Henry Thiessen. One of the most influential American Arminian theologians of the twentieth century was Henry C. Thiessen, who taught a generation of budding young Christian scholars at Wheaton College. His *Lectures in Systematic Theology* was compiled by his son and was used as the primary textbook in doctrine and theology courses in numerous Christian colleges, universities and seminaries around North America during the 1950s and 1960s. Thiessen was apparently not aware that he was an Arminian! But his pattern of thought is clearly Arminian. Thiessen's first principle was that "God cannot hate any-

---

[35]Ibid., pp. 345-46.
[36]Ibid., p. 357.
[37]John Miley, *Systematic Theology* (Peabody, Mass.: Hendrickson, 1989), p. 264.
[38]Ibid.

thing He has made (Job 14:5), only that which has been added to His work. Sin is such an addition."[39] Thus he could not countenance the Calvinist idea that God hates the reprobate and passes by them when choosing to save some out of the mass of perdition. Thiessen described the decrees of God in the moral or spiritual realm (redemption) as beginning with permission of sin (God is not the author of sin), continuing with overruling sin for the good, saving from sin through Christ and rewarding his servants and punishing the disobedient.[40] Election is "that sovereign act of God in grace, whereby from all eternity He chose in Christ Jesus for Himself and for salvation, all those whom He foreknew would respond positively to prevenient grace. . . . It is a sovereign act in grace."[41] It does not rest on human merit even though it is based on God's foreknowledge of faith and is not (as Thiessen saw in Calvinism) capricious or arbitrary.[42] Finally, in concert with Arminius, the Wheaton professor affirmed that God produces repentance and faith in those who respond positively to prevenient grace: "Thus God is the Author and Finisher of Salvation. From beginning to end we owe our salvation to the grace of God which He has decided to bestow upon sinful men."[43]

H. Orton Wiley. Nazarene theologian H. Orton Wiley provides another example of a conservative Arminian theologian of the twentieth century who remained close to Arminius and the early Remonstrants as well as to Wesley (except in his doctrine of the atonement). Wiley first noted that election, as affirmed by Arminians, is conditional, especially as it applies to individuals.[44] He rejected modified Calvinist "single election" (to salvation) as logically impossible and points out that double predestination (including reprobation) is implied by "single election." Then he declared his own Arminian view of predestination:

> In opposition to this, Arminianism holds that predestination is the gracious purpose of God to save mankind from utter ruin. It is not an arbitrary, indiscriminate act of God intended to secure the salvation of so many and no more. It includes provisionally, all men in its scope, and is conditioned solely on faith in Jesus Christ.[45]

---

[39]Henry C. Thiessen, *Lectures in Systematic Theology* (Grand Rapids: Eerdmans, 1949), p. 131.
[40]Ibid., pp. 153-55.
[41]Ibid., p. 156.
[42]Ibid., p. 157.
[43]Ibid., p. 158.
[44]H. Orton Wiley, *Christian Theology* (Kansas City, Mo.: Beacon Hill, 1941), 2:335.
[45]Ibid., p. 337.

Who are the elect? "Those who hear the proclamation and accept the call are known in the Scriptures as the elect."[46] Can a person who never hears the explicit proclamation of the gospel believe and be saved? "God's Word is in some sense universally uttered, even when not recorded in a written language."[47] Like Wesley before him, Wiley was an inclusivist, at least in theory; he held out the hope that those never reached with the gospel message might nevertheless receive God's word and respond with faith. Who are the reprobate? They are those who resist the call of God to their utter destruction.[48] Wiley and most twentieth-century evangelical Arminians did not reject predestination as either election or reprobation; they defined election and reprobation corporately and conditionally, and thus guard the character of God as loving and just.

Ray Dunning. Nazarene theologian Ray Dunning, writing well after Wiley, relegates the subject of predestination to a brief paragraph in *Grace, Faith and Holiness*. This is unfortunate not only for its brevity but also for some confusion of terms. According to Dunning, predestination "is the gracious purpose of God to save mankind from utter ruin, and election is God's universal choice of all men, which awaits their uncoerced response."[49] The first part of that statement is a quotation from Wiley, but the second part introduces some confusion into the concept of election. Most Arminians have said that election is God's predestination of groups to service and salvation; regarding individuals, election is based on God's foreknowledge of who will respond in faith to his initiative. Dunning seems to confuse election with "calling." Still, the basic Arminian pattern regarding predestination can be discerned in Dunning's work.

Thomas Oden. Another twentieth-century Arminian theologian is evangelical and ecumenical Methodist Thomas Oden. Without explicitly wearing the Arminian label, his *The Transforming Power of Grace* exudes Arminian hermeneutics and logic. Like previous Arminians Oden rejects unconditional election and irresistible grace. "If grace compels free will, all appeals and exhortations to the will would be absurd."[50] Rather, free will is itself enabled by grace: "The power with which one cooperates with grace is grace

[46]Ibid., p. 343.
[47]Ibid., p. 341.
[48]Ibid., p. 344.
[49]H. Ray Dunning, *Grace, Faith and Holiness* (Kansas City, Mo.: Beacon Hill, 1988), p. 435.
[50]Thomas C. Oden, *The Transforming Power of Grace* (Nashville: Abingdon, 1993), p. 114.

itself."[51] Oden argues this is the ancient ecumenical consensus of the church.[52] If God absolutely and pretemporally decrees that particular persons will be saved and others damned, apart from any cooperation of human freedom, then God cannot in any sense intend that all will be saved, as 1 Timothy 4:10 declares. The promise of glory is conditionally based on grace being received by faith and active in love.[53]

For Oden, election is conditional; it requires willing cooperation. This is no limitation of divine sovereignty because God allows it to be so. God grants people the power to say no to grace.[54] Oden is aware that Calvinists point to Romans 9 to prove that election is unconditional and grace irresistible, but he offers an alternative interpretation that is completely consistent with Arminius's own reading of that chapter:

> The subject of the discourse in Romans 9-11 was not the eternal election or reprobation of particular individual persons to eternal life or death, as individualistic exegesis has sometimes argued, but rather the election of the Gentiles to be recipients of the promise equally with the descendents of Abraham, based on faith's free response to grace.[55]

Finally, Oden faces the Calvinist objection that if election is based on foreseen faith, faith becomes a meritorious good work that establishes the person's own righteousness. In that case salvation, Calvinists claim, is not a free gift of God. Oden's response is typically Arminian:

> Faith is not a meritorious cause of election, but it is constantly attested as the sole condition of salvation. Faith merely receives the merit of atoning grace, instead of asserting its own merit. God places the life-death option before each person, requiring each to choose. The *elektos* are those who by grace freely believe. God does not compel or necessitate their choosing.[56]

Conclusion. Other twentieth-century Arminian theologians could be quoted as witnesses to the fact that classical Arminianism does include doctrines of predestination and election. Even reprobation is accounted for by Arminian theology. Jack Cottrell, Leroy Forlines, I. Howard Marshall, Robert Shank, William Klein, Bruce Reichenbach and many more evangelical

---

[51]Ibid., p. 145.
[52]Ibid., p. 132.
[53]Ibid., p. 135.
[54]Ibid., p. 144.
[55]Ibid., pp. 142-43.
[56]Ibid., p. 140.

Arminian scholars have written about these topics with eagerness and even passion. The idea that Arminianism preaches free will against predestination is simply false; it preaches predestination *and* free will as an instrument for inclusion in either election or reprobation, which are corporate and conditional.[57]

Arminianism, Predestination, Middle Knowledge and Open Theism

Two topics have arisen around contemporary Arminianism and created controversy about it. One is the use of divine middle knowledge to reconcile God's foreknowledge with free will; the other is open theism, which qualifies divine foreknowledge in order to support free will. Both concepts arose in relation to Arminianism because of a perceived difficulty with classical Arminianism. Can God (or anyone) know the future exhaustively and infallibly if the future contains free decisions and actions not yet determined by anyone or anything? In other words, if free will is libertarian, such that persons exercising it could choose to do something other than what they actually do, how is it possible even for God to foreknow how free will will be used? If God foreknows that subject X will do Y at time Z in the future, how can X's decision and action be truly free in the strong sense of incompatibilist free will? Thus is there really anything to know of libertarian free will? Wouldn't knowing such a future free decision or action be something like knowing the DNA of unicorns? Can the omniscient God know unicorn DNA even though it does not exist and (presumably) has not even been imagined?

Classical Arminianism assumes and asserts libertarian free will that is not compatible with determinism. It does not say that everyone has such free will all of the time; it only says that in spiritual matters, and especially pertaining to salvation, human beings have free will as a gift from God. At least some of the time, especially when confronted by the message of the gospel and the call to repent and believe, and enabled by prevenient grace, humans can freely choose to believe or turn away in rejection. This is bedrock belief for Arminians. However, many critics have pointed out the logical difficulty of reconciling that kind of free will with absolute foreknowledge. The claim is not that foreknowledge causes anything, but only that if someone

---

[57]An excellent study of corporate election that is fully consistent with Arminianism and supports its view of predestination is William W. Klein, *The New Chosen People* (Eugene, Ore.: Wipf & Stock, 2001).

such as God knows what will happen with absolute certainty, it cannot happen otherwise. Even Arminius seemed to open the door to a limitation of God's foreknowledge while holding onto an unlimited view of it. According to Arminius scholar William Witt:

> For Arminius, the creation of the world means that the future of history is open. The unfallen human being is genuinely free (given God's prevenient and sustaining grace) to remain faithful to its creator. However it is also free to sin if it wills. . . . If the creature sins, then not only the creature's future, but also (in some sense) God's future, will be different. For without sin, there is no need for redemption.[58]

Did Arminius perceive the problem of apparent incompatibility of God's foreknowledge and libertarian free will? We do not know. But he was already in enough trouble with the authorities; doubtless he did not want to tread into deeper waters. Still, according to some Arminians, had Arminius lived long enough, he may have sought a solution to the apparent inconsistency through either Molinism (middle knowledge) or open theism (self-limiting divine foreknowledge).

Middle knowledge. Arminian advocates of middle knowledge sometimes claim that Arminius does make use of the concept and that it is implicit in his own thinking about the future and free will. Christian philosopher William Lane Craig has written extensively on the subject of middle knowledge as the key to unlocking the problem. He has even suggested that Molinism might be the key to a Calvinist-Arminian rapprochement.[59] So-called middle knowledge (if it exists) is God's knowledge of what any free creature would freely do in any given set of circumstances. In other words, as God envisions every possible world, he knows intuitively what person X, who is endowed with libertarian free will, would do at any given moment and in any given situation. This concept, first developed in detail by Luis Molina (1535-1600), was applied to the controversy within Roman Catholic theology between those who believed in predestination (such as Blaise Pascal) and those who believed in libertarian freedom (such as the Jesuits). Craig points out how divine middle knowledge could reconcile divine foreknowledge and predestination with libertarian free will:

[58]Witt, *Creation, Redemption and Grace,* p. 366.
[59]William Lane Craig, "Middle Knowledge a Calvinist-Arminian Rapprochement?" in *The Grace of God the Will of Man,* ed. Clark H. Pinnock (Grand Rapids: Zondervan, 1989), pp. 141-64.

Prior to the determination of the divine will, God knows how every possible free creature would respond in all possible circumstances, including the offer of certain gracious helps that God might provide [prevenient grace]. In choosing to create a certain order God commits himself, out of his goodness, to offering various graces to all people—graces that are sufficient for their salvation. He knows, however, that many will in fact freely reject his aids and be lost. But those who assent to his grace render it efficacious in procuring their salvation. Given God's immutable determination to create a certain order, those who God knew would respond to his grace are predestined to be saved. It is absolutely certain that they will respond to and persevere in God's grace; and, indeed, in the composite sense it is impossible that they should be lost. Nevertheless, in the divided sense they are entirely free to reject God's grace; but were they to do so, then God would have had different middle knowledge than he does and so they would not be predestined [to salvation].[60]

Most classical Arminians are wary of this approach. The claim that Arminius himself assumed God's middle knowledge and its role in providence and predestination is dubious. No one questions that Arminius occasionally but rarely said things that could be interpreted as Molinist.[61] Witt is right that in general, however, the Dutch theologian rejected middle knowledge, especially as it might be used by God to predetermine decisions and actions of human persons. The logic of Arminius's account of free will steers away from any determinism, but one use of middle knowledge is to explain how the actual world is determined by God using knowledge of what free creatures would do in any given world, including the one God ultimately decided to create—this one. Arminius averred repeatedly that determined acts cannot be sinful. This can be found in virtually every one of his treatises. Furthermore, as Witt points out, middle knowledge seems incompatible with libertarian free will:

> Not even God could know with certainty what a rational creature *would* do in a given situation prior to its free-will decision, not because God's knowledge is limited, but because (logically and temporally) prior to the actual decision of the creature's will, the outcome of the creature's act is inherently uncertain.[62]

---

[60]Ibid., p. 158.

[61]For example, in his "Public Disputation IV," on the knowledge of God, Arminius mentioned "middle knowledge" (in *Works*, 2:124), but the context does not seem to support the contention that he meant the same as Molina's or Craig's version of middle knowledge.

[62]Witt, *Creation, Redemption and Grace*, p. 363.

Witt is correct that Molinism leads to determinism and is therefore incompatible with Arminianism. He also argues correctly that in the final analysis Arminius himself realized this and backed away from using middle knowledge.[63] The only free will that would be compatible with God's use of middle knowledge in creation is a compatibilist free will—one compatible with determinism. Individuals possessing and using such free will would not be able to do other than what they in fact do. After all, God created them and placed them in the particular circumstances in which they find themselves so that his detailed, meticulous plan for history could be fulfilled. Even though the Molinist says such persons have libertarian free will, it does not seem possible. And it makes God look like the ultimate manipulator. Philosophers debate whether counterfactuals of freedom are logically possible. That is, is it logically possible to know what a genuinely free person (i.e., one possessing libertarian freedom) would do in any given set of circumstances? What would person X do in a different world than this one? Many philosophers are convinced that middle knowledge is illogical because counterfactuals of freedom are illogical.

Open theism. Open theists jump on the problem of reconciling divine foreknowledge and libertarian free will by suggesting that the two cannot be reconciled, so God must not know the future exhaustively and infallibly insofar as it contains decisions and actions not yet determined or caused by anything or anyone. Arminius did seem to view the future and God as in some sense open. At the same time, though, he believed in God's exhaustive and infallible foreknowledge. Open theists are Arminians who reject middle knowledge as a solution. They argue that God's foreknowledge is limited *because God has decided it should be.* Perhaps a better way of putting it is that God does know the future infallibly as a realm of both settled *and* yet unsettled (thus open) events. For open theists God knows it as both open and settled because some future decisions and actions are already determined by God (or something or someone else). But some of it is not yet settled because humans have ability to do otherwise and therefore will yet decide, for example, between options A and B. Until they decide, even God cannot know with absolute certainty which will be chosen. This view was first suggested among evangelical Protestants by Methodist (and therefore Arminian) evangelist and theologian Lorenzo McCabe in the 1890s. It be-

---

[63]Ibid., pp. 365-66.

gan to grow in popularity among evangelicals in the 1990s under the influence of the book *The Openness of God,* which contained essays on God's foreknowledge by Arminians Clark Pinnock, John Sanders, Richard Rice, David
Basinger and William Hasker.[64]

Open theists argue that their view is consistent Arminianism. As they
see it, they have fixed classical Arminianism's logical inconsistency between divine foreknowledge and human free will.[65] But at what cost? Most
Arminians have not jumped on the open-theist bandwagon because they
are committed to the doctrine of predestination! Now, there is an irony!
Calvinists accuse classical Arminians of not believing in predestination,
but most classical Arminians reject open theism precisely because they believe in predestination. If open theism is true, election and reprobation
can only be corporate. But classical Arminianism bases a great deal on Romans 8:29, which seems to refer not to classes or groups but to individuals.
God does not justify and glorify groups, but individuals. Classical Arminian theology includes corporate election *and* individual (conditional)
election based on God's foreknowledge of future faith (or lack thereof).
Open theism has to reduce predestination (election and reprobation) to
its indefinite, corporate dimension; predestination of individuals gets lost.
Some classical Arminians, such as Jack Cottrell, reject open theism because they believe it undermines God's providential governance of history, but that assumes that foreknowledge gives God a providential advantage, which is debatable.[66] It remains to be seen whether many Arminians
will adopt open theism. Few Arminians are willing to denounce their open
theist brothers and sisters as heretics, but most are unwilling at present to
give up belief in absolute divine foreknowledge, because the Bible seems
to assume it everywhere.

   Conclusion. The upshot is that classical Arminianism may involve a para-

---

[64]Clark Pinnock et al., *The Openness of God* (Downers Grove, Ill.: InterVarsity Press, 1994). Later,
   theologian and pastor Gregory A. Boyd chimed in with published support for open theism.
[65]This claim has been communicated to me by several open theists even though it is not often
   found in their writings; open theists want to keep classical Arminians on their side, hoping
   that the classical Arminians will defend them in the current climate of controversy. I consider
   open theism a legitimate evangelical and Arminian option even though I have not yet
   adopted it as my own perspective.
[66]Jack Cottrell, *What the Bible Says About God the Ruler* (Eugene, Ore.: Wipf & Stock, 2000). In
   chapter five, "Special Providence and Free Will," the Church of Christ theologian ties divine
   foreknowledge of free decisions and actions together with God's providential control. In later
   articles he criticizes open theism for undermining the latter. (The volume cited here was orig-
   inally written in 1984, before open theism became the subject of controversy.)

dox: God's exhaustive and infallible foreknowledge (simple foreknowledge) together with libertarian free will. Middle knowledge is no help because it assumes the possibility of counterfactuals of freedom and leads to determinism. Open theism takes too much away from the biblical doctrine of predestination. Just as Calvinists often claim that they are biblically warranted to believe in both unconditional foreordination of sin and human responsibility for sin, so Arminians claim they are justified in embracing both exhaustive and infallible divine foreknowledge and libertarian free will because both are necessary for a sound biblical worldview. And, not all philosophers believe they are necessarily logically incompatible.[67]

---

[67]See, for example, Alvin C. Plantinga, *God, Freedom, and Evil* (Grand Rapids: Eerdmans, 1974). Some readers may wonder if I am affirming a logical contradiction here. I am not intentionally and certainly not comfortably doing so. I acknowledge a difficulty but am not convinced it is a sheer contradiction. Because I feel the weight of the open theist critique of classical Arminianism I remain open to open theism while remaining a classical Arminian awaiting help to relieve the paradox from philosophy.

MYTH 9

Arminian Theology Denies Justification by Grace Alone Through Faith Alone

Classical Arminian theology is a Reformation theology. It embraces divine imputation of righteousness by God's grace through faith alone and preserves the distinction between justification and sanctification.

ONE OF THE MOST DAMAGING MISCONCEPTIONS about Arminianism is that it is not truly Protestant; critics say it is not a Reformation theology but is closer to Catholic soteriology. The claim is that Arminius and his followers defected from the article by which, according to Luther, the Christian faith stands or falls—salvation as a free gift of grace received by faith alone—and subtly reintroduced salvation by works of righteousness. More specifically, so it is said, Arminians deny that Christ's righteousness is imputed to believers on account of faith alone, replacing it with faith as a meritorious achievement that earns God's favor. All of this is false. Michael Horton is representative of those Calvinist critics of Arminianism who simply get it wrong at this point. In *Modern Reformation* he says, "The Arminians denied the Reformation belief that faith was a gift and that justification was a purely forensic (legal) declaration. For them, it included a moral change in the believer's life and faith itself, a work of humans, was the basis for God's declaration." And, "This imputation or crediting of faith as our righteousness, rather than Christ's active and passive obedience, is precisely the doctrine articulated by Arminius, rendering faith a work which achieves righteousness before God."[1]

---

[1] Michael Horton, "Evangelical Arminians," *Modern Reformation* 1 (1992): 16, 18.

Clearly, Horton (and other critics who raise the same objection) has laid down the gauntlet; this is a serious charge, because Arminians do consider themselves Protestants in the Reformation tradition. Horton concludes that "An evangelical cannot be an Arminian any more than an evangelical can be a Roman Catholic."[2] This accusation of implicit Catholicism was made against Arminius in his own lifetime, and he strove to counteract it. It has dogged Arminianism ever since; conservative Calvinists especially keep it alive in their polemics against Arminianism. Is there any truth to it? What is the Arminian doctrine of justification? Is it consistent with Luther and Calvin, or does it import works righteousness into Protestant thought? Notice that Horton did not simply level a charge of serious theological error against popular Arminianism; his accusation was that Arminius *himself* denied justification by grace through faith alone as imputation of Christ's righteousness. So it is important to look carefully at what Arminius and his followers did and did not say about this crucial theological matter.

Arminians have always been uncomfortable with a purely forensic (declaratory) righteousness and have attempted to balance that with an inward, imparted righteousness that actually begins to transform a sinner into a righteous person. However, Luther himself sought this balance in his essay "Two Kinds of Righteousness" where he taught both alien, imputed righteousness (forensic) and inward, transforming righteousness, with the latter attendant upon the former.[3] Arminius, Wesley and all true Arminians have done nothing in this area of soteriology different than Luther. However, Arminians have not always been perfectly clear about the nature of imputed righteousness (Luther's first righteousness). Is it Christ's active and passive obedience (to use Reformed language) that is imputed to believers on account of faith, or is faith itself credited to believers as righteousness? A formula that appears in Arminius's writings, and in some later Arminian theologians, is "faith imputed for righteousness." This is apparently what stirred up Horton and other Reformed critics. And it has been controversial among Arminians for centuries. What does it mean? Is it a sufficient expression of the righteousness of justification?

All real Arminians have always confessed that justification is a gift of

---

[2]Ibid., p. 18.
[3]Martin Luther, "Two Kinds of Righteousness," in *Martin Luther's Basic Theological Writings*, ed. Timothy Lull (Minneapolis: Fortress, 1989), pp. 155-64.

God's grace that cannot be merited or earned. They also have always declared that the grace of justification is received only by faith and that faith is not a good work. Many Arminians even say that faith itself is a gift of God. Finally, we will see that the formula "faith imputed for righteousness" is ambiguous and does not necessarily replace the imputation of Christ's righteousness. Many Arminians affirm that Christ's righteousness is imputed to believers on account of their faith, and this imputed righteousness is the sole ground of their acceptance by God. Furthermore, at the heart of Arminianism is a denial that faith is the efficacious or meritorious cause of justification; it is always only the instrumental cause of justification. Whether these clarifications of Arminian doctrine will satisfy Horton and other monergistic evangelicals is doubtful, because they seem to believe that only monergism—God as the sole active agent in salvation—does justice to the Protestant doctrine of justification by grace through faith alone. However, that seems arbitrary to Arminians. If it can be shown that Arminianism does not make faith the efficient or meritorious cause of justification and that it does affirm that justification is always only a free gift of grace, which does not depend on works, I believe that is enough to rescue Arminianism's Protestant credentials from those who would take them away.

Arminius and Justification

The previous chapters of this book have already demonstrated that Arminius believed salvation is of grace alone and not at all of works. He attributed every good in every human being solely to the grace of God; his main concern was to protect God's character by abstaining from any doctrine that would make God the author of sin. Therefore, he said that humans are the cause of evil, but God is the sole cause of good. What about justification? Did Arminius teach it in a way that is consistent with classical Protestantism? Was he a Reformation thinker? As astute and authoritative a Reformed theologian as Alan P. F. Sell, former theological secretary of the World Alliance of Reformed Churches, declared, "On the question of justification, Arminius finds himself at one with all the Reformed and Protestant Churches."[4] Arminius scholar A. Skevington Wood concurred and said that Arminius "was not aware of having in any way departed from the reformed doctrine relating to justification."[5] Howard Slaatte agrees by saying that

---

[4]Alan P. F. Sell, *The Great Divide* (Grand Rapids: Baker, 1983), p. 12.

"Arminius was a confirmed product of the Protestant Reformation" and not a Pelagian or a moralist.[6] According to Carl Bangs, Arminius affirmed the strongest view possible of justification, to the point of accepting Luther's *simul justus et peccator* (righteous and sinner at the same time) on the basis that real righteousness is imputed as a forensic act of God.[7] These and many more witnesses testify that Arminius was firmly rooted in Reformation theology and did not depart from the classical Protestant doctrine of justification by grace alone through faith alone.

What did Arminius say? In his "Declaration of Sentiments" he responded to the accusation of heresy regarding justification:

> I am not conscious to myself, of having taught or entertained any other sentiments concerning *the justification of man before God,* than those which are held unanimously by the Reformed and Protestant Churches, and which are in complete agreement with their expressed opinions.[8]

He even expressed agreement with Calvin's own view of justification: "My opinion is not so widely different from his as to prevent me from employing the signature of my own hand in subscribing to those things which he has delivered on this subject, in the Third Book of his *Institutes;* this I am prepared to do at any time, and to give them my full approval."[9]

Arminius delivered his own brief statement of the doctrine of justification to turn aside the claim that his was heretical by Protestant standards:

> I believe that sinners are accounted righteous solely by the obedience of Christ; and that the righteousness of Christ is the only meritorious cause on account of which God pardons the sins of believers and reckons them as righteous as if they had perfectly fulfilled the law. But since God imputes the righteousness of Christ to none except believers, I conclude, that in this sense it may be well and properly said, *To a man who believes Faith is imputed for righteousness through grace,*—because God hath set forth his Son Jesus Christ to be a propitiation, a throne of grace [or mercy-seat,] through faith in his blood.[10]

What more do critics want? What could Arminius have said that would

---

[5]A. Skevington Wood, "The Declaration of Sentiments: The Theological Testament of Arminius," *Evangelical Quarterly* 65, no. 2 (1993): 128.

[6]Howard A. Slaatte, *The Arminian Arm of Theology* (Washington, D.C.: University Press of America, 1979), p. 23.

[7]Carl Bangs, *Arminius* (Grand Rapids: Zondervan, 1985), pp. 344-45.

[8]Arminius, "A Declaration of the Sentiments of Arminius," *Works,* 1:695.

[9]Ibid., p. 700.

[10]Ibid.

make him more Protestant? In this pithy statement he clearly affirmed justification as pardon and imputation of Christ's obedience and righteousness by grace through faith in the blood of Jesus Christ. He also confessed Christ's righteousness as the only meritorious cause of justification, and justification as a forensic act in which God declares sinners righteous and reckons or accounts Christ's righteousness to them. Apparently, his formula "To the man who believes faith is imputed for righteousness through grace" remains a stumbling block for critics regardless of how Arminius explained it! He denied in the clearest way possible that it signifies anything other than classical Protestant theology.

First, Arminius considered justifying faith a sheer gift which is not a good work that earns or merits salvation. If that was his opinion, then clearly he also considered justification itself a free gift and not something we must earn or merit. In "Certain Articles to Be Diligently Examined and Weighed," he defined justifying faith as "that by which men believe in Jesus Christ, as in the Saviour of those universally who believe, and of each of them in particular, even the Saviour of him who, through Christ, believes in God who justifies the ungodly."[11] This faith is a gift of God through grace:

> No man believes in Christ except him who has been previously disposed and prepared by preventing or preceding grace to receive life eternal, on that condition on which God wills to bestow it, according to the following passage of Scripture, "If any man will execute his will, he shall know of the doctrine, whether it be of God, or whether I speak of myself" (John vii, 17).[12]

He also said:

> Faith is a gracious and gratuitous gift of God, bestowed according to the administration of the means necessary to conduce to the end; that is, according to such an administration as the justice of God requires either towards the side of mercy or towards that of severity. It is a gift which is not bestowed according to an absolute will of saving some particular men: For it is a condition required in the object to be saved, and it is in fact a condition before it is the means for obtaining salvation.[13]

Arminius clarified this in his "The Apology or Defence of James Arminius," where he distinguished between faith as a quality and faith as an act.

---

[11]Arminius, "Certain Articles to Be Diligently Examined and Weighed," *Works,* 2:723.
[12]Ibid., p. 724.
[13]Ibid., p. 723.

Faith as a quality is bestowed graciously by God, and it is this that brings justification; faith as an act is mere yielding to the gospel, and that is the sole condition of justification.[14] Then, in a letter to his friend Uitenbogard dated 1599, Arminius said that "justification by faith" actually is a kind of shorthand for being justified by that which faith apprehends—Jesus Christ's righteousness. To those who accused him of replacing Christ with faith as the meritorious cause of justification, he said, " '*The righteousness of Christ* is imputed to us,' and '*Faith* is imputed for righteousness.' "[15] In other words, the two are the same, or they are two sides of the same coin. At the very least, in light of these statements by Arminius, critics should now see that he did not deny justification as imputation of Christ's righteousness or make human faith the meritorious cause of justification, replacing the grace of Jesus Christ.

Second, Arminius believed in the forensic doctrine of justification; that is, he believed that righteousness is declared and imputed, and not owned by the believer who is justified. There is no hint in Arminius that God's acceptance of individuals is based in any part on their own righteousness. For Arminius, "The Justification . . . of a man before God is that by which, when he is placed before the tribunal of God, he is considered and pronounced, by God as the Judge, righteous *[justus]* and worthy of the reward of righteousness; whence also the recompense of reward itself follows by consequence."[16] In other words, in justification God declares a person righteous and then gives the gift of actual righteousness. This is entirely consistent with Luther's doctrine in "Two Kinds of Righteousness." Lest anyone misunderstand him Arminius continued:

> The cause of this [justification] is, not only God who is both just and merciful, but also Christ by his obedience, offering, and intercession according to God through his good pleasure and command. But it may thus be defined, "It is a Justification by which a man, who is a sinner, yet a believer, being placed before the throne of grace which is erected in Christ Jesus the Propitiation, is accounted and pronounced by God, the just and merciful Judge, righteous and worthy of the reward of righteousness, not in himself but in Christ, of grace, according to the Gospel, to the praise of the righteousness and grace of God,

---

[14]Arminius, "The Apology or Defence of James Arminius, D.D.," *Works*, 2:50.
[15]Ibid., p. 45.
[16]Arminius, "Disputations of Some of the Principal Subjects of the Christian Religion," *Works*, 2:254.

and to the salvation of the justified person himself."[17]

In a nutshell, "Justification . . . is . . . purely the imputation of right-eousness through mercy from the throne of grace in Christ the propitiation made *[factum]* to a sinner, but who is a believer."[18] What more could anyone say to satisfy those who want to know whether a doctrine of justification is Protestant? Arminius made absolutely clear in every way possible that justi-fication is a declaration of God concerning the sinner who believes and that it is based solely on Christ and his grace, and received by faith alone, which is itself a gift of grace.

Third, one charge frequently laid against Arminius's (and Arminian-ism's) doctrine of justification is that it makes faith the efficient and meri-torious cause of justification, thus resulting in justification as a reward for a work of righteousness. How did Arminius regard the causes of justification? First, he stated clearly and repeatedly that faith itself is a work of the Holy Spirit and not a work of autonomous humans. "Evangelical faith is an assent of the mind, produced by the Holy Spirit, through the Gospel, in sinners, who through the law know and acknowledge their sins, and are penitent on account of them."[19] Thus the Holy Spirit is the efficient cause of justifica-tion. Second, he asserted that "the Meritorious Cause of justification is Christ through his obedience and righteousness; who may therefore be justly called the principal or outwardly-moving cause."[20] He left no doubt about the nature of justification as imputation of Christ's righteousness and obedience, and not reward for human obedience:

> In his obedience and righteousness, Christ is also the Material Cause of our
> justification, so far as God bestows Christ on us for righteousness, and imputes
> his righteousness and obedience to us. In regard to this two-fold cause, that is,
> the Meritorious and Material, we are said to be constituted righteous through
> the obedience of Christ.[21]

Faith is only the instrumental cause of justification and not the meritori-ous or material (efficient) cause: "Faith is the Instrumental Cause, or act, by which we apprehend Christ proposed to us by God for a propitiation and for righteousness."[22] As to whether Arminius countenanced any good work

---

[17]Ibid., p. 256.
[18]Ibid., pp. 256-57.
[19]Arminius, "The Private Disputations of James Arminius," *Works*, 2:400.
[20]Ibid., p. 406.
[21]Ibid.

as a part of justification (as ground or cause), his own statement should settle the question: "That faith and works concur together in justification, is a thing impossible," and

> Christ has not obtained *[promeritum]* by his merits that we should be justified by the worthiness and merit of faith, and much less that we should be justified by the merit of works: But the merit of Christ is opposed to justification by works; and, in the Scriptures, Faith and Merit are placed in opposition to each other.[23]

Finally, Arminius distinguished sharply between justification and sanctification in good Protestant fashion. The former is the application of Christ's expiation or propitiation of sins through his blood; the latter is the purifying of the sinner by the blood of Christ. "In justification, this sprinkling [of Christ's blood] serves to wash away sins that have been committed; but in sanctification, it serves to sanctify men who have obtained remission of sins, that they may further be enabled to offer worship and sacrifices to God through Christ."[24] There is no hint in Arminius that justification is in any way dependent on sanctification; remission of sins and imputation of Christ's righteousness is independent of inward cleansing and growth in righteousness although the latter always follows the former.

William Witt correctly concludes that "while those who sought reasons to distrust Arminius were able to pounce on statements which could be misrepresented, there is actually nothing in Arminius' conception of justification which is contrary to orthodox Protestant theology."[25] That is because for Arminius

> justification is a forensic reckoning by which a sinner who has faith in Christ is pronounced righteous by God acting as a judge. It is not itself an act which makes the sinner righteous but is an imputation of the righteousness of Christ to the one who has faith not in his own merit, but in Christ's.[26]

Without doubt, Arminius's formula that in justification "faith is imputed for righteousness" is infelicitous, but he explained it adequately to clear up any doubts or concerns. He did not mean that faith itself is righteousness or

---

[22]Ibid., p. 407.
[23]Ibid., pp. 407, 408.
[24]Ibid., p. 409.
[25]William Gene Witt, *Creation, Redemption and Grace in the Theology of Jacob Arminius* (Ph.D. diss., University of Notre Dame, 1993), p. 599.
[26]Ibid., p. 594.

that God considers it so. Nor did he mean that faith is the meritorious cause
of justification. Rather, as he made absolutely clear, the righteousness of justification is forensic; it is Christ's obedience imputed to the believer's account because of faith, which is itself God's gracious gift. All a sinner must
do is receive it by not resisting prevenient grace.

Justification in Remonstrant Theology and in Wesley

Simon Episcopius. Like his mentor, Arminius, early Remonstrant leader Simon Episcopius distinguished strongly between justification and sanctification. The former is the free remission of sins by faith in Jesus Christ apart
from the merit of works.[27] The latter is God's transforming work within a
person by the Holy Spirit, conforming him or her to Jesus Christ. Sanctification is no ground or cause of justification, which is "a liberal and munifi-
cent imputation of faith itself for righteousness."[28] There again is the trou-
bling formula, but Episcopius meant nothing sinister by it; in his theology,
as in Arminius's, faith imputed for righteousness means only that faith is the
instrumental cause that appropriates the declaration of Christ's righteousness to the sinner's account, making him or her a believer. For Episcopius, as for Arminius, justification is all of God's mere and pure grace,
and by faith only in Jesus Christ.[29] It is not at all a reward or an inward work;
it is pure gift and forensic pronouncement of God the judge regarding the
sinner who receives the gift of faith.

Philip Limborch. Later Remonstrant Philip Limborch departed significantly from Arminius and Episcopius in developing his doctrine of justification. This is no doubt the source of later confusion about "the Arminian
doctrine of justification." Many English and American Calvinists only read
Limborch and theologians influenced by him, and impute his idea of justification to Arminius and Arminianism generally. Limborch, however, was a
revisionist Arminian at best and a pseudo-Arminian at worst. He started out
right in his description of justification as declaration of righteousness: "In a
judicial sense it denotes a declaration of righteousness, that is, absolving a
man from guilt, and treating him as one that is righteous."[30] He noted that

---

[27]Simon Episcopius, *Confession of Faith of Those Called Arminians* (London: Heart & Bible, 1684),
    pp. 210-11.
[28]Ibid., p. 211.
[29]Ibid.
[30]Philip Limborch, *A Complete System, or, Body of Divinity*, trans. William Jones (London: John
    Darby, 1713), p. 835.

the formula "faith imputed for righteousness," which he embraced and used, caused consternation and controversy, so he attempted to clarify it as meaning "that a man is esteemed by God as righteous upon account of his faith."[31] Then he caused no end of trouble for Arminians (whom he poorly represented) by adding:

> To let this dispute pass, we say "that justification is the merciful and gracious act of God, whereby he fully absolves from all guilt the truly penitent and be-
> lieving soul, through and for the sake of Christ apprehended by a true faith,
> or gratuitously remits sins upon the account of faith in Jesus Christ, and gra-
> ciously imputes that faith for righteousness."[32]

Lest anyone misunderstand, he added that Christ's righteousness is *not* imputed to us, but our own faith is imputed to us for righteousness for the sake of Christ.[33] This is exactly what Arminius and Episcopius did *not* say or mean! Limborch fell into serious theological error by saying that saving faith is an act of our own obedience and our own work. The damage was done even though he tried to undo it by saying inconsistently that this work of faith is not meritorious.[34] Clearly, Limborch is responsible for the critics' confusion about Arminianism and justification. They would be right *if* later Arminians agreed with Limborch, but for the most part they did not. The Arminians of the heart (evangelical Arminians) follow Arminius, whereas the Arminians of the head (rationalist and liberal Arminians) follow Limborch.

Limborch scholar and critic John Mark Hicks is right about Limborch's problem and the distance between his view and Arminius's: "Limborch regards faith as forming part of that righteousness that belongs to Christ," and "Limborch must escape the charge that man partially merits his salvation by his obedience."[35] In fact, however, according to Hicks, Limborch does not escape the charge. Arminius does. For Arminius, he notes, "It is not that there is a righteousness inherent within faith, but that faith is the condition upon which God bestows the merit [of] Christ's obedience," and for Arminius, "faith is both a gift of God and a condition of salvation which involves a

---

[31]Ibid., p. 836.
[32]Ibid.
[33]Ibid., p. 837.
[34]Ibid., p. 838.
[35]John Mark Hicks, *The Theology of Grace in the Thought of Jacobus Arminius and Philip van Limborch* (Ph.D. diss., Westminster Theological Seminary, 1985), pp. 209, 219.

human response," but there is no merit in the response.[36]

Arminius and the Remonstrants after him used the formula "faith imputed for righteousness." It is an unfortunate formula because it is open to possible misinterpretation. However, if critics would simply read Arminius (and perhaps also Episcopius), they would see what he meant by it. The contexts make it clear. Wherever he used that phrase, Arminius clarified it by referring to God's gracious imputation of Christ's obedience by his grace on account of faith, which is a gift of God. Faith is the instrument that receives Christ's imputed righteousness, and there is no merit in that reception because even it is a work of God within the sinner who is becoming a believer by not resisting prevenient grace. For Arminius, faith is clearly not a substitute for Christ's righteousness, nor is it considered righteous by God. Limborch took the phrase "faith imputed for righteousness" and turned it into what it sounds like: that faith is a work that forms part of the process of justification and on account of which God imputes righteousness (but not Christ's obedience) to people. Their own faith is counted by God as righteousness. That is not what Arminius meant! Why did Arminius use a formula so open to distortion? Some have suggested that the answer hangs on the preposition *for*.

When Arminius said that faith is imputed to us "for righteousness," he was trying to distinguish the role of faith from the role of Christ and his obedience in justification. He was denying that Christ's righteousness is imputed to us "for righteousness" because that implies it is not itself the righteousness imputed to us. Rather, Christ's righteousness is simply imputed to us. *For* implies "as if." There is no "as if" (a legal fiction) in the imputation of Christ's righteousness to us. That our faith is imputed "for righteousness" means that it is not actually righteousness; it is only the instrument of righteousness. According to Witt, "Our faith is imputed to us 'for righteousness' because it is not righteousness, properly speaking, but the act by which we apprehend the alien righteousness of Christ."[37] This may seem convoluted, but it is the only possible interpretation given all that Arminius said about justification, faith and righteousness. Unfortunately, Limborch meant what the phrase "faith imputed for righteousness" sounds like. He thereby began a chain reaction that has led to the widespread misconception that Arminius and all Arminians believe Christ's righteousness is not imputed to believers in justification but that faith, as an act of human obedience and substi-

---

[36]Ibid., pp. 88, 97.
[37]William Gene Witt informed me in private correspondence, August 5, 1999.

tute for Christ's obedience, is counted as righteousness by God.

John Wesley. The notion that John Wesley did not fully and wholeheart-edly embrace and teach the Protestant doctrine of justification by grace through faith alone is simply mistaken. A. Skevington Wood notes that "Wesley claimed that, with respect to the central Protestant doctrine of jus-tification, he concurred entirely with the teaching of Calvin."[38] Wesley was too good a scholar to be mistaken about something like that. He knew Calvin's theology well. In *John Wesley's Scriptural Christianity* Wesleyan scholar Thomas Oden proves beyond any doubt that Wesley's doctrine of justification was entirely consistent with classical Protestant teaching. Wes-ley followed Arminius rather than Limborch. Wesley has sometimes been found guilty by association because of his high regard for William Law, who authored *A Serious Call to a Devout and Holy Life,* which strongly influ-enced Wesley. But Oden points out Wesley's deep dissatisfaction with Law, who tended to conflate justification and sanctification. Wesley clearly dis-tinguished them, regarding sanctification "not the cause but the effect of justification."[39]

Oden also mentions problems with the description of justification in the Doctrinal Minutes of early Methodist meetings, over which Wesley presided (1744-1747). The early Methodists wanted to reconcile James and Paul, and overcome any idea that true salvation can exist without good works. So they defined justification as "to be pardoned and received into God's favor; into such a state, that if we continue therein, we shall be finally saved."[40] In other words, a particular stress was laid on continuing in God's favor. Neverthe-less, those who jump on this or other statements in the Minutes without re-gard to what Wesley said in his sermons and letters miss the larger picture. Oden demonstrates conclusively that in general Wesley held firmly to justi-fication as imputation of Christ's righteousness that cannot be improved but only received by faith. For Wesley, in contrast to Limborch, "It is not that faith as such is imputed for righteousness, but that 'faith in the right-eousness of Christ' is so imputed that the believer is clothed in a right-eousness not his own, a glorious dress that enables and calls him to 'put off the filthy rags' of his own righteousness."[41] Wesley made clear that both

---

[38]Arthur Skevington Wood, "The Contribution of John Wesley to the Theology of Grace," *Grace Unlimited,* ed. Clark H. Pinnock (Minneapolis: Bethany House, 1975), p. 219.
[39]Thomas C. Oden, *John Wesley's Scriptural Christianity* (Grand Rapids: Zondervan, 1994), p. 200.
[40]Ibid., p. 201.
[41]Ibid., p. 207.

Christ's active and passive obedience are imputed to believers by God on account of their faith, but that once imputed righteousness is given, God also implants righteousness so that they begin to be conformed to Jesus Christ. But implanted righteousness is not the basis of imputed righteousness. Wesley's account of these matters in the sermon "The Lord Our Righteousness" is no different from Luther's in "The Two Kinds of Righteousness."

Two sermons by Wesley especially reveal his Protestant commitment to the doctrine of justification by grace alone through faith alone: "Salvation by Faith" and "Justification by Faith." Critics trip over his emphasis on sanctification, but they need to take into account the Methodist founder's heightened concern to counteract antinomianism among some who claimed free grace as license to sin. Wesley's typical way of expressing the subject was that salvation is by grace alone through faith alone, but true faith is never alone. In other words, justification as imputed righteousness always results in inward transformation that produces works of love. In "Salvation by Faith" Wesley put to rest any notion that any part of salvation could be based on human merit: "All the blessings which God hath bestowed upon man, are of his mere grace, bounty, or favor; his free, undeserved favor; favor altogether undeserved; man having no claim to the least of his mercies."[42] All good works are unholy and sinful apart from grace. Grace is the source of salvation, and faith is its only condition. "None can trust in the merits of Christ till he has utterly renounced his own."[43]

If for Wesley faith is not a meritorious work, what is it? "Christian faith is then, not only an assent to the whole gospel of Christ, but also a full reliance on the blood of Christ; a trust in the merits of his life, death, and resurrection; a recumbency upon him as our atonement and our life, *as given for us,* and *living in us.*"[44] For Wesley even faith is a gift of God, just as it was for Arminius.[45] It is first and foremost an empty reception of the gift of faith itself. Faith is *both* a human act and the gift of a divine quality. The process of salvation (on the human side) begins with a decision to accept God's gift of faith and continues with trust in Christ alone, which is the gift received. A person can no more trust in Christ without God's help than save him- or

---

[42]John Wesley, "Salvation by Faith," in *John Wesley,* ed. Stephen Rost (Nashville: Thomas Nelson, 1989), p. 91.
[43]Ibid., p. 99.
[44]Ibid., p. 94.
[45]John Wesley, "Justification by Faith," in *John Wesley,* ed. Stephen Rost (Nashville: Thomas Nelson, 1989), p. 187.

herself. "Neither is salvation of the works we do when we believe: for *it is then God that worketh in us*, and, therefore, that he giveth us a reward for what he himself worketh, only commendeth the riches of his mercy, but leaveth us nothing whereof to glory."[46] Faith is the condition of salvation but not a human achievement.

According to Wesley, "The plain scriptural notion of justification is pardon, the forgiveness of sins."[47] Justification is reconciliation with God by God's grace on account of faith. It is the nonimputation of sins. In his sermon "Justification by Faith" Wesley seemed to deny the doctrine of imputed righteousness, but that cannot be his meaning because in "The Lord Our Righteousness" he gave it a ringing endorsement. Wesley was not a systematic thinker; like Luther he never produced a system of theology. In one sermon he criticized imputed alien righteousness and in another spoke warmheartedly of every believer being "clothed in Christ's righteousness" that is not his or her own. Wesley was often reacting to contexts; his theology often was ad hoc—determined by perceived errors and imbalances that needed correcting. Nevertheless, it would be highly unfair and improper to say that Wesley did not believe in the classical Protestant doctrine of forensic justification as imputed righteousness. What he did reject was justification as a legal fiction whereby people were left by God without transformation through inward righteousness. Wesley liked to simplify doctrines that he thought were overlaid with speculation. Wesley scholar Kenneth Collins notes rightly that while Wesley was at times ambivalent about justification as imputation because of its possible misuses, he did most heartily embrace a simplified form of it: "Simply put, for Wesley, the righteousness of Christ is imputed to believers in the sense that they are now accepted by God not for the sake of anything that they have done, whether it be works of charity, mercy or the like, but *solely* because of what Christ has accomplished through His life and death on their behalf."[48]

Justification in Nineteenth-Century Arminianism

The old problem of justification as forensic imputation of Christ's right-

---

[46]Wesley, "Salvation by Faith," p. 98.
[47]Wesley, "Justification by Faith," p. 182.
[48]Kenneth J. Collins, *The Scripture Way of Salvation: The Heart of John Wesley's Theology* (Nashville: Abingdon, 1997), pp. 92-93.

eousness (Arminius and Episcopius) versus justification as faith reckoned as righteousness (Limborch and later Remonstrants) appeared again in nineteenth-century Methodist theology, which was the main location for the outworking of modern Arminianism. Some of the nineteenth-century Arminian Methodist theologians warmly embraced and endorsed forensic justification and imputed righteousness; others rejected that in favor of justification as primarily nonimputation of sin. That some followed Limborch more closely than Arminius hardly means, however, that Arminianism in general denies justification as imputation of Christ's righteousness. Many Arminians follow Arminius, as they should. However, in spite of disagreements, the nineteenth-century Methodist theologians Richard Watson, William Burton Pope, Thomas O. Summers and John Miley all adhered to the basic Protestant doctrine that justification is by God's grace alone through faith alone, and eschewed any hint of works righteousness or confusing justification with sanctification. They all affirmed that justification is imputation of righteousness, even if not of Christ's obedience.

Richard Watson. Unfortunately, Watson misunderstood the formula "imputation of faith for righteousness" and interpreted justification primarily as nonimputation of sin resulting in reconciliation with God. He left no doubt, however, that he regarded justification, whatever its exact nature, as a gift and not something that can be merited. Faith that brings justification is "the entire trust and reliance of an awakened and penitent sinner, in the atonement of Christ alone, as the meritorious ground of his pardon."[49] This is not in any sense a virtue or good work, however, as faith is impossible apart from prevenient grace.[50] Faith is the sole condition for justification; all meritorious works have no value for being reconciled to God. Justification and sanctification are radically distinct, and the latter can never be the formal cause of the former.[51] Watson affirmed that "justification by faith alone [without works] is thus clearly the doctrine of the Scriptures."[52]

For Watson, justification includes two aspects: nonimputation of the guilt of sin, and imputation of righteousness. Justification is first and foremost forgiveness for sins and is an act of God's grace and mercy received by faith.

---

[49]Richard Watson, *Theological Institutes* (New York: Lane & Scott, 1851), 2:248.
[50]Ibid., p. 253.
[51]Ibid., p. 251.
[52]Ibid., p. 246.

Secondarily, God counts the believer in Christ righteous also, on account of faith. However, justification is not imputation of Christ's active and passive obedience; it is not imputation of Christ's righteousness:

> The Scriptural doctrine is . . . that the death of Christ is accepted in the place of our personal punishment, on condition of our faith in him; and, that when faith in him is actually exerted, then comes in, on the part of God, the act of imputing, or reckoning righteousness to us; or, what is the same thing, accounting faith for righteousness, that is, pardoning our offences through faith, and treating us as the objects of his restored favor.[53]

Watson, like Limborch, regarded the doctrine of imputation of Christ's obedience to believers who are still sinners a fiction and thus repugnant to God's character: "This whole doctrine of the imputation of Christ's personal and moral obedience, as their own personal moral obedience, involves a fiction and impossibility inconsistent with the Divine attributes."[54] At least, however, Watson did not follow Limborch in treating faith as meritorious, but it would have helped had he asserted more forcefully that faith is a gift. In the end, the shadow of Limborch hovers over Watson and raises doubts about the fullness of his agreement with the classical Protestant doctrine of justification as imputation of Christ's righteousness to believers. Whether this is necessary for authentic evangelical Protestantism is open to debate.

William Burton Pope. Pope followed the traditional Protestant pattern of treating justification as an act of God in grace and mercy accepting penitent and believing sinners as if they had not sinned and imputing righteousness to them on account of their faith. He defined justification as

> the Divine judicial act which applies to the sinner, believing in Christ, the benefit of the Atonement, delivering him from condemnation of his sin, introducing him into a state of favour, and treating him as a righteous person. . . . It is the imputed character of justification which regulates the New Testament use of the word.[55]

For him, justification is always declaratory and of grace alone. Faith that appropriates the justifying grace of God is not a work but the act of renounc-

---

[53]Ibid., p. 242.
[54]Ibid., p. 216.
[55]William Burton Pope, *A Compendium of Christian Theology* (New York: Phillips & Hunt, n.d.), 2:407.

ing all trust in human ability. Faith is merely the instrumental cause and
never the meritorious cause of justification, which is Christ's atoning obedience. What did Pope believe about imputation of Christ's obedience to believers? This is a major question Reformed critics ask of Arminians. Whether
everything hangs on it is another issue; many Arminians (and Anabaptists
and others) would urge that it not be made a test of orthodoxy or fellowship. The crucial issue is whether justification includes forensic righteousness (whether imputation of Christ's obedience or simply of God's reconciling favor) based on faith alone without merit. Pope was ambiguous
about whether God's declared righteousness was imputation of Christ's obedience or simply God's reckoning of the believer as righteous. His statement of the matter is ultimately not satisfying: "The ungodly who in peni-
tence believes has the virtue or efficacy of Christ's obedience reckoned to
him without having that obedience itself imputed: he is *made the righteousness
of God in Him,* which is different from having the righteousness of Christ set
to his account."[56] We can only ask how. But critics should at least pay attention to the fact that Pope, a true Arminian, believed that the virtue or efficacy of Christ's obedience is reckoned to the believer in justification, who is
made the righteousness of God in Christ by God's grace on account of faith.
Isn't it splitting hairs to claim that this is not a Protestant account of justification?

Thomas Summers. Summers's account of justification follows Watson's
and Pope's closely. He rejected any meritorious work, including faith, and
attributed all saving efficacy to grace received by faith. Justification is by
grace through faith alone apart from works of righteousness.[57] His explanation of justification denies imputation of Christ's obedience to believers but
upholds imputation of righteousness: "In justification we are *accounted, accepted*—dealt with—as if we were righteous, just as pardoned culprits, who
are not by their pardon made innocent, are dealt with as if they were not
criminals."[58] This reckoning is faith imputed for righteousness, but faith was
not treated by Summers as a work rewarded with God's favor. Rather, faith
is simply the instrumental condition of the gift of salvation, which is completely of God's grace.[59]

---

[56]Ibid., p. 413.
[57]Thomas O. Summers, *Systematic Theology* (Nashville: Publishing House of the Methodist Epis-
    copal Church, South, 1888), 2:120.
[58]Ibid., p. 121.
[59]Ibid., p. 120.

John Miley. Miley stuck closely to the other nineteenth-century Methodist thinkers. For him, justification is by grace alone through faith alone without works.[60] The only condition for justification is faith in Christ, which means simple trust in Christ as Savior. Repentance for sins is there presupposed. Justification is extrinsic; it effects no interior moral change, which is the work of sanctification. It is complete and sets the sinner right with God as if he had never sinned.[61] But Miley rejected justification as forensic declaration of alien (Christ's) righteousness:

> There can be no strictly forensic justification of a sinner except by a mistaken or a corrupt judgment, neither of which is possible with God. Yet this forensic term is appropriated for the expression of his act in the forgiveness of sin. Of course, it is used in a qualified sense, and yet not in a sense which is alien to its primary meaning.[62]

This is a confusing statement to say the least. Miley accepted that in justification "we are . . . as completely right with the law as we could be from a purely forensic justification."[63] His alternative to forensic justification is not as clear as we would wish. What is important, however, is that for Miley, as for the other nineteenth-century Arminian theologians, justification is not at all based on good works or merits, but is a sheer gift of God by his mercy and grace in response to faith. It is not coterminous with sanctification and depends not at all on any inward goodness or righteousness in the believer. Its only condition and instrumental cause is faith, its meritorious cause is Christ (atonement), and its efficient cause is the Holy Spirit.

Twentieth-Century Arminians and Justification
H. Orton Wiley. One of the leading Arminian theologians of the twentieth century was Nazarene H. Orton Wiley, whose three-volume *Christian Theology* set the gold standard for theologians in the Holiness tradition for many years. For him, salvation is completely gift and requires no meritorious work on a human's part. Faith is its only condition, and faith is both God's gift and human free response to prevenient grace.[64] Wiley laid out a clear and understandable order of salvation, beginning with prevenient grace and

---

[60]John Miley, *Systematic Theology* (Peabody, Mass.: Hendrickson, 1989), 2:318.
[61]Ibid., p. 323, 312, 313.
[62]Ibid., p. 311.
[63]Ibid., p. 312.
[64]H. Orton Wiley, *Christian Theology* (Kansas City, Mo.: Beacon Hill, 1941), 2:369.

conversion, which is composed of repentance and faith—both of which are gifts of God in the sense that they are only possible because of prevenient grace.[65] Conversion is followed (logically, not temporally) by regeneration and justification, which are God's responses to conversion. In contrast to Calvinism Wiley expressed what virtually every modern evangelical Arminian believes about the order of salvation:

> Calvinism . . . holds that man is regenerated by absolute decree, and then turns to God; Arminianism holds that through grace, preveniently bestowed, man turns to God and is then regenerated. Thus conversion in its truest scriptural meaning, is the pivotal point, wherein through grace, the soul turns from sin, and to Christ, in order to regeneration [and justification].[66]

For Wiley justification is the judicial act of God that precedes and is entirely distinct from sanctification. It is more than mere forgiveness; it includes imputation of righteousness: "The one act of justification when viewed negatively is the forgiveness of sins; when viewed positively, is the acceptance of the believer as righteous."[67] Justification is a once and for all work of God (although it can be rejected) and is instantaneous; it is not a work or a sentence extending over years. Its sole ground (meritorious cause) is Jesus Christ's propitiatory sacrifice received by faith.[68] Wiley excluded any form of moralism that bases God's acceptance on a person's inward holiness.

Like some of his nineteenth-century Arminian forebears, Wiley waffled on the nature of imputed righteousness. He affirmed it unequivocally and noted that Arminius agreed entirely with Calvin on imputation of Christ's righteousness.[69] However, he cautioned against antinomian implications and interpretations of the Reformed doctrine of imputed righteousness where Christ's active and passive obedience are said to be put to the believer's account by God. After seeming to sympathize with the Reformed formula (in spite of some dangers) Wiley ended up favoring the formula "the imputation of faith for righteousness" as better than imputation of Christ's active and passive obedience, but he did not fully explain why.[70] What is clear, however, is

---

[65]Ibid., pp. 373-76.
[66]Ibid., p. 378.
[67]Ibid., p. 393.
[68]Ibid., p. 395.
[69]Ibid., p. 397.
[70]Ibid., pp. 400-401.

that Wiley did not consider justification dependent on good works or inward righteousness, and did believe it includes (along with pardon for sins) God's imputation of righteousness to the believer on account of faith. For him "faith is not to be identified with righteousness in the . . . sense that faith constitutes righteousness." And "faith itself, as a personal act of the believer, and not the object of that faith . . . is imputed for righteousness."[71]

No doubt some Calvinist critics will find these two statements mutually contradictory or at least in tension. If it is not Christ's righteousness that is imputed to the believer in justification, whose righteousness is it? And doesn't the idea that faith is imputed for righteousness imply that faith is righteousness? No doubt Wiley would have answered that it does not have to be any particular person's righteousness; God simply regards the person of faith as obedient, not because faith is goodness but because God decides it will count as righteousness. And nothing in that decision makes it actual righteousness. Nevertheless, I generally agree with Arminius and Reformed theology that it must be Christ's obedience that is reckoned as the believer's; otherwise what Christ accomplished for us in his life and death is left separate from the righteousness imputed to us. Why would that be the case? Surely if he fulfilled all righteousness and we are "in Christ" by faith, it would be his righteousness that would be imputed to us.

Henry Thiessen. Henry C. Thiessen's account of predestination is thoroughly Arminian. (Though, like many evangelicals he did not understand Arminianism correctly and so repudiated it by identifying it with semi-Pelagianism.) Thiessen regarded justification as imputation of Christ's righteousness.[72] According to him the righteousness of a believer is always (and only) forensic righteousness, and its sole cause is grace and the sole condition is faith.[73] He wrote, "The believer is now clothed in a righteousness not his own, but provided for him by Christ, and is therefore accepted into fellowship with God."[74] Thiessen proves that at least some Arminians do affirm the imputation of Christ's righteousness in justification.

Thomas Oden. Contemporary Methodist theologian Thomas Oden affirms forensic justification as a sheer gift received by faith apart from merit: "*Justification* is a term that derives from the legal sphere: hence it is called a

---

[71]Ibid., p. 400.
[72]Henry C. Thiessen, *Lectures in Systematic Theology* (Grand Rapids: Eerdmans, 1949), p. 363.
[73]Ibid., p. 366.
[74]Ibid., pp. 366-67.

forensic or judicial metaphor. Accordingly, one is justified who is made up-right with the Lawgiver."[75] For Oden, justification includes imputation of Christ's righteousness. He sees no conflict between this and Arminianism, and indeed there is none.

> The benefits of Christ's obedience (active and passive) are accounted or reck-oned to the believer, but this does not imply that the believer actually and im-mediately lives with perfect uprightness or acts precisely as Christ acted. . . . Justification remains a declarative act of God external to human willing, as dis-tinguished from sanctification, which is an efficacious act of God the Spirit within a sinner's will, to change that will."[76]

It is hard to see how any Reformed Christian could quibble with Oden's thoroughly Arminian expression of justification, except perhaps by claim-ing it is inconsistent with even evangelical synergism.[77] A true Arminian can only disagree; there is no logical inconsistency between the two.

Conclusion

The facts simply show that Arminianism does not exclude or undermine jus-tification by grace alone through faith alone. Classical Arminians all affirm it. The only area where some Arminians differ from Reformed theology on justification has to do with whose or what righteousness is imputed to believ-ers. I believe it would be best for all Arminians to return to Arminius on this matter and, with Oden, embrace the idea of imputation of Christ's right-eousness. It is implied by Scripture (2 Cor 5:21) and arises most naturally out of the dual and linked ideas of being "in Christ" by faith, and being con-sidered righteous by God. Nevertheless, it is not certain that one must con-fess imputation of Christ's righteousness in order to be fully Protestant or evangelical so long as one affirms justification as imputed righteousness rather than imparted righteousness and regards faith as its sole instrumen-tal (not meritorious) cause.

---

[75]Thomas C. Oden, *Life in the Spirit: Systematic Theology* (San Francisco: HarperSanFrancisco, 1992), 3:109.

[76]Ibid., pp. 116-17.

[77]Oden does not call himself an Arminian; he prefers to be known as a follower of the early Christian ecumenical consensus, which he calls "paleo-orthodoxy." However, he is a Method-ist and a perusal of the footnotes of his systematic theology (especially vol. 3 on soteriology) reveals heavy use of Arminian sources. His *Transforming Power of Grace* expresses a distinctively Arminian soteriology, and he even says that the Arminian and Remonstrant movement recov-ered the early patristic consensus.

MYTH 10

All Arminians Believe
in the Governmental Theory
of the Atonement

There is no one Arminian doctrine of Christ's atonement.
Many Arminians accept the penal substitution theory
enthusiastically, but others prefer the governmental theory.

MANY CRITICS OF ARMINIANISM ACCUSE IT of departing from the strong substitutionary atonement doctrine of the Reformers and of most of post-
Reformation evangelicalism. Calvinists especially have several issues with
Arminianism's doctrine of the atonement. First, high Calvinists accuse
Arminianism of leading either to universalism or to belief that Christ's
death on the cross actually saved no one. The first of these charges arises
from high Calvinism's doctrine of limited atonement. This is the idea,
spelled out and declared by the Synod of Dort, that Christ's death, though
sufficient for the salvation of all of humanity, was actually intended by God
only for the elect. Arminians call this "limited atonement" because it limits
the scope of Christ's substitutionary sacrifice to the elect only. Calvinists,
though, prefer "definite" or "particular" atonement because they say that
Christ died for those God intended to save—a definite group of particular
people. Along with Lutherans and most other Christians (Eastern Orthodox, Roman Catholic and many others), Arminians reject this doctrine in
favor of general or universal atonement, that Christ's death was for everyone even if only actually applied to those who believe.

Calvinist critics often say that this universal atonement leads inevitably
to universal salvation because if Christ paid the penalty or suffered the

punishment for every person, then every person must be saved. Why would anyone have to pay the penalty or suffer the punishment for sins if Christ already paid or suffered for them? Calvinist Edwin Palmer declared that "if He [Christ] died for all—then no one is lost. All are reconciled and redeemed."[1] On the other had, Calvinists often claim, if Arminians reject universalism—which they know most Arminians do—then Christ's death must not have actually saved anyone; people are saved by their own choices to appropriate Christ's death by faith. Calvinist Kim Riddlebarger charged that in Arminianism "the death of Christ does not actually save sinners but merely renders people savable if they exercise their freedom to choose and to follow Christ."[2] He went even further: "If you follow . . . the logic of the Arminian system, then you can no longer affirm . . . that it is God who saves sinners, and not sinners who save themselves with God's help."[3] Palmer chimed in: "Because the Arminian believes in an atonement that is unlimited in its extent, it is necessarily a vague, indefinite, poverty stricken atonement that does not actually save anyone."[4] In other words, Riddlebarger and Palmer, echoing many other Calvinists, claimed that consistent, nonuniversalist Arminianism must teach that sinners save themselves with God's help. This is, of course, not what Arminians believe. Nor does Arminianism lead there.

Arminianism says that salvation is solely and exclusively by the blood of Jesus Christ; his atoning death on behalf of all sinners is what saves. The Calvinist critics overlook two important points in Arminian theology. First, there is a universal aspect to salvation because of the atonement. Arminians believe that the guilt of original sin (Adamic sin) is set aside by God for Christ's sake on account of his death for all (Rom 5). That is why children are not condemned even though, apart from Christ's death for them, they are children of wrath. Some Calvinists agree. Second, Arminians believe that Christ's death on the cross provided *possible* salvation for everyone, but it is actualized only when humans' accept it through repentance and faith. The situation is analogous to a blanket amnesty. After the Vietnam war, conscientious objectors and resisters who fled to Canada were offered pardon upon returning to the United States. Some returned and accepted the am-

---

[1]Edwin H. Palmer, *The Five Points of Calvinism* (Grand Rapids: Baker, 1972), p. 47.
[2]Kim Riddlebarger, "Fire and Water," *Modern Reformation* 1 (1992): 9.
[3]Ibid., p. 10.
[4]Palmer, *Five Points of Calvinism*, p. 48.

nesty and some did not. Those who returned simply took advantage of the amnesty declared by the U.S. government; they did not create it. Those who stayed in Canada (or other countries) did not nullify the amnesty; it was still there for them. In contrast, Edwin Palmer accused Arminianism of believing in wasted blood of Jesus: "To them the atonement is like a universal grab-bag: there is a package for everyone, but only some will grab a package. . . . Some of [Christ's] blood was wasted: it was spilled."[5]

Arminians like to point out that these particular objections to their theology seem to rely on questionable assumptions and raise more serious problems for their critics. These objections assume that Christ's death by itself and without any acceptance automatically saves some people. Doesn't this imply that human repentance and faith are superfluous? Why does God command them? The elect presumably are saved by the cross before and apart from their responses to the gospel. Furthermore, these objections to Arminian belief about the atonement are based on faulty reading of Arminian theology. Arminians do believe that Christ died for everyone, but the benefit of his death (setting aside condemnation for actual sins, in contrast to Adamic sin) is applied by God only to those who repent and believe. Does that mean some of Christ's blood is wasted? That is a gross distortion. Was some of the amnesty for objectors to the Vietnam war wasted because not all accepted it? What would that even mean? And Arminians wish to turn the tables and examine high Calvinism's belief in limited atonement. Doesn't the Bible reveal God's universal love for humanity? Why would God send Christ to die for only some people when Scripture clearly says that he loved the whole world and is not willing that any should perish but that all should come to repentance (Jn 3:16; 2 Pet 3:9)? Palmer anticipated this Arminian objection and stated bluntly that in these passages "*All* is not *all*."[6] And Palmer (and some other Calvinists) accuses Arminians of not doing justice to the clear meaning of the Bible!

That Arminians do not believe Christ's death is what really saves people is a vicious calumny that hardly requires serious response. A fair-minded reading of any Arminian book of theology will recognize that all evangelical Arminians, from Arminius to Wesley, Wiley and Oden, believe that *all* the saved are saved by the death of Christ and not by any act of the will or work of righteousness. The free response to the gospel results in the mercy of God,

---

[5]Ibid., p. 41.
[6]Ibid., p. 53.

through the cross of Jesus Christ, being applied to the sinner's life so that he or she is no longer a sinner in God's sight but a forgiven and reconciled person. The decision of faith is not the meritorious or efficient cause of salvation; that alone is Christ and his death. The decision of faith is only the instrumental cause of salvation; like cashing a check, it activates the gift. But it does not add to the gift or make the gift any less gratuitous. Arminians believe people are saved only by Christ's death and not by their own decisions or actions.

Another misconception is that all Arminians hold to the governmental theory of the atonement rather than the substitutionary atonement. In many books of Calvinist theology the governmental theory, first articulated by early Remonstrant leader Hugo Grotius, is called the "Arminian theory." It is not. Arminius did not believe in it, neither did Wesley nor some of his nineteenth-century followers. Nor do all contemporary Arminians. Additionally, many Calvinist treatments of the governmental theory distort it. The governmental theory includes an element of substitution! The only significant difference between it and the penal substitution theory (often said to be the orthodox doctrine of the atonement, especially by conservative Reformed theologians) is that the governmental theory does not say that in their place Christ bore the actual punishment of sinners; it says that he bore suffering as an alternative to punishment in their place. In other words, according to those Arminians who do hold to the governmental theory, God inflicted pain on Christ for the sins of the world in order to uphold his justice and holiness. Christ's suffering was equivalent to any sinner's deserved punishment so that God could forgive while at the same time being wholly just and holy. But Christ did not take the actual punishment deserved by every person. To say that the governmental theory denies substitution is simply false. It differs from the traditional Reformed theory of the atonement only at that one point. Readers can decide for themselves whether Calvinist critics' rejection of it as serious theological error is fair.

Thus, not all Arminians embrace the governmental theory, and those who do nevertheless believe in Christ's substitutionary sacrifice for sins. Calvinist critics of Arminianism Robert Peterson and Michael Williams admit that Wesley "clearly and strongly affirms substitutionary atonement, especially in the language of penal satisfaction." But they continue to say that most of his theological descendents "have not followed his lead."[7] Furthermore:

---

[7]Robert A. Peterson and Michael D. Williams, *Why I Am Not an Arminian* (Downers Grove, Ill.: InterVarsity Press, 2004), pp. 193, 198.

Matters are complicated by the fact that Arminians teach that Christ suffered as our representative, even as our substitute, but not our *penal* substitute. These distinctions are best understood in light of the view that Arminians have adopted instead of Wesley's view—the governmental view of the atonement. This view, first articulated by Arminius's student Hugo Grotius, claims that Jesus did not receive the specific punishment due our sins. Rather, his death was in the best interests of God's moral government and provided a powerful example of God's hatred of sin.[8]

Several things must be pointed out by way of response. First, not all Arminians have adopted the governmental theory, and certainly Arminius himself did not hold it. Therefore, it is wrong to identify it as *the* Arminian theory or attribute it to Arminians without qualification. Second, the authors begin by saying that the governmental theory stands in contrast to the substitutionary theory. Then they admit that it teaches that Christ died as our substitute! Apparently, they will only allow their own version of the penal substitution theory to count as a substitutionary theory. In fact, however, even the governmental theory holds that Christ's death was a substitution for sins. The authors have to narrow their disagreement with the governmental theory more specifically by saying that in it Jesus did not "receive the specific punishment due our sins," failing to note what the atoning work did accomplish in this view. Finally, they write "his death was in the best interests of God's moral government and provided a powerful example of God's hatred of sin." What is wrong with that? Are they suggesting that the death of Christ was *not* in the best interests of God's moral government and did *not* provide a powerful example of God's hatred of sin? Peterson and Williams's critique of the governmental theory is fraught with problems, as are, in my experience, all Calvinist treatments of it.

Arminius's and the Remonstrants' Views of the Atonement
Arminius. Is it possible to consider the governmental theory "the Arminian doctrine of the atonement" when it was foreign to Arminius's own thought? That would be like calling something "the Calvinist doctrine" when Calvin clearly and explicitly taught an alternative view. Critics who claim that Arminianism includes the governmental theory should read Arminius! William Witt is correct that Arminius accepted and embraced a variation of the Anselmic satisfaction theory not very different (if at all) from the Reformed

---

[8]Ibid., pp. 198-99.

penal substitution theory.[9] For Arminius, Christ's death was a substitutionary, expiatory and propitiatory sacrifice for sins that perfectly fulfilled the
law and established a new covenant of faith.[10] Arminius explained his own
view of the atonement in his treatise "Examination of Dr. Perkins's Pamphlet on Predestination." There he argued that, according to the Scriptures, Christ died for all people without prejudice to anyone and that his
death satisfied the demands of justice for those who believe. He made much
of 2 Corinthians 5:19, where Paul wrote that God was in Christ reconciling
the world to himself. Arminius also wrote of many other passages where the
"world" is mentioned as the object of God's love and redeeming will in
Christ: John 1:29; 3:16; 4:42; 6:51; 1 John 2:2; 4:14. Arminius concluded that

> It is manifest, as well from these passages as from the usage of Scripture, that
> by the word "world" in those places is meant simply the whole body of man-
> kind. But, in my opinion, there is no place in all Scripture in which it can be
> shown beyond all controversy that the word "world" signifies *the elect.* Christ is
> said to have died *for all.* (Heb. ii. 9, and elsewhere.) He is called "the Saviour
> of *all men,* specially of those that believe;" (1 Tim. iv. 10;) which expression
> cannot, without twisting and injury, be explained respecting conservation in
> this life.[11]

Of the opinion that Christ represented on the cross the elect only,
Arminius wrote, "Scripture nowhere says this; nay, it says the contrary in very
many places."[12] Clearly then Arminius believed in and taught the universality of the atonement.

Arminius explained the reason for and the effect of the atonement by appealing to God's compassion and justice. God's main motive in sending
Christ was compassion, but justice played a role as well. The two cannot be
separated. God wanted to remit the sins of fallen people and reconcile them
to himself, but he could not do it without satisfaction to his justice, which
sin injured. In other words, before God could reconcile fallen people to
himself he needed to reconcile himself to fallen people. God had the *right*
simply to forgive sinners without satisfaction paid to his justice, but he
would not do so because of his holiness:

---

[9]William Witt, *Creation, Redemption and Grace in the Theology of Jacob Arminius* (Ph.D. diss., University of Notre Dame, 1993), p. 555.
[10]Ibid., pp. 557-62.
[11]Arminius, "Examination of Dr. Perkins's Pamphlet on Predestination," *Works*, 3:329.
[12]Ibid., p. 328.

There remains with God His right entire to impart those benefits—which are His by nature, which He desired from compassion to communicate to sinful men, but, justice withstanding, could not carry into effect, and which, now that His justice is pacified by the blood and death of Christ, He can actually bestow—to whom He thinks fit, and under those conditions which He shall prescribe: because He, as the injured party, could prescribe the mode of reconciliation, which also He did prescribe, consisting in the death and obedience of His own Son; and because He Himself gave to us Him who was to perform the functions of a Mediator for us.[13]

If Christ's death satisfied God's justice for all, why aren't all saved? Arminius answers: "For the sins of those for whom Christ died were in such manner condemned in the flesh of Christ, that they by that fact are not delivered from condemnation, unless they actually believe on Christ."[14] In other words, God decided that the sins of all people would be expiated by Christ's death in such a way that only if people believe on Christ would their sins actually be forgiven. But Christ's death actually did reconcile God to sinful humanity; however the communication of the benefits of that reconciliation—reconciliation of persons to God, pardon and justification, regeneration—depend on human belief:

These two functions and operations of Christ—to wit, the recovering, through the blood of Christ, of the salvation lost by sin; and the actual communication or application, by the Holy Spirit, of the salvation obtained by that blood—are distinct from each other. The former is antecedent to faith; the latter requires faith preceding, according to the decree of God.[15]

Arminius confronted the charge that his teaching on the atonement implied that humans are their own saviors because they have to believe on Christ in order for Christ's obedient sacrifice to be applied to them for reconciliation with God. He appealed to God's sovereign will to place conditions on the application of the blessing of the atonement to people and to the fact that anyone who meets those conditions does so only by grace:

Who has merited that the blessing [of the atonement] should be offered to himself? Who has merited that any grace whatsoever should be conferred on

---

[13]Ibid., p. 331.
[14]Ibid., p. 335.
[15]Ibid., p. 336.

himself to embrace that? Do not all those things proceed from gratuitous Divine favour? And if they do, is not God to be celebrated on account thereof with perpetual praises by those who, being made partakers of that grace, have received the blessing of God?[16]

To those critics who point to Romans 9:16, which says that salvation is not of him that wills or runs but only of God who shows mercy, Arminius responded that this passage rules out salvation by works but not salvation by God's mercy to those who believe with the help of God's grace.[17]

But did Arminius believe that Christ's death on the cross was a *penal substitution* for sins? Did he teach that Christ suffered the punishment deserved by humanity for rebellion against God? He did. In his theological orations he approached the atonement by first laying the groundwork in federal theology.[18] That is, God appointed Adam as the federal head or true representative of the human race in the covenant of works. Arminius affirmed that in Adam's fall into sin, his entire posterity fell with him.[19] He then discovered the cause of God's appointment of Christ as mediator of a new covenant (of grace) in God's justice and mercy: "First, in the conflict between justice and gracious mercy; and, Afterwards, in their amicable agreement, or rather their junction by means of wisdom's conciliating assistance."[20] In other words, God wanted to show mercy toward fallen humanity but could do so only in a way that would at the same time satisfy his justice. In his wisdom, God brought the two together in the decision to provide Christ as mediator through his life and death. Wisdom required, Arminius argued, that the mediator be both human and blameless, so the Word of God was appointed to undertake the office of priest "to offer his own flesh to God as a sacrifice for the life of the world."[21] God required Christ, who voluntarily agreed, to "lay down his soul as a victim in sacrifice for sin . . . [and] give his

---

[16]Ibid., p. 445.

[17]Ibid., p. 450.

[18]Anyone who doubts Arminius's embrace of federal theology must consider this Arminian statement: "There are two methods or plans by which it might be possible for man to arrive at a state of righteousness before God and to obtain life from him,—the one is according to righteousness through the law, by works and 'of debt;' the other is according to mercy through the gospel, 'by grace, and through faith:' These two methods are so constituted as not to allow both of them to be in a course of operation at the same time; but they proceed on the principle, that when the first of them is made void, a vacancy may be created for the second" (Arminius, "Oration IV," *Works*, 1:417).

[19]Ibid., p. 409.

[20]Ibid., p. 413.

[21]Ibid., p. 415.

flesh for the life of the world . . . [and] pay the price of redemption for the sins and the captivity of the human race."[22] Finally, Arminius made clear the penal nature of Christ's sacrifice by saying that he died on the cross, "thus paying the price of redemption for sins by suffering the punishment due to them."[23] Clearly, for Arminius Christ's death was not merely an example of how much God abhors sin! It was a propitiation of God's wrath arising out of his mercy, and it consisted of suffering the punishment humanity deserves for sin. In this way Christ became the new head of the race by establishing a new covenant between God and people:

> Such a covenant could not be contracted between a just God and sinful men, except in consequence of a reconciliation, which, it pleased God the offended party, should be perfected by the blood of our High Priest to be poured out on the altar of the cross. He who was at once the officiating priest and the Lamb for sacrifice, poured out his sacred blood, and thus asked and obtained for us a reconciliation with God.[24]

Christ's death, for Arminius, was no mere demonstration of justice to uphold God's moral government as he forgave sinners. It was the infliction of the just punishment for human sin upon Christ so that the demands of righteousness could meet the desire of mercy and reconciliation be accomplished.

Hugo Grotius. Hugo Grotius (1583-1645) was one of the early supporters of the Remonstrants, but he was not a minister or theologian. He was a Dutch lawyer, diplomat and statesman. In some of his writings he attempted to explicate the doctrine of the atonement in order to make it more rational in terms of the jurisprudence of his day. His theory has come to be known as the governmental theory of the atonement. It has often been read back into Arminius, who does not seem to have known anything about it, and it is found in some of the Remonstrants' theological writings. According to the governmental theory of Grotius, God could have simply forgiven humanity's sins without any sacrifice, but he decided to offer the death of Christ as a display of how seriously he takes sin in order to uphold his moral government of the universe. Christ bore *a* punishment, but not *the* punishment due humanity; his suffering and death were the nonnecessary demonstration of justice for the sake of God's holiness and righteousness. They vin-

---

[22]Ibid., p. 416.
[23]Ibid., p. 419.
[24]Ibid., p. 423.

dicated God's glory as he forgave humanity's sinfulness. Nineteenth-century Methodist theologian John Miley explained it in great detail in his *Systematic Theology*, which borrows heavily in this doctrine from Grotius: "The vicarious sufferings of Christ are an atonement for sin as conditional substitute for penalty, fulfilling, on the forgiveness of sin, the obligation of justice and the office of penalty in moral government."[25] In the governmental theory of Grotius, then, Christ did not suffer the actual penalty for sins; he suffered a substitute for penalty for sins. It was a "rectorally compensatory measure for the remission of penalty."[26] It was a "provisory substitute for penalty, and not the actual punishment of sin."[27] The reason for it and its effect was to render divine forgiveness consistent with moral government by showing God's horror at sin.

That Arminius himself did not teach this, which is often mistakenly called "the Arminian theory of the atonement," is attested by Miley and other authorities: "Arminius himself maintained both penal substitution and a real conditionality of forgiveness."[28] John Mark Hicks agrees and says that in Arminius's theology "Christ suffered both the temporal and the eternal punishments of sin for all sinners and satisfied those penalties."[29] Some early Arminian theologians, however, were influenced by Grotius, and they deviated from Arminius's own understanding under that influence.

Simon Episcopius. Simon Episcopius, perhaps the first true Arminian theologian after Arminius, offered an account of the atonement that fell short of the robust doctrine of Arminius. In his *Confession of Faith of Those Called Arminians* Episcopius said only that Christ fulfilled the offices of prophet, priest and king, and by his obedience merited reconciliation of all sinners to God and opened the door to salvation by faith for those who accept it. He did not discuss the issue of punishment for sins, and he avoided any detailed theory of how Christ's death made God's forgiveness possible and just.

Philip Limborch. Later Remonstrant theologian Philip Limborch, however, embraced the governmental theory of the atonement wholeheartedly.

---

[25]John Miley, *Systematic Theology* (Peabody, Mass.: Hendrickson, 1989), 2:68.
[26]Ibid., p. 96.
[27]Ibid.
[28]Ibid., p. 121. Miley, who believed in a version of Grotius's governmental theory, thought these two elements inconsistent with each other.
[29]John Mark Hicks, *The Theology of Grace in the Thought of Jacobus Arminius and Philip van Limborch* (Ph.D. diss., Westminster Theological Seminary, 1985), p. 75.

According to him, God did not have to punish sins; God could forgive sins without any satisfaction to his justice. But God's character propels him to act justly, and salvation ought to be consistent with (retributive) justice, so God offered Christ as a blameless sacrifice to suffer a substitute or alternative penalty to the one deserved by sinners. The purpose was to uphold God's just government of the universe. Thus, Christ's death satisfied the public justice of God. "God, in his grace, accepted the physical death of Christ as a sufficient payment for sin with regard to the physical demands of the Law."[30] Hicks well summarizes Limborch's theory of the atonement:

> According to Limborch's theory of the atonement, Christ paid a real, but not a full, price to the justice of God. The price was his physical death which demonstrated that God hated evil and loved justice. The price had no relation to the eternal penalty of sin except that it opens the way of reconciliation by the suspension of the Father's wrath. Since this wrath was publicly displayed through Jesus, the Father is appeased and the way is now open for reconciliation with man. The Father has opened the way of salvation by the establishment, through his Son, of a new covenant in which the forgiveness of sins is proffered upon the condition of faith and repentance.[31]

To what extent Episcopius and the first generation of Remonstrants were influenced by Grotius is unclear, but Limborch obviously drank deeply at Grotius's well and fell into it. In this account of the atonement Christ did not actually bear the sins of humanity; he did not suffer the punishment for human sin. Rather, he suffered a substitute or alternative penalty that shows God's wrath against sin. His suffering and death were his alone and not really humanity's.

John Wesley's and the Nineteenth-Century Methodist Theologians' Views of the Atonement

John Wesley. Even the harshest Calvinist critics of Arminianism admit that John Wesley believed in the penal substitution theory of the atonement and not the governmental theory. And yet Wesley was an unapologetic Arminian! He even named his magazine for Methodists *The Arminian Magazine.* The title was only changed decades after his death. Wesley rooted the atonement in God's love for humanity as well as in God's justice and wrath toward

---

[30]Ibid., p. 202.
[31]Ibid., p. 206.

sin. It was a universal atonement, but its blessings (reconciliation with God, justification, sanctification) are applied conditionally to those who repent and believe. According to Wesley scholar Thomas Oden, the Methodist founder followed the views of Tertullian, Cyprian and Anselm closely so that

> Christ's work is understood as the payment of ransom or satisfaction. The sinner is up to his neck in debts that can never be paid. Christ's work pays all the debts. He suffered for all humanity, bore our punishment, paid the price of our sins for us. Thus, we have nothing to offer God but the merits of Christ.[32]

Wesley never tired of describing the great sacrifice of Christ and called it a propitiation of God's wrath, bearing the curse of the law and freeing humans from condemnation by paying the price for sins. These images and metaphors abound in Wesley's sermons. Believers are justified freely by God, Wesley declared, because of the atonement:

> His sins, all his past sins, in thought, word, and deed, are covered, are blotted out, shall not be remembered or mentioned against him any more than if they had not been. God will not inflict on that sinner what he deserved to suffer because the Son of his love hath suffered for him. And from the time we are "accepted through the beloved," "reconciled to God through his blood," he loves and blesses and watches over us for good, even as if we had never sinned.[33]

Clearly, Wesley did believe in the substitutionary death of Christ; there is no hint of the governmental theory in his sermons, letters or essays. Even Calvinists Peterson and Williams admit it: "Wesley clearly and strongly affirms substitutionary atonement, especially in the language of penal satisfaction."[34]

After exonerating Wesley of teaching "the Arminian theory of the atonement," the governmental theory, Peterson and Williams write, "Our thesis is that Wesley was correct to teach substitutionary atonement and that his heirs have erred to depart from it."[35] Peterson and Williams write as if *all* Arminians after Wesley adopted the governmental theory in place of something they call the "substitutionary atonement." Is that correct? And are governmental theory and substitutionary atonement really antithetical to each other? Doesn't

---

[32]Thomas C. Oden, *John Wesley's Scriptural Christianity* (Nashville: Abingdon, 1994), p. 187.
[33]John Wesley, "Justification by Faith," in *John Wesley* (Nashville: Thomas Nelson, 1989), p. 182.
[34]Peterson and Williams, *Why I Am Not an Arminian*, p. 193.
[35]Ibid.

the governmental theory include some element of substitution? Before delving into Wesley's nineteenth-century followers—Richard Watson, William Burton Pope, Thomas Summers and John Miley—it should be said that all of them, like all Arminians, rejected limited atonement vociferously. They all argued that the high Calvinist view that Christ represented only the elect in his suffering violates the character of God and the clear meaning of Scripture. Furthermore, they argued that the atonement's universality does not lead to universalism, because it contains an element of conditionality; God declares it to be effective only for those who believe. Watson spoke for all Arminians when he declared that Christ's sacrifice is a restoration of righteousness that must be accepted by faith, but faith does not restore righteousness; only the death of Christ can restore it. And Christ's death was necessary for humans' salvation.[36] Why was it necessary? The nineteenth-century Arminians did not fully agree on that. But they were far from united in rejecting penal substitution and adopting the governmental theory.

Richard Watson. Watson was the first Wesleyan Methodist systematic theologian and his *Theological Institutes* served as the standard instructional manual for Methodist theological training for generations. He considered and rejected Grotius's governmental theory as inadequate by itself to explain why Christ had to die and how his death made salvation possible. Contrary to the idea that Christ suffered a penalty other than ours, Watson wrote of New Testament atonement passages: "These passages . . . prove a *substitution, a suffering in our stead.* The chastisement of offences was laid upon him, in order to our peace; and the offenses were ours, since they could not be his 'who did no sin, neither was guile found in his mouth.' "[37] He explicitly called Christ's death a "penal substitution," a "propitiation," and an appeasement of the "wrath of God." According to Watson, there is no reconciliation apart from Christ's atoning sacrifice as propitiation of God's wrath by means of vicarious suffering:

> Thus, then, for us to be reconciled to God is to avail ourselves of the means by which the anger of God toward us is to be appeased, which the New Testament expressly declares to be generally "the sin offering," of him "who knew no sins," and instrumentally, as to each individual personally, "faith in his blood."[38]

---

[36]Richard Watson, *Theological Institutes* (New York: Lane & Scott, 1851), 2:102, 104.
[37]Ibid., p. 111.
[38]Ibid., p. 121.

Watson found points of value and problems in both the satisfaction and governmental theories. Both stand against the "Socinian view," by which he meant the belief that Christ's death was only a demonstration of God's love and a moral example, and not at all a satisfaction of the demands of justice. He appealed to Grotius against Socinus and his followers, and found in Grotius an ally for promoting a kind of satisfaction view of the atonement in which Christ's death was more than an example but also a real satisfaction. However, Watson criticized those versions of the traditional satisfaction theory that insist Christ's suffering was the exact equivalent of the suffering deserved by every sinner; he could see no sense in that. Rather, Christ's suffering was enough to satisfy the demands of justice. At the same time he criticized the governmental theory for reducing the reason for the atonement to expediency (i.e., that God saw it as fitting even if not necessary). Watson explained the governmental theory of Grotius:

> In a word, Christ is supposed, in this opinion, to have made satisfaction for our sins, not because his death is to be accounted an adequate compensation, or a full equivalent for the remission of punishment, but because his suffering in our stead maintained the honour of the Divine law, and yet gave free scope to the mercy of the lawgiver.[39]

The reason this is an inadequate account of the atonement, according to Watson, is because it appears

> to refer the atonement more to wisdom and fitness as an *expedient* than to wisdom and fitness in close and inseparable connection with justice; and it is defective in not pointing out what that connection between the death of Christ and that honouring of the law of God is, which allows of the remission of punishment to offenders, of which they speak.[40]

Watson insisted that, contrary to the governmental theory, Christ's death must be understood as having an effect on God himself. It "satisfies the rectitude of his character" in the face of sin, which dishonors him and does not merely display and uphold his moral government:

> The satisfaction of Divine justice by the death of Christ, consists, therefore, in this, that this wise and gracious provision on the part of the Father having been voluntarily carried into effect by the Son, the just God has determined it to be consistent with his own holy and righteous character and the ends of law

---

[39]Ibid., p. 137.
[40]Ibid., pp. 137-38.

and government, to forgive all who have true "faith in the blood of Christ," the appointed propitiation for sins, as though they had all been personally punished for their transgressions.[41]

Clearly, for Watson the governmental theory cannot stand on its own two feet, although its emphasis on God's moral government upheld by Christ's death is helpful. It only supplements and cannot replace the satisfaction theory (or penal substitution theory), which regards Christ's death also as the vicarious payment, penalty or suffering of punishment for the sake of God's righteousness and holiness, which have been offended by sin.

William Burton Pope. Pope was also an influential Arminian theologian of the nineteenth century who rejected the governmental theory of the atonement as inadequate, but he incorporated elements of it into his own doctrine of the atonement. Critics who suppose that all Arminians after Wesley adopted the governmental theory may be charmed by their use of governmental themes and motifs, but they miss their criticisms of the Grotian theory as flawed. Pope attempted to hold together three themes about Christ's death: substitutionary, governmental and moral influence.[42] For him, God's moral government was vindicated by the atonement, but that was a result of the atonement rather than its sole purpose or effect.[43] The main purpose of the atonement was propitiation through substitute punishment. Pope criticized Grotius's view of the atonement:

> Grotius founded what has been called the Rectoral or Governmental theory of the Atonement, which dwells too exclusively on its necessity for the vindication of God's righteousness as the Ruler of all. Not to speak of the invisible repugnance felt by every reverent mind to the thought that our Lord was thus made a spectacle to the universe, this theory errs by making a subordinate purpose extreme.[44]

Pope explained his thoroughly Arminian theory of the atonement:

> Our Savior's sacrifice on the cross finished a perfect obedience which He offered in His Divine-human Person. This was His own obedience, and therefore of infinite value or worthiness; but it was vicarious, and its benefit belongs absolutely to our race, and, on certain conditions, to every member of it. As

---

[41]Ibid., p. 139.

[42]William Burton Pope, *A Compendium of Christian Theology* (New York: Phillips & Hunt, n.d.), 2:314.

[43]Ibid., p. 276.

[44]Ibid., p. 313.

availing for man, by the appointment of God, it is no less than the satisfaction, provided by Divine love, of the claims of Divine justice, upon transgression: which may be viewed, on the one hand, as an expiation of the punishment due to the guilt of human sin; and, on the other, as a propitiation of the Divine displeasure, which is thus shown to be consistent with infinite goodwill to the sinners of mankind. But the expiation of guilt and propitiation of wrath are one and the same effect of the Atonement. Both suppose the existence of sin and the wrath of God against it. But, in the mystery of the Atonement, the provision of eternal mercy, as it were, anticipates the transgression, and love always in every representation of it has the pre-eminence. The passion is the exhibition rather than the cause of the Divine love to man.[45]

Pope considered what Christ did on the cross a substitutionary suffering of the wrath of God against sin that assuages wrath and makes possible loving and just forgiveness, which is the main motive behind the cross.

Thomas Summers. Summers was yet another important nineteenth-century Arminian theologian who opposed the governmental theory as an insufficient account of why Christ died and what effect his death had on God and humanity. In fact, Summers spoke out against the Grotian theory as "superficial, sentimental heresy!"[46] Like Pope, he tied together three necessary aspects of the atonement: propitiatory, governmental and moral.[47] Each makes its own unique contribution to a holistic understanding of the atonement, but none can say everything about Christ's death that needs to be said. Against the Grotian theory, Summers said: "We challenge that both in the New Testament and in Christian experience the cross of our Lord Jesus Christ is infinitely more than the embodiment of the forces of moral government."[48] Rather, the propitiatory sacrifice of Christ really reconciled the Father to humanity and provided for the consequent reconciliation of humanity to God.[49]

The atonement is the satisfaction made to God for the sins of all mankind, original and actual, by the mediation of Christ, and especially by his passion and death, so that pardon might be granted to all, while the divine perfections are kept in harmony, the authority of the Sovereign is upheld.[50]

---

[45]Ibid., p. 264.
[46]Thomas O. Summers, *Systematic Theology* (Nashville: Publishing House of the Methodist Episcopal Church, South, 1888), 1:258.
[47]Ibid., p. 265.
[48]Ibid., p. 270.
[49]Ibid., p. 268.
[50]Ibid., pp. 258-59.

Summers argued that the governmental theory is not the one true Arminian theory of the atonement and said that though it may approve itself to a "shallow rationalism," it does not offer an adequate interpretation of Scripture because of its profound misrepresentations of propitiation and reconciliation.[51] Nevertheless, Summers found some value in that theory because it displays the "rectoral goodness of the universal Sovereign who is righteous in all his ways" and thus "will deter men from sinning."[52]

Charles Finney. Almost without doubt two nineteenth-century theologians stand out as primarily responsible for the myth that the governmental theory is "the Arminian theory" of the atonement. They are Charles Finney and John Miley. Finney, though, was not an Arminian (see pp. 26-28). His theology was closer to semi-Pelagianism; it was without classical Arminian roots and may have been influenced by the late Remonstrant Philip Limborch (as mediated to Finney by Nathaniel Taylor). At least their patterns of thought are similar. Finney rejected the satisfaction and penal-substitution theories of the atonement in favor of the governmental theory: "The atonement of Christ was intended as a satisfaction of public justice."[53] For him, Christ's suffering and death justified God's pardoning of sin and dispensing with retributive justice toward sinners. It upheld God's moral government of the universe but was in no way an actual bearing of punishment due sinners.

John Miley. An Arminian and a leading Methodist theologian of the late nineteenth century, John Miley embraced and promoted the governmental theory of the atonement. He argued that "the vicarious sufferings of Christ are an atonement for sin as a conditional substitute for penalty, fulfilling, on the forgiveness of sin, the obligation of justice and the office of penalty in moral government."[54] For him, Christ bore no punishment or penalty for sins. The purpose and effect of the atonement was purely and simply to preserve moral government as God forgives those who repent.[55] Miley's argument, persuasive to some later Arminians, was that there lies an inconsistency between the universality and conditionality of the atonement in the

---

[51]Ibid., p. 273.

[52]Ibid., p. 283.

[53]Charles Finney, *Finney's Systematic Theology*, ed. J. H. Fairchild, abr. ed. (Minneapolis: Bethany House, 1976), p. 207.

[54]Miley, *Systematic Theology*, 2:68.

[55]Ibid., p. 69.

satisfaction and penal substitution theories.[56] He averred that if Christ died
for all in the sense of bearing their punishment or paying their penalty, then
all are saved. This is also an argument used by Calvinists against Arminians.
Miley accepted the argument and offered the Grotian theory of the atonement as the solution. He need not have done this. There is no inconsistency
between Christ's representation of all in his suffering and death, and the
condition that in order to benefit from that representation individuals have
to avail themselves of its benefits by faith.

Conclusion. Critics who claim that the governmental theory of the atonement is "the Arminian theory" of the atonement have simply not done their
homework. Of the four major nineteenth-century Arminian theologians
only one—John Miley—clearly and uncritically accepted that view, and incorporated it into his theology without major alteration. The others either
rejected it (Summers) or accepted parts or aspects of it while holding primarily to the satisfaction or penal substitution theory (Watson and Pope).
Clearly then the identification of the governmental theory, with Arminianism is wrong. Arminius did not teach it. Episcopius does not seem to have
held it. Limborch, the pseudo-Arminian Remonstrant, taught a version of
it. Wesley rejected it, as did most of his nineteenth-century followers.

How do myths like this one begin, and why do they take on a life of their
own so that it is almost impossible to refute them? One theory is that many
twentieth- and twenty-first-century Calvinist critics of Arminianism know it
primarily (if not exclusively) from Princeton theologian B. B. Warfield's
caustic attack on John Miley's *Systematic Theology*.[57] However, some Calvinists
have bothered to read some twentieth-century Arminian theologians and
have found the governmental theory there.

Twentieth-Century Arminians and the Atonement
H. Orton Wiley. The seminal evangelical Arminian theologian of the twentieth-century Holiness movement is H. Orton Wiley, who was influenced by
John Miley. He attempted to combine the governmental theory with the penal substitution theory but ended up adopting the former lock, stock and
barrel. Wiley seemed to be convinced by Miley's argument that the penal
substitution or satisfaction theory of the atonement required universalism

---

[56]Ibid., p. 193.
[57]B. B. Warfield, "A Review of Systematic Theology," in *Selected Shorter Writings of Warfield*, vol. 2,
ed. John E. Meeter (Phillipsburg, Penn.: Presbyterian & Reformed, 1980).

or limited atonement. He mistakenly attributed the beginning of the governmental theory to Arminius.[58] He relied very heavily on Miley's account of the doctrine: "The atonement is thus determined to consist in the sufferings of Christ, as a provisory substitute for penalty in the interest of moral government."[59] Christ did not suffer the actual punishment due sinners, but suffered a punishment accepted by God in place of that penalty:

> The governmental theory of the atonement . . . makes prominent the sacrifice of Christ as a substitute for penalty. It maintains that the death on the cross marked God's displeasure against sin, and therefore upholds the divine majesty and makes possible the forgiveness of sins. On this theory, the sacrifice of Christ is regarded as a substitute for public rather than retributive justice.[60]

Wiley correctly noted that the penal substitution theory (or satisfaction theory) does not have a monopoly on substitution. The governmental theory holds it as well.[61] It is wrong for critics of the governmental theory, such as Peterson and Williams, to pit it against substitutionary atonement. In it Christ suffers and dies in sinners' place. It may not be their own punishment (i.e., the punishment they deserve), but it is a substitute suffering for that punishment. Even for those who hold the governmental theory, Christ was our substitute. He suffered an infliction for sin that God accepted as adequate to meet the demands of divine justice. The only real difference between that and the traditional satisfaction or penal-substitution theory is that Christ did not suffer everyone's deserved punishment or penalty.

R. Larry Shelton. Another twentieth-century Arminian-Wesleyan theologian who finds some merit in the governmental theory of the atonement is R. Larry Shelton. He seems to accept Miley's and Wiley's belief that penal substitution conflicts with conditionality of salvation within the Arminian universality of the atonement. He finds some value in Anselm's satisfaction motif and in Abelard's moral example model, but he leans heavily toward the governmental view:

> The governmental model opens up a more personal concept for understanding Christ's work than is found in the penal substitutionary judicial or transactional concepts. As modified by the Wesleyan-Arminians [Miley and Wiley?], the governmental idea is enhanced and the necessity for faith-union

---

[58]H. Orton Wiley, *Christian Theology* (Kansas City, Mo.: Beacon Hill, 1941), 2:252.
[59]Ibid., p. 258.
[60]Ibid., p. 295.
[61]Ibid., p. 245.

with Christ as a condition for salvation is more strongly grounded.[62]

F. Leroy Forlines. It should not be supposed that all twentieth-century Arminian theologians have embraced the governmental theory of the atonement. Free Will Baptist theologian F. Leroy Forlines considers the governmental theory and rejects it on the grounds that

> all of the valid principles that the governmental view proposes to uphold are done better by the satisfaction view. The satisfaction view more successfully shows the importance of holiness and the seriousness of sin. It gives a much higher view of the love of God. It creates a more solid foundation for respect for God's government.[63]

He gives a ringing endorsement to the penal-substitution theory:

> When Jesus Christ went to the cross, all the sins of all the world that ever had been committed, were being committed, and ever would be committed were laid on Him. With our sins upon Him, He took our place under the righteous wrath of God. God poured out His wrath upon Him as if He were guilty of all the sins of the whole race. . . . In a very real and literal sense, Jesus took the place of every sinner.[64]

Thomas Oden. Another contemporary Arminian theologian who holds to something like the penal substitution theory as opposed to the governmental theory is Methodist Thomas Oden. In his magisterial *Systematic Theology* he summarizes the three decisive points of Jesus' atoning death in good Arminian fashion: "(1) its *necessity,* there is no salvation except through the meritorious death of Christ; (2) it is *unlimited in extent,* it avails for all sinners and for all sin; and (3) it is *conditional* in its application, it is efficacious only for the penitent and believing sinner."[65] According to Oden, Christ

> bore the guilt of others and paid their penalties. By his suffering and death, Christ removed the discord between God and humanity. . . . By this means he rendered a satisfaction fully sufficient for and available to all. . . . His passive obedience consisted primarily in his dying act of paying the penalty due oth-

---

[62]R. Larry Shelton, "Initial Salvation," in *A Contemporary Wesleyan Theology,* ed. Charles W. Carter (Grand Rapids: Zondervan, 1983), p. 505.

[63]F. Leroy Forlines, *The Quest for Truth* (Nashville: Randall House, 2001), p. 203.

[64]Ibid., p. 187.

[65]Thomas C. Oden, *Systematic Theology:* vol. 2, *The Word of Life* (San Francisco: Harper & Row, 1989), p. 357.

ers. He took their punishment, atoning for their sins. By his obedience, Christ freed us from the curse of the law (Gal. 3:13, John 1:29, Rom. 8:32).[66]

Like Wesley before him, Methodist Oden adheres to the classical satisfaction theory in its penal substitution form. There is no hint of the governmental theory in his thought, unless it is simply in affirmation that the atonement upholds God's righteousness and justice. That he is an Arminian is displayed in his strong affirmation of the universality and conditionality of the atonement as well as in his ringing endorsement of Arminius's theology as the recovery in a post-Reformation context of the early Christian ecumenical consensus.[67]

We can only hope that critics who impute the governmental theory of the atonement to all Arminians and call it "the Arminian theory of the atonement" will reconsider this charge as well as the temptation to pit the Arminian view against substitutionary models of the atonement. For all its flaws, the governmental theory does portray Christ's death as a substitution for divine retributive justice against sinners. Nevertheless, many Arminians, including Arminius himself, have avoided it; some have even harshly attacked and condemned it without compromising their Arminian credentials.

---

[66]Ibid., p. 361.
[67]Thomas C. Oden, *The Transforming Power of Grace* (Nashville: Abingdon, 1993), p. 152.

CONCLUSION

Rules of Engagement for Evangelical Calvinists and Arminians

BASED ON THE EXPOSITION OF REAL Arminianism in this book, I confidently assert that Arminianism is a legitimate evangelical theological option and that Arminians should not be ashamed to wear that label proudly. The stigma attached to it is unwarranted and should disappear. But what of the claim that Arminianism inevitably leads to unitarianism, universalism and liberal theology? In the infamous 1992 Arminianism issue of *Modern Reformation,* Michael Horton declared, "Wherever Arminianism was adopted, unitarianism followed, leading to the bland liberalism of present mainline denominations."[1] That too is a myth. First, it ignores the fact that the father of liberal theology—Friedrich Schleiermacher, who was a Calvinist—was untouched by Arminianism. It also overlooks the fact that today's evangelical scene is filled with Arminians who are thoroughly orthodox theologically, and there have always been orthodox Arminians among evangelicals. Whatever their particularities that appear peculiar to outsiders, Pentecostals, Holiness believers, many Baptists and free-church evangelicals who are Arminians are just as biblically and theologically conservative as most Calvinists. The claim that these churches are riddled with or are on a slippery slope toward heresy is nothing other than vicious calumny. But the same can and should be said about the other side: Arminians who point the finger at Calvinists and denounce their theology as heresy, unbiblical or tantamount to pagan fatalism should learn to appreciate the great contributions of Reformed theology to Protestantism, and they should recognize and acknowl-

---

[1]Michael S. Horton, "Evangelical Arminians," *Modern Reformation* 1 (1992): 16.

edge evangelicalism's debt to Calvinism.

Adherents of both sides within evangelicalism should agree on some basic rules of discourse. First, before speaking or writing about another theology, we must be sure we have read it and are able to describe it as its own best representatives describe it. In short, before saying "I disagree" we must be able to truly say "I understand." Calvinists who attack Arminianism should have at least a passing acquaintance with Arminius and two or three solid evangelical Arminian theologians. Arminians should refrain from criticizing Calvinism until they have read Calvin and some Reformed theologians who follow him closely.

Second, critics should always be sure they are not assaulting a straw man. That happens whenever Calvinist critics of Arminianism aim their polemical weapons not at real Arminianism but at evangelical folk religion, which sometimes vaguely resembles Arminianism in a very distorted way. The cover of the May-June 1992 issue of *Modern Reformation* displayed a ballot on which God votes for and Satan votes against the salvation of a certain individual, and the final box on the ballot says "A TIE! Your vote must decide the issue." No doubt this was taken from a real gospel tract, but it is not true Arminianism. Such folk-religion tripe should not be used to illustrate it. True Arminians would never say "God votes for your soul; the devil votes against it; you cast the deciding vote." Such clichés are unworthy of Arminianism and of critics who charge them to Arminianism's account. Calvinists bristle when detractors describe Calvinism as stoic fatalism. They should avoid doing the same kind of thing to Arminianism.

Third, both Calvinists and Arminians should admit the weaknesses of their own theologies and not pretend that the other one alone contains tensions, apparent inconsistencies, difficulties explaining biblical passages and mysteries. We should strictly avoid double standards. If we point out apparent inconsistencies in the other party's theology and argue that inconsistency shows weakness, we should not pretend our own theology is free of such flaws.

Finally, both Calvinists and Arminians should strictly avoid attributing beliefs to adherents of the other side that those adherents explicitly reject. This often happens because critics think they see where certain beliefs of the others must logically lead and then attribute the "good and necessary consequence" (as they see it) of a belief to the others even though the others deny it. For example, Calvinists often say that Arminians believe the free will decision of faith is the decisive factor in salvation. That is how Calvinists see it, but Arminians neither say nor believe this. Similarly, Arminians sometimes say that Calvinists believe in fatalism, but Calvinists reject fatalism. Both sides should learn to say, "This is the logical consequence of their belief," and follow up with, "But they don't follow the logic there." There is nothing wrong with arguing against a viewpoint on the basis of where it seems to inevitably lead. Arminians reject high Calvinism because it seems to lead inevitably to God as the author of sin and evil. In other words, it is fair to say, "If I were a Calvinist, I would have to believe that God is the author of sin and evil, and that I can't believe." It is also fair to say, "Based on logic, Calvinists should say that God is the author of sin and evil, because that is the only claim consistent with everything else they believe." However, it is unfair to say those things about Calvinism without also saying, "But most Calvinists do not believe that God is the author of sin and evil." Calvinists who argue against Arminianism should follow this same rule of fairness, admitting that Arminians do not believe that the prevenient-grace-enabled free decision of faith is the decisive factor in salvation.

If both sides would follow some simple, commonsense rules of fairness, they could coexist and cooperate peacefully—evangelicalism would be stronger and its mission enhanced. But this requires good will and dialogue. But apparently some Calvinists and some Arminians do not care about fairness. This is demonstrated on the Internet, where websites put up by passionate followers of both theologies have included articles viciously attacking the other point of view and its adherents. One website describes "the Christ of Arminianism" as a false Christ worse than the Christ of any cult. Commonly found at Calvinist Internet sites are charts and quizzes identifying Arminianism with semi-Pelagianism if not Pelagianism. These tactics ought to stop, and well-intentioned Calvinists and Arminians should expose these errors and dishonest tactics. It should not be up to Calvinists alone to clear the good name of Calvinism from slander by overly zealous Arminians; nor should it be up to Arminians alone to defend true Arminianism against distortions and false accusations.

One irenic evangelical Calvinist scholar occasionally contacts me to get an Arminian description of some point of Arminian theology, because he knows self-description is always better than a description by an outsider. He once asked why Arminians object when Calvinists say that Arminianism makes the decision of faith the "decisive factor" in salvation. He probably still believes it does, but after dialogue he could better see why Arminians do not like that charge. I routinely contact Calvinist friends and acquaintances to clarify points of Calvinist theology. None of this is to say that the debate should cease; the differences do matter! But an irenic and honest debate should be fair.

Can Calvinists and Arminians peacefully coexist and cooperate under the large tent of evangelicalism? When they recognize each other as authentically evangelical, they can. It is distressingly strange to find some Calvinists saying, for example, that Arminianism is "on the precipice of heresy" or that Arminians are "barely Christians," and then wondering why Arminians are offended. Within their own denominations Calvinists and Arminians can and probably should emphasize their particularities, allowing no slippage into the other theology. But evangelicalism is a multi-denominational and transdenominational movement; it has no headquarters and no firm boundaries. Evangelicals have much in common, including a mission to proclaim Jesus Christ to the world. They can fulfill that mission better together than apart. When they are in contexts where neither Calvinism nor Arminianism is the norm (as in the National Association of Evangelicals [NAE] and similar organizations), they should stress their common ground and avoid casting aspersions on each other. Unfortunately, some evangelical Calvinists have worked hard to make Reformed theology the norm for evangelical faith. Arminians are marginalized if not quietly excluded. Arminians, however, are not Johnny-come-latelies to the evangelical scene. They were there at the founding of the NAE and most other evangelical organizations, including transdenominational seminaries that now avoid hiring them.

In spite of their common ground and equally evangelical commitments and spirit, many Calvinists and Arminians probably cannot peacefully coexist in the same churches without reducing theology and worship to shallowness. That does not mean they cannot cooperate and accept each other as equals within the broader evangelical movement that includes so many theological differences. For example, only rarely and in very unusual circumstances can those who hold to infant baptism and believer's baptism coexist within a single congregation, but within the broader evangelical coalition they have worked together without rancor or competition for many years. The situation will probably be the same for passionate Calvinists and Arminians. They will seek out churches where their distinctive views of

God's sovereignty and human freedom will be valued and taught, and will shape worship and pastoral care. But that should be no barrier to their embracing as brothers and sisters fellow evangelicals of the other persuasion who are equally committed to the basics of the gospel.

I hope this book contributes to a better understanding of Arminianism. If it does, evangelical Arminians will come out of the theological closet and claim their Arminianism without shame or fear of exclusion; Calvinists will see that much of what they have been told about Arminianism is simply false, and thus they will begin to spread the good message that Arminians are not so different in their basic theological convictions. After all, Arminians also emphasize the grace of God and attribute no spiritual goodness to human endeavor; they too stress the sovereignty of God and strictly avoid giving humans autonomous status over God. Even though Arminians give these great doctrines their own distinctive spin, based on their reading of Scripture, they stand on the same ground of Protestant orthodoxy with Calvinists, pointing away from themselves and to the glory and love of God revealed in Jesus Christ.

Name Index

Subject Index

alien righteousness, 210, 213

Alliance of Confessing Evangelicals, 93-94, 139

Anabaptists, 22, 33, 80, 94-95, 216

antinomianism, 212

Arian, Arianism, 5, 23-24, 79-80, 88-91

Armenia, 13

Arminianism, Arminian
 contemporary representatives of, 29
 definition of, 16
 doctrine of God and, 88-93
 Jacob Arminius and, 22
 of the head, 17, 23, 26, 87, 91, 116, 209
 of the heart, 17, 24, 87, 209
 overview of, 31-39
 Pelagianism and, 80-82, 142-45, 152
 Reformed Theology and, 44-60
 Scripture and, 69-71, 82-88
 semi-Pelagianism and, 10, 30-31, 40-43, 56, 79-81, 95, 139-52, 158-66, 244

Athanasian Creed, 92-93

atonement, 6, 31, 34-35, 63-70, 153, 221-41
 governmental, 221-41
 limited, 15-16, 66, 77, 221-23, 233, 239
 penal, 221-42

Baptist, Baptists, 8-9, 29, 187, 242

Belgic Confession, 44, 84

Calminianism, 61, 67-69, 76-77

Calvinism, Calvinist
 Arminian criticism of, 47, 63-67, 99-100, 103-5, 136, 181-83, 187
 definition of, 15
 Friedrich Schleiermacher and, 23-24, 150, 242
 John Wesley and, 55, 108-10
 sin and evil and, 99-102

canon, 85

Chalcedonian Definition, 91-92

Christian Reformed Church, 7, 69n.

Christianity Today magazine, 8-9

Christology, 88-93

Church of Christ, 7, 87

Church of England, 23

common grace. *See* grace

compatibilism, compatibilist. *See* free will

conditional predestination. *See* predestination

Congregationalism, Congregational churches, 23, 44, 87

covenant theology, 52-54. *See also* federal theology

deism, 26, 117, 122, 132

determinism, 63, 73-75, 98-101, 119-21, 135-37, 174, 179-80, 194-99

divine sovereignty, 115-36

double predestination. *See* predestination

Eastern Orthodoxy, Eastern Orthodox, 90

enabling grace. *See* grace

Enlightenment, 17, 23, 76, 87, 91, 96, 99, 147, 174

Episcopalians, 87, 94

eternal life, 16, 63, 166, 193

Eternity magazine, 8-9

evangelical, evangelicalism, 8, 10, 21, 41, 78-96, 139-40, 221, 242-46

Evangelical Free Church of America, 69

evangelical synergism. *See* synergism

federal theology, 51, 53, 228. *See* covenant theology

folk religion, 58, 179, 243

free will, 14, 75-76, 97-114, 125, 164, 174
 compatibilist, 20, 75-76, 108, 129
 incompatibilist, 20, 75-76, 98, 135

Free Will Baptists, 87, 93

General Baptists, 14

governmental atonement. *See* atonement

grace, 158-78, 200-220
 common, 41-42, 144, 148, 177
 enabling, 35, 66
 irresistible, 63-66, 155-57, 185, 192-93
 prevenient, 20, 27-28, 35-37, 66, 76, 95, 138, 141-49, 159-78, 180-81, 244

Heidelberg Catechism, 44, 48, 84

humanism, 9, 79, 82, 87

imputed righteousness, 31, 154, 200-202, 204, 210, 212-20